Ordinary National Certificate Mathematics

Volume 1

by the same author

ORDINARY NATIONAL CERTIFICATE MATHEMATICS

Volume 2

Ordinary National Certificate Mathematics
Volume I

Second Edition in SI Units

H. A. HORNER
M.A. (Cantab), F.I.M.A.

Head of Department of Mathematics and Computing
Luton College of Technology

HEINEMANN EDUCATIONAL BOOKS · LONDON

Heinemann Educational Books Ltd

LONDON EDINBURGH MELBOURNE AUCKLAND TORONTO
SINGAPORE HONG KONG KUALA LUMPUR
IBADAN NAIROBI JOHANNESBURG
LUSAKA NEW DELHI

ISBN 0 435 71082 6

Published by
Heinemann Educational Books Ltd
48 Charles Street, London W1X 8AH

Reproduced and printed by photolithography and bound in
Great Britain at The Pitman Press, Bath

To
EDNA, my wife and
PATRICIA, my daughter
for
their patience and
understanding during
many trying months.

Preface to Second Edition

All teachers and students will be aware of the change-over that is taking place in the system of units.

Whilst the period of transition from the Imperial System to the Système International (SI) may not be complete, some examining bodies have already proposed the use of SI units only. In view of this, it was felt that this volume should be reprinted with SI units only.

Because of their extensive use, decimal points have been preserved; but as far as possible digit groupings (separated by spaces) are generally in groups of three, i.e. the comma, as a separator, is deleted. (Groups of four digits in certain cases are not broken up). In addition, *because of its convenient size*, the centimetre is retained as a unit although eventually this may be eliminated. Otherwise, as far as possible the units used are SI units as recommended.

For reference purposes a short list of SI units is given below. This list is intended to cover the text in this volume. (Currency units are not referred to).

SI UNITS OF MEASURE

1. *Basic SI units* (six)
   length—metre (m); mass—kilogramme (Kg);
   time—second (s); electric current—ampere (A);
   temperature—degree Kelvin (°K); luminous intensity—candela (cd).

2. *Derived units* (*special names*)
   force—newton (N); work, energy—joule (J);
   power—watt (W); electric potential—volt (V);
   luminous flux—lumen (lm); illumination—lux (lx).

3. *Derived units* (*complex names*)
   area (m^2); volume (m^3); frequency c/s; density (Kg/m^3);
   velocity (m/s); acceleration (m/s^2); pressure (N/m^2).

4. *Multiples and sub-multiples* (*prefix in brakets*)
   1 000 000—10^6—mega (M); 1 000—10^3—Kilo (K); 100—10^2—hecto (h);
   10—10^1—deca (da); 0·1—10^{-1}—deci (d); 0·01—10^{-2}—centi (c);
   0·001—10^{-3}—milli (m); 0·000 001—10^{-6}—micro (μ).

5. *Units used in this volume*
   length—mm, cm, m, Km; area—mm^2, cm^2, m^2;
   volume—cm^3, m^3; time—S, minute (min); angle—rad, degrees, minutes;
   mass—g; temperature—degrees Celsius (°C);
   density—g/cm^3; density (surface)—g/cm^2;
   moments of inertia—$g\ cm^2$, $Kg\ cm^2$;
   force, pressure—w/m^2, KN/m^2; work, energy—Nm, KNm, J, KJ;
   acceleration due to gravity—9·81 m/s^2 (unless otherwise specified).

Preface to First Edition

The introduction of the new form of Ordinary National Certificate has given the opportunity to introduce a new type of text book. There are many good books based on the old National Certificate schemes but a need has arisen for books tailored to the new requirements. No credit is taken for the various mathematical methods introduced in the present book as these have been known for generations.

This is the first volume of a two volume series for years one and two of the new ONC syllabus and covers the first year. An attempt has been made to present the book in a form such that students can make the fullest use of it. Each chapter will present an amount of theory which can be dealt with in a standard two-hour period. Clearly, if class periods are longer, it will be possible to absorb the material more comfortably.

Students are reminded that, in order to acquire a proper understanding of the subject and its applications, it is necessary to learn a number of sound basic rules and methods. If these are practised, using the examples provided, the interpretation and breakdown of practical problems will be less difficult. The number of unworked examples provided in each chapter is not excessive, so that it should be possible for students to attempt them all. It will be found that, provided all the unworked examples are attempted conscientiously, he necessary skills in analysis, manipulation and computation will be acquired.

Throughout the text, emphasis is on correct methods of

computation, correct methods for dealing with the rearrangement (transposition) of formulae, logical setting out of solutions, neatness and clarity of arrangement of material, and the systematic use of all the normal mathematical tables found in books of standard four-figure tables.

It cannot be stressed too highly that students who are seriously concerned to develop their mathematical approach and skills must work steadily at the subject. No scientific or engineering subject can be fully comprehended and satisfactorily studied without a sound mathematical background.

As this first book in the series is being written at the start of the operation of the new National Certificate scheme, it should be appreciated that the greatest importance is laid on methods of analysis and computation. The questions used are of a suitable standard, but the usual practice of quoting questions from public examination bodies and technical college examinations is not followed.

The final stages of the book will provide a few specimen papers of O.1 level for students to attempt prior to their examination.

It is sincerely hoped that the books in the series will be useful to students and the new approach will help to promote confidence.

The presentation of material is based on teaching, by the author, to Ordinary National Certificate students over a period of about twenty years, and it is hoped that the experience will be helpful to both students and lecturers.

I would like to record my grateful thanks to my typist Mrs G. Clifford for her careful and methodical work. Without her help this book could not have been prepared so well and so soon.

In addition I would like to thank Macmillan and Co. Ltd. for permission to include the tables in Appendix C.

Finally thanks are due to all the many students who, in the past have indirectly contributed to the presentation of the text.

Whilst every effort has been made to avoid errors, I would be grateful to receive the corrections of any which may be found.

A few errors discovered in the first printing have been corrected in the second and third impressions.

H. A. HORNER

Contents

CONTENTS

19	Approximate Numerical Methods	187
20	Tabulation of Polynomial Functions	200
21	Tabulation of Functions and Increments	207
22	Slopes and Gradients of Graphs	213
23	Plots of Functions and Derivatives from First Principles	220
24	Derivatives of x^n	228
25	Derivatives of Functions by Substitution	237
26	Integration	245
27	Revision Examples	254
	Answers to Examples	261
Appendix A	Specimen Papers	273
Appendix B	Table of Constants, Conversion Factors, and Formulae	276
Appendix C	Mathematical Tables	279
Index		289

1

Indices and Logarithms

1.1 Revision of Index Laws

Using the base a, if a number N is expressed as $N = a^x$, then x is the index (or power) to which the base is raised in order to give the number N. In general a (the base) will be a positive number, but x may be positive or negative (whole number or fraction). Since x is essentially a 'power', the following rules of indices apply when multiplication and division occur.

1.1.1 Rules of indices

(i) $\qquad a^x \times a^y \times a^z = a^{x+y+z}$ (*Fundamental law*)

This will apply for any number of multiplications so long as the base is the same.

(ii) $\qquad (a^x)^y = a^{xy}$

(iii) $\qquad \dfrac{a^x}{a^y} = a^{x-y}$

(iv) $\qquad \dfrac{a^x}{a^x} = a^0 = 1$

(v) *Negative index*

If a number is expressed as a^{-x}, using the rules (i) and (iv) it follows that

$$a^x \times a^{-x} = a^{x-x} = a^0 = 1$$

$$\therefore \ a^{-x} = \frac{1}{a^x} \quad \text{and also} \quad a^x = \frac{1}{a^{-x}}$$

Hence a negative index indicates that the *reciprocal* of a number is being evaluated.

1.1.2 Application of the rules when different bases occur

Care must be taken when using indices, to ensure that the rules are applied strictly.

Example:

$$\frac{a^3b^2c^2}{abc^4} \times \frac{a^2b^3c}{a^4b^2} \quad (\textit{Note: } c = c^1)$$

$$= a^{3+2-1-4} \times b^{2+3-1-2} \times c^{2+1-4}$$

$$= a^0 \times b^2 \times c^{-1}$$

$$= 1 \times b^2 \times \frac{1}{c^1} = \frac{b^2}{c}$$

Note that the indices are collected together, using the previous rules, bases a, b, and c being kept separate. Normally results are given with positive indices only.

1.1.3 Meaning of a fractional index

Consider $a^{\frac{1}{2}}$.

Using rule (i) $\qquad a^{\frac{1}{2}} \times a^{\frac{1}{2}} = a^{\frac{1}{2}+\frac{1}{2}} = a^1 = a$

But also a square root is defined as

$$\sqrt{a} \times \sqrt{a} = a$$

Therefore it follows that $a^{\frac{1}{2}}$ and $\sqrt{a}$ mean the same, i.e.

$$a^{\frac{1}{2}} = \sqrt{a}$$

Similarly $\quad a^{1/n} \times a^{1/n} \times a^{1/n} \ldots (n \text{ times}) = a^{n \times (1/n)} = a^1 = a$

Therefore $\qquad a^{1/n} = \sqrt[n]{a}$ (The nth root of a)

Finally combining this last result and rule (ii), it follows that

$$a^{m/n} = \{a^{1/n}\}^m = (\sqrt[n]{a})^m$$

and $\qquad a^{m/n} = (a^m)^{1/n} = \sqrt[n]{a^m}$

(This rule would normally only be used when m and n are positive integers.)

1.2 Laws of Logarithms

1.2.1 Logarithms

If a number N is expressed as $N = a^x$, then x is the logarithm to the base a of the number N. It follows that *logarithms are indices*. The result is written as

$$\log_a N = x$$

Any number may be chosen as a base for a table of logarithms. However, since any number can be used, the base a chosen is normally one of two numbers, i.e. 10 or e.

Common logarithms. These are tabulated values of logarithms (indices) to base 10. It is assumed that students are familiar with the tables and are able to write down any required logarithm.

Natural (Naperian or hyperbolic) logarithms. These are tabulated to base e (e = 2·718) and will be dealt with in the next chapter.

1.2.2 Antilogarithms

These are the values of $N = a^x$, where x is the logarithm. Separate tables are *not essential* but are provided for common logarithms. They are not usually provided for natural logarithms, unless tables of e^x are given.

Example:

$$\text{Antilogarithm of } 0{\cdot}5678 \text{ to base } 10 = 3{\cdot}697$$
$$\text{This means that } 10^{0{\cdot}5678} \qquad\qquad = 3{\cdot}697$$

1.2.3 Rules of logarithms

Since logarithms are indices, by using a standard base calculations can be done by using logarithms (indices) only. Based on the results for indices, the following rules of logarithms follow:

(i) $\qquad \log (A \times B \times C) = \log A + \log B + \log C$

(ii) $\qquad \log \left(\dfrac{A}{B}\right) = \log A - \log B$

(iii) $\qquad \log (a^x) = x \times \log a = x \log a$

(iv) $\qquad \log \sqrt[n]{a} = \dfrac{1}{n} \times \log a = \dfrac{1}{n} \log a.$

Students will be familiar with the use of logarithms for multiplication and division. Examples are given in 1.3 of the use of logarithms to evaluate a^x.

1.3 Evaluation of a^x

The methods are illustrated by the following worked examples.

Examples:

(i) Evaluate (find the numerical value of) $(1 \cdot 286)^{1 \cdot 3}$

Let $N = (1 \cdot 286)^{1 \cdot 3}$

Then $\quad \log_{10} N = 1 \cdot 3 \times \log_{10} (1 \cdot 286)$

$= 1 \cdot 3 \times 0 \cdot 1092$

$= 0 \cdot 1419$

$\therefore \ N = (1 \cdot 286)^{1 \cdot 3} = \text{antilog}_{10} \ 0 \cdot 1419$

$= 1 \cdot 387$

No.	Log
$1 \cdot 3$	$0 \cdot 1139$
$0 \cdot 1092$	$\bar{1} \cdot 0382$
$0 \cdot 1419$	$\bar{1} \cdot 1521$

(ii) Evaluate $(10 \cdot 86)^{0 \cdot 58}$

Let $\qquad\qquad\qquad N = (10 \cdot 86)^{0 \cdot 58}$

Then $\log N = 0.58 \times \log 10.86$

$\qquad = 0.58 \times 1.0358$

$\qquad = 0.6009$

$\therefore N = (10.86)^{0.58} = \text{antilog } 0.6009$

$\qquad = 3.989$

No.	Log
0·58	$\bar{1}$·7634
1·0358	0·0154
0·6009	$\bar{1}$·7788

(*Note:* (i) In reading the tables 1·0358 was taken as 1·036 to the nearest 4th figure

(ii) 0·58 × 1·0358 could have been multiplied out arithmetically and obtained to 4 decimal places. However, in general, this would only affect the 4th significant figure, so no appreciable increase in accuracy is obtained).

Further examples are included below.

WORKED EXAMPLES (read carefully)

(*a*) Simplify:

$$\frac{a^{\frac{1}{2}}b^3c^3}{abc^2} \times \frac{a^{-\frac{1}{2}}b^{-2}c^{\frac{1}{2}}}{b^{\frac{3}{2}}c^{\frac{3}{2}}} \qquad (\text{remember } a = a^1)$$

$$= a^{\frac{1}{2}-\frac{1}{2}-1} \times b^{3-2-1-\frac{3}{2}} \times c^{3+\frac{1}{2}-2-\frac{3}{2}}$$

$$= a^{-1} \times b^{-\frac{3}{2}} \times c^0 = \frac{1}{a} \times \frac{1}{b^{\frac{3}{2}}} \times 1 = \frac{1}{ab^{\frac{3}{2}}}$$

(*b*) Simplify and then evaluate:

$$X = \frac{2^{\frac{3}{2}} \times 3^{-\frac{3}{2}} \times 3^4 \times 2^{-\frac{1}{2}}}{3 \times 2^{\frac{5}{2}} \times 3^3 \times 2^2}$$

$$= 2^{\frac{3}{2}-\frac{1}{2}-\frac{5}{2}-2} \times 3^{-\frac{3}{2}+4-1-3}$$

$$= 2^{-\frac{7}{2}} \times 3^{-\frac{3}{2}} = \frac{1}{2^{\frac{7}{2}}} \times \frac{1}{3^{\frac{3}{2}}}$$

$$= \frac{1}{2^3 \times 2^{\frac{1}{2}} \times 3^1 \times 3^{\frac{3}{2}}} = \frac{1}{2^3 \times 3 \times \sqrt{2} \times \sqrt{3}}$$

$$= \frac{1}{24\sqrt{6}}$$

(Note the use of multiplication sign to separate bases when they are arithmetical values.)

Now multiply numerator and denominator by $\sqrt{6}$ (this is called *rationalizing* the fraction)

$$X = \frac{1 \times \sqrt{6}}{24 \times \sqrt{6} \times \sqrt{6}} = \frac{\sqrt{6}}{24 \times 6} = \frac{\sqrt{6}}{144} = \frac{2 \cdot 449}{144}$$

$$= 0 \cdot 017$$

(c) Given $p_1 v_1^n = p_2 v_2^n$ obtain an expression for the ratio of v_1 to v_2, i.e. $\dfrac{v_1}{v_2}$.

[This example involves index laws and some *transposition* (rearrangement) of formulae.]

$$p_1 v_1^n = p_2 v_2^n$$

(Note the index refers to v_1 and v_2 *not* p_1 and p_2)

Divide each side by p_1 and v_2^n

$$\frac{v_1^n}{v_2^n} = \frac{p_2}{p_1}$$

Since the index is the same for both v_1 and v_2, we may write

$$\frac{v_1^n}{v_2^n} = \left(\frac{v_1}{v_2}\right)^n$$

$$\therefore \left(\frac{v_1}{v_2}\right)^n = \frac{p_2}{p_1}$$

Take the nth root of each side (or raise each side to the power of $1/n$)

then $\dfrac{v_1}{v_2} = \left(\dfrac{p_2}{p_1}\right)^{\frac{1}{n}} \cdot \left(\text{could be written } \sqrt[n]{\dfrac{p_2}{p_1}} \cdot \right)$

(d) Evaluate $W = a^{4/n}\sqrt{(a^m a^{3p})}$ when $a = 2$, $m = 3$, $n = 2$, $p = 3$.

Substituting the given values

$$W = (2)^{\frac{4}{2}}\sqrt{(2^3 \times 2^9)}$$

Clearly all the numbers involved can be expressed in powers of 2.

$$\therefore W = (2)^2 \times (2^3 \times 2^9)^{\frac{1}{2}}$$
$$= 2^2 \times 2^{12 \times \frac{1}{2}}$$
$$= 2^2 \times 2^6 = 2^8 = \underline{256}$$

(e) Using logarithms, evaluate $(0 \cdot 657)^{1 \cdot 41}$.

Let $\qquad N = (0 \cdot 657)^{1 \cdot 41}$

then $\qquad \log N = 1 \cdot 41 \times \log (0 \cdot 657)$
$$= 1 \cdot 41 \times \bar{1} \cdot 8176$$

Now $\bar{1} \cdot 8176$ is a *mixed number* and must be written as

$$\bar{1} \cdot 8176 = -1 + 0 \cdot 8176 = -0 \cdot 1824$$
$$\therefore \log N = 1 \cdot 41 \times (-0 \cdot 1824)$$
$$= -1 \cdot 41 \times 0 \cdot 1824$$

Logarithms are only used to multiply positive numbers
$\therefore$ Logarithms are used to find the value of $1 \cdot 41 \times 0 \cdot 1824$

$$\therefore \log N = -0 \cdot 2571$$

No.	Log
1·41	0·1492
0·1824	$\bar{1}$·2610
0·2571	$\bar{1}$·4102

To find N this logarithm must be put in mixed number form

$$-0 \cdot 2571 = -1 + 0 \cdot 7429 = \bar{1} \cdot 7429$$
$$\therefore \log N = \bar{1} \cdot 7429$$
$$\therefore N = \text{antilog } \bar{1} \cdot 7429 = \underline{0 \cdot 5533}$$

(f) Using logarithms evaluate

$$P = 17 \cdot 2 x^m y^n$$

when $x = 1 \cdot 87$, $y = 0 \cdot 286$, $m = 1 \cdot 35$, $n = 2 \cdot 3$.
Substituting the given values

$$P = 17 \cdot 2 \times (1 \cdot 87)^{1 \cdot 35} \times (0 \cdot 286)^{2 \cdot 3}$$

(*Note:* The introduction of the multiplication signs when the numerical values are substituted in the formula.)

Taking logarithms of each side of the expression

$$\log P = \log 17 \cdot 2 + \log (1 \cdot 87)^{1 \cdot 35} + \log (0 \cdot 286)^{2 \cdot 3}$$
$$= \log 17 \cdot 2 + [1 \cdot 35 \times \log 1 \cdot 87] + [2 \cdot 3 \times \log 0 \cdot 286]$$
$$= 1 \cdot 2355 + [1 \cdot 35 \times 0 \cdot 2718] + [2 \cdot 3 \times \bar{1} \cdot 4564]$$
$$= 1 \cdot 2355 + [1 \cdot 35 \times 0 \cdot 2718] + [2 \cdot 3 \times (-0 \cdot 5436)]$$
$$= 1 \cdot 2355 + [1 \cdot 35 \times 0 \cdot 2718] - [2 \cdot 3 \times 0 \cdot 5436]$$

The values of the products in square brackets must now be obtained by using logarithms.

$$\therefore \ \log P = 1 \cdot 2355 + 0 \cdot 3669 - 1 \cdot 2500$$
$$= 1 \cdot 6024 - 1 \cdot 2500 = 0 \cdot 3524$$
$$\therefore \qquad P = \text{antilog } 0 \cdot 3524 = \underline{2 \cdot 251}$$

No.	Log
1·35	0·1303
0·2718	$\bar{1}$·4343
0·3669	$\bar{1}$·5646

No.	Log
2·3	0·3617
0·5436	$\bar{1}$·7353
1·2500	0·0970

Examples 1

1. Simplify and evaluate

$$\frac{2^5 \times 3^2 \times 5^{\frac{3}{2}}}{2^3 \times 3^{-2} \times 5^2}$$

2. Simplify the expression

$$\frac{\sqrt{(a^3)} \times \sqrt[3]{(b^4)}}{\sqrt[3]{(a^5)} \times (b^{\frac{1}{2}})^5}$$

expressing the result with positive indices.

3. Using the rules of indices simplify the expression

$$\frac{p^{2x}q^{5y}r^z}{p^x q^y} \div \frac{p^{3x}q^{4y}r^{3z}}{q^{2y}r^{2z}}$$

4. If

$$P = \frac{WL^2 X^4}{YZ^2}$$

transpose the formula to find an expression for L.

5. Transpose the formula
$$f = \frac{1}{2\pi\sqrt{(LC)}}$$
to obtain an expression for L.

6. Simplify and evaluate
$$\sqrt{\left(\frac{10^6 \times 10^3}{10^2}\right)}$$

7. If $xy^5 = XY^5$ obtain an expression for the ratio of y to Y.

8. If $V = 2d^2\sqrt{P}$, transpose the formula to find P.

9. Use logarithms to evaluate $(2\cdot31)^{-1\cdot56}$.

10. Use logarithms to evaluate $\sqrt[3]{[(3\cdot2)^7 + (5\cdot5)^4]}$.

11. Evaluate $(0\cdot587)^{1\cdot61}$.

12. Evaluate $(0\cdot0852)^{-1\cdot51}$.

13. Evaluate
$$\frac{(37\cdot63)^3 \times (0\cdot059)^2 \times (49\cdot63)^{0\cdot13}}{15\cdot2 \times 0\cdot007\,63}$$

14. If $pv^n = c$, calculate the value of c when $p = 15$, $v = 6\cdot6$ and $n = 1\cdot5$.

15. Using substitution of the values given and logarithms, find the value of
$$E = \tfrac{1}{2}(1 - e^2)\frac{Mm}{M + m}(V - U)^2 \quad \text{when} \quad M = 257\cdot5, \quad m = 201\cdot6, \quad V = 11,$$
$U = 9$ and $e = 0\cdot66$.

16. If $Q = 3\cdot1 \times L^{1\cdot03} \times H^{1\cdot47}$, calculate the value of Q when $L = 17\cdot8$ and $H = 4\cdot75$.

17. Transpose the formula $n = KH^{1\cdot25} P^{-0\cdot5}$ to find K, and evaluate K when $n = 200$, $P = 80$ and $H = 12$.

18. A certain constant c is found from the formula $c = Pn^{-3\cdot5} d^{-5\cdot5}$. Calculate c when $P = 0\cdot1$, $d = 4$ and $n = 500$.

19. Use logarithms to evaluate:

(i) $(0\cdot25)^{0\cdot25}$, (ii) $(92\cdot01)^{-1\cdot3}$, (iii) $\dfrac{1}{(0\cdot080\,72)^{0\cdot75}}$

20. Evaluate
$$\frac{(82\cdot64)^{-1\cdot2}}{\log_{10}2\cdot718}$$

21. Evaluate $(0\cdot03)^{0\cdot6}$.

22. Evaluate (a) $(0\cdot87)^{1\cdot3}$, (b) $(0\cdot0714)^{-1\cdot56}$.

23. A formula relating tensions at different positions in a rope wrapped round a cylinder is $T = T_1 e^{\mu\theta}$. Calculate T when $T_1 = 75$, $e = 2\cdot718$, $\mu = 0\cdot168$ and $\theta = 10$.

24. A formula giving the current i at time t in terms of the initial current I is $i = Ie^{-t/CR}$. Calculate the value of i when $I = 5\cdot8$, $e = 2\cdot718$, $t = 5\cdot1$, $C = 2 \times 10^{-6}$ and $R = 5 \times 10^6$.

25. In calculating the work done when a gas expands, the work done W (units) is given by
$$W = \frac{c}{n - 1}\left(\frac{1}{v_1^{n-1}} - \frac{1}{v_2^{n-1}}\right)$$
Calculate W when $c = 12\,500$, $n = 1\cdot41$, $v_1 = 5$ and $v_2 = 9$.

2

Exponential Equations

2.1 Solution of Equations of Type $a^{x+1} = b^{2x-1}$

Examples:

(i) Consider the equation $5^{2x+1} = 3^{2x-1}$.

The equation will be solved if a value of x can be found to satisfy the equality. This statement is equivalent to a statement like $X = Y$, from which it follows that $\log X = \log Y$. Similarly using logarithms to base 10 it can be stated that

$$\log_{10}(5^{2x+1}) = \log_{10}(3^{2x-1})$$

(*Note:* $(2x + 1)$ is the complete index of 5, $(2x - 1)$ is the complete index of 3.)

$$\therefore \ (2x + 1)\log_{10} 5 = (2x - 1)\log_{10} 3$$

A simple equation to calculate x has now been found.

Now substitute the values of $\log_{10} 5$ and $\log_{10} 3$

$$(2x + 1) \times 0.6990 = (2x-1) \times 0.4771$$

Remove the brackets:

$$1.3980x + 0.6990 = 0.9542x - 0.4771$$

$$1.3980x - 0.9542x = -0.4771 - 0.6990$$

$$x(1.3980 - 0.9542) = -1.1761$$

$$x(0.4438) = -1.1761$$

$$x = \frac{-1.1761}{0.4438}$$

No.	Log
1·176	0·0704
0·4438	$\bar{1}$·6472
2·650	0·4232

$$x = -2.650$$

(*Note:* The nearest 4-figure values are used to read the tables.)

10

(ii) If $pv^n = c$, calculate n when $c = 150$, $p = 3.8$, $v = 12$.

The value of n can be found by transposing the formula first and then substituting the given numerical values *or* substituting the values and solving the equation obtained.

(*Note:* pv^n means $p \times v^n$.)

Taking logarithms of both sides of the equation

$$\log_{10}(pv^n) = \log_{10} c$$

$$\therefore \log p + \log v^n = \log c$$

$$\log p + n \log v = \log c$$

Substitute the numerical values for p, v and c.

$$\log 3.8 + n \times \log 12 = \log 150$$

$$0.5798 + n \times 1.0792 = 2.1761$$

$$n \times 1.0792 = 2.1761 - 0.5798$$

$$n \times 1.0792 = 1.5963$$

$$n = \frac{1.5963}{1.0792}$$

$$n = \underline{1.479}$$

No.	Log
1·596	0·2031
1·079	0·0330
1·479	0·1701

2.2 Naperian Logarithms (Hyperbolic Logarithms)

These are logarithms to base e where e is a special base, and e = 2·718 to four significant figures. Logarithms to this base can be read from tables provided in standard books of tables.

Logarithms provided are only for numbers between 1 and 10.

(*Note:* From tables $\log_e 1 = 0$, $\log_e 10 = 2.3026$.)

The tables are used to find logarithms to base e as illustrated:

Examples:

(i) $\log_e 5.783 = \underline{1.7549}$

(ii) $\log_e 578.3 = \log_e (5.783 \times 10^2)$

$$= \log_e 5.783 + \log_e 10^2$$

Usually $\log_e 10^n$ is found from the foot of the table for $n = 1, 2, 3, \ldots$

$$\therefore \ \log_e 578 \cdot 3 = 1 \cdot 7549 + 4 \cdot 6052$$
$$= \underline{6 \cdot 3601}$$

(iii) $\log_e 0 \cdot 057\,83 = \log_e \left(\dfrac{5 \cdot 783}{10^2} \right)$

$$= \log_e 5 \cdot 783 - \log_e 10^2$$
$$= 1 \cdot 7549 - 4 \cdot 6052$$
$$= -(4 \cdot 6052 - 1 \cdot 7549)$$
$$= \underline{-2 \cdot 8503}$$

This could be expressed as a mixed number $\bar{3} \cdot 1497$, but the $\bar{3}$ has *not the same significance as $\bar{3}$ used with common logarithms*.

Alternatively (iii) could be found as follows:

$$\log_e 0 \cdot 057\,83 = \log_e (5 \cdot 7\,83 \times 10^{-2})$$
$$= \log_e 5 \cdot 783 + \log_e 10^{-2}$$
$$= 1 \cdot 7549 + \bar{3} \cdot 3948$$
$$= \bar{3} \cdot 1497 = \underline{-2 \cdot 8503}$$

2.2.1 Antilogarithms to base e

When antilog$_e$ x is found, the value is e^x.

Examples:

(i) To find antilog$_e$ $2 \cdot 0795$
Since the tables give values up to $2 \cdot 3026$, this can be found directly from the table

$$\text{antilog}_e\ 2 \cdot 0795 = 8 \cdot 001$$

(ii) To find antilog$_e$ $6 \cdot 7832$
From the foot of the table $\log_e 10^2 = 4 \cdot 6052$
Subtract this from $6 \cdot 7832$: $6 \cdot 7832 - 4 \cdot 6052$ giving $2 \cdot 1780$
Now antilog$_e$ $2 \cdot 1780 = 8 \cdot 829$
Since $\log_e 10^2$ was subtracted this was equivalent to dividing the answer by 100

$$\therefore \ \text{Antilog}_e\ 6 \cdot 7832 = 100 \times 8 \cdot 829 = \underline{882 \cdot 9}$$

(iii) Antilog$_e$ (−5·6783)

Add 6·9078 (equivalent to multiplying by 10^3)

This gives 6·9078 − 5·6783 = 1·2295

antilog$_e$ (1·2295) = 3·420 (nearly)

∴ antilog$_e$ (−5·6783) = 3·420 ÷ 10^3 = 0·003 42

OR antilog$_e$ (−5·6783) = antilog$_e$ ($\bar{6}$·321$\bar{7}$)

Subtract $\bar{7}$·9022 (equivalent to dividing by 10^{-3})

This gives $\bar{6}$·3217 − $\bar{7}$·0922 = 1·2295

antilog$_e$ (1·2295) = 3·420 (nearly)

∴ antilog$_e$ (−5·6783) = 3·420 × 10^{-3} = 0·003 42

2.3 Change of Base of Logarithms

It is possible (though not generally necessary) to obtain logarithms of numbers to any base. Since tables are only provided for logarithms to, at the most, two bases, a conversion formula is required.

Let
$$a^x = b^y = N$$

then
$$\log_a N = x, \log_b N = y$$

Take logs to base a of each side

$$x = y \times \log_a b$$

$$\therefore \log_a N = (\log_b N) \times \log_a b$$

$$\therefore \log_b N = \frac{1}{\log_a b} \times \log_a N = \frac{\log_a N}{\log_a b}$$

This is a standard formula for the conversion of logarithms.

Examples:

$$\text{(i) } \log_5 17 = \frac{\log_{10} 17}{\log_{10} 5} = \frac{1·2304}{0·6990} = \underline{1·760}$$

$$\text{(ii) } \log_3 58 = \frac{\log_{10} 58}{\log_{10} 3} = \frac{1·7634}{0·4771} = \underline{3·696}$$

(*Note:* that base chosen is usually $a = 10$.)

2.3.1 Calculation of logarithms to base e using base 10

This is the most important application of the change of base formula.

$$\log_e N = \frac{\log_{10} N}{\log_{10} e} = \frac{\log_{10} N}{\log_{10} 2 \cdot 718} = \frac{\log_{10} N}{0 \cdot 4343}$$

Now if the reciprocal of $0 \cdot 4343$ is calculated, it is found to be $2 \cdot 3026$. (This is the same as $\log_e 10$—see tables.)

Hence $\underline{\log_e N = 2 \cdot 3026 \log_{10} N}$ (approx. $2 \cdot 203 \log_{10} N$)

Examples:

(i) $\log_e 17 \cdot 6 = 2 \cdot 303 \log_{10} 17 \cdot 6$

$2 \cdot 303$	$0 \cdot 3623$
$1 \cdot 245$	$0 \cdot 0953$
$2 \cdot 868$	$0 \cdot 4576$

$\qquad\qquad = 2 \cdot 303 \times 1 \cdot 2455$

$\qquad\qquad = \underline{2 \cdot 868}$

(If this is read from Naperian tables it is found to be $2 \cdot 8679$.)

(ii) $\log_e 0 \cdot 176 = 2 \cdot 303 \times \log_{10} 0 \cdot 176$

$\qquad\qquad = 2 \cdot 303 \times \bar{1} \cdot 2455$

$\qquad\qquad = -2 \cdot 303 \times 0 \cdot 7545$

$\qquad\qquad = \underline{-1 \cdot 738}$

WORKED EXAMPLES

(*a*) Solve the equation $(3 \cdot 8)^{3x+1} = (11 \cdot 7)^{x+2}$.

$$(3x + 1) \log_{10} 3 \cdot 8 = (x + 2) \log_{10} (11 \cdot 7)$$

$$(3x + 1) \times 0 \cdot 5798 = (x + 2) \times 1 \cdot 0682$$

$$1 \cdot 7394x + 0 \cdot 5798 = 1 \cdot 0682x + 2 \cdot 1364$$

$$(1 \cdot 7394 - 1 \cdot 0682)x = 2 \cdot 1364 - 0 \cdot 5798$$

$$0 \cdot 6712x = 1 \cdot 5566$$

$$\therefore \; x = \frac{1 \cdot 5566}{0 \cdot 6712}$$

$$\therefore \; \underline{x = 2 \cdot 319}$$

$$\begin{array}{r} 0 \cdot 1922 \\ \bar{1} \cdot 8268 \\ \hline 0 \cdot 3654 \end{array}$$

(b) If $y = ax^n$, find a and n if $y = 1{\cdot}75$ when $x = 3{\cdot}1$ and $y = 9{\cdot}7$ when $x = 4{\cdot}2$.

$$\log y = \log a + n \times \log x$$
$$\therefore \log 1{\cdot}75 = \log a + n \times \log 3{\cdot}1$$
$$\log 9{\cdot}7 = \log a + n \times \log 4{\cdot}2, \quad \text{substitute logarithms}$$
$$\therefore 0{\cdot}2430 = \log a + n \times 0{\cdot}4914$$
$$0{\cdot}9868 = \log a + n \times 0{\cdot}6232$$

$\qquad\qquad\qquad\qquad\qquad\qquad\qquad\qquad\quad \overline{1}{\cdot}8715$
$\qquad\qquad\qquad\qquad\qquad\qquad\qquad\qquad\quad \overline{1}{\cdot}1199$

Subtract $\qquad\qquad\qquad\qquad\qquad\qquad\qquad\quad \overline{0{\cdot}7516}$

$$0{\cdot}7438 = n \times 0{\cdot}1318$$

$\qquad\qquad\qquad\qquad\qquad\qquad\qquad\qquad\quad 0{\cdot}7516$

$$\therefore n = \frac{0{\cdot}7438}{0{\cdot}1318} = \underline{5{\cdot}644} \qquad\qquad\qquad \overline{1}{\cdot}7946$$

$\qquad\qquad\qquad\qquad\qquad\qquad\qquad\qquad\quad \overline{0{\cdot}5462}$

$$\log a = 0{\cdot}9868 - 5{\cdot}644 \times 0{\cdot}6232$$
$$= 0{\cdot}9868 - 3{\cdot}5180$$
$$= \overline{3}{\cdot}4688$$
$$\therefore a = \text{antilog } \overline{3}{\cdot}4688 = \underline{0{\cdot}002\ 943}$$

Hence $\qquad\qquad\qquad y = 0{\cdot}002\ 94 x^{5{\cdot}644}$

(c) Given $p_1 = 585$, $v_1 = 3{\cdot}7$, $v_2 = 15{\cdot}6$, evaluate W, if

$$W = p_1 v_1 \log_e \left(\frac{v_2}{v_1}\right).$$

$$W = 585 \times 3{\cdot}7 \times \log_e \left(\frac{15{\cdot}6}{3{\cdot}7}\right)$$

$\qquad\qquad\qquad\qquad\qquad\qquad\qquad\qquad\quad 2{\cdot}3026$
$\qquad\qquad\qquad\qquad\qquad\qquad\qquad\qquad\quad 0{\cdot}4447$

$$= 585 \times 3{\cdot}7 \times (\log_e 15{\cdot}6 - \log_e 3{\cdot}7) \qquad \overline{2{\cdot}7473}$$

$$= 585 \times 3{\cdot}7 \times (2{\cdot}7473 - 1{\cdot}3083)$$

$$= 585 \times 3{\cdot}7 \times 1{\cdot}4390 \qquad\qquad\qquad 2{\cdot}7672$$

$\qquad\qquad\qquad\qquad\qquad\qquad\qquad\qquad\quad 0{\cdot}5682$

$$= \text{antilog } 3{\cdot}4935 \qquad\qquad\qquad\qquad 0{\cdot}1581$$

$$\underline{W = 3116.} \qquad\qquad\qquad\qquad\qquad \overline{3{\cdot}4935}$$

(d) Using logarithms to base 10, find the value of

$$P = mt \log_e \left(\frac{ab}{c}\right)$$

when $m = 176$, $t = 0.52$, $a = 11.5$, $b = 3.4$, $c = 2.3$.

$$P = 176 \times 0.52 \times \log_e \left(\frac{11.5 \times 3.4}{2.3} \right)$$

$$= 176 \times 0.52 \times 2.303 \log_{10} \left(\frac{11.5 \times 3.4}{2.3} \right)$$

$$= 176 \times 0.52 \times 2.303 \times (\log_{10} 11.5 + \log_{10} 3.4 - \log_{10} 2.3)$$

$$= 176 \times 0.52 \times 2.303 \times (1.0607 + 0.5315 - 0.3617)$$

$$= 176 \times 0.52 \times 2.303 \times 1.2305$$

$$= \text{antilog } 2.4138$$

$$\therefore \underline{P = 259.3}$$

$$2.2455$$
$$\bar{1}.7160$$
$$0.3623$$
$$0.0900$$
$$\overline{2.4138}$$

Examples 2

1. Solve the equation $3^x = 5^{2x-1}$.
2. Find the value of x which satisfies $7^{3x-2} = e^{x+1}$ ($e = 2.718$).
3. Solve the equation $(7.16)^y = (1.92)^{y+2}$.
4. If $3^{2x-1} = e^{x+1}$ and $e = 2.718$, find the value of x.
5. Use logarithms to solve the equation $10^{5-3t} = 2^{7-2t}$.
6. Solve $(0.7)^n = 0.4$.
7. Solve the equation $2^x \times 15^x = 5$.
8. Find p when $5^{p+1} = 8^p$.
9. In a gas expansion the law connecting pressure p and volume v is $pv^n = c$. Calculate n when $c = 30\,000$, $p = 110$, $v = 17$.
10. A law connecting current I amps required to fuse a wire of diameter d thousandths of an inch is $I = Kd^m$. Calculate K and m if $I = 2.1$ when $d = 22$, and $I = 5.8$ when $d = 36$.
11. If the law connecting two quantities s and t is $s = ae^{bt}$, find a and b given $s = 2$ when $t = 1$, and $s = 1$ when $t = 2$. (It is preferable to use logs to base e.)
12. If the law connecting the two variables x and y is of the form $y = ax^n$, determine a and n given $y = 7.08$ when $x = 1.2$, and $y = 56$ when $x = 4.6$.
13. Obtain the values of a and b to satisfy the law $y = ac^{bx}$ given $y = 1$ when $x = 1$, and $y = 1.2$ when $x = 1.5$ ($e = 2.718$). (It is preferable to use logs to base e.)
14. The law connecting the tension T in a rope lapped round a cylinder is $T = T_1 e^{\mu\theta}$, where T_1 is the initial tension, μ the coefficient of friction, θ the angle of lap in radians. If $T = 20$ when $\theta = 3$, and $T = 100$ when $\theta = 23$, find the values of T_1 and μ. (It is preferable to use logs to base e.)

15. Using Naperian logarithm tables, find the values of (i) $\log_e 7\cdot285$, (ii) $\log_e 532\cdot6$, (iii) $\log_e 0\cdot0534$.

16. Using Naperian logarithm tables, find the value of (i) $\text{antilog}_e 1\cdot9687$, (ii) $\text{antilog}_e 8\cdot3562$, (iii) $\text{antilog}_e (-6\cdot3285)$.

17. Using logarithms to *base* 10, calculate the values of (i) $\log_e 15\cdot62$, (ii) $\log_e 1762$, (iii) $\log_e 0\cdot138$.

18. If $P = 5ab \log_e \left(\dfrac{x}{y}\right)$, calculate the value of P, given $a = 3\cdot7$, $b = 17\cdot6$, $x = 17$, $y = 5$.

19. Calculate θ from the formula

$$\theta = \frac{1}{\mu} \log_e \left(\frac{T_2}{T_1}\right)$$

when $\mu = 0\cdot15$, $T_2 = 125$, $T_1 = 17$.

20. Calculate W, the work done in Joules by a gas expanding isothermally,

if
$$W = p_1 v_1 \log_e \left(\frac{v_2}{v_1}\right)$$

when $p_1 = 2160$, $v_1 = 1\cdot5$, $v_2 = 8\cdot2$.

21. The time, t seconds, for a voltage to drop from E to V is given by

$$t = CR \log_e \left(\frac{E}{V}\right).$$

Calculate t when $C = 2 \times 10^{-6}$, $R = 1\cdot5 \times 10^6$, $E = 20$, $V = 13$.

22. Evaluate $\log_8 19$.

23. Evaluate $\log_5 38\cdot2$.

24. Evaluate $\log_e (13\cdot1 \times 7\cdot6)$.

25. Evaluate $\log_e \left(\dfrac{39\cdot6}{8\cdot5}\right)$.

3

Algebraic Revision

3.1 Products, Factors and Fractions

3.1.1 Removal of brackets

This process is often used during the simplification of expressions, necessary when solving equations and transposing formulae.

Examples:

(i) $3x(2x + 4y - z) = 6x^2 + 12xy - 3xz$

(ii) $-5ab(2a + 3b - 4c) = -10a^2b - 15ab^2 + 20abc$

(iii) $2x(3x + y) - 3y(3x + 2y) = 6x^2 + 2xy - 9xy - 6y^2$
$$= 6x^2 - 7xy - 6y^2$$

(iv) $(5a + 2b)(3a - 4b) = 5a(3a - 4b) + 2b(3a - 4b)$
$$= 15a^2 - 20ab + 6ab - 8b^2$$
$$= 15a^2 - 14ab - 8b^2$$

(v) $(X + Y)(X + Y) = X(X + Y) + Y(X + Y)$
$$= X^2 + 2XY + Y^2$$

(vi) $(X - Y)(X - Y) = X(X - Y) - Y(X - Y)$
$$= X^2 - 2XY + Y^2$$

(vii) $(X - Y)(X + Y) = X(X + Y) - Y(X + Y)$
$$= X^2 - Y^2$$

(v), (vi) and (vii) are of particular importance and should be memorized as:

$$(X + Y)^2 = X^2 + 2XY + Y^2$$
$$(X - Y)^2 = X^2 - 2XY + Y^2$$
$$(X - Y)(X + Y) = X^2 - Y^2$$

These results may be applied more widely.

Examples:

(i) $(4a + 3b)^2 = (4a)^2 + 2(4a)(3b) + (3b)^2$
$$= 16a^2 + 24ab + 9b^2$$

(ii) $(7p - 2q)^2 = (7p)^2 - 2(7p)(2q) + (2q)^2$
$$= 49p^2 - 28pq + 4q^2$$

(iii) $(3l - 4m)(3l + 4m) = (3l)^2 - (4m)^2$
$$= 9l^2 - 16m^2$$

3.1.2 Factorization

This is a process which is the reverse of bracket removal. It may often be required when dealing with transposition of formulae.

Examples:

(i) $3a^2b + 9b^2a - 15abc = 3ab(a + 3b - 5c)$

(ii) $20x^2 + 12xy - 5xy - 3y^2 = 4x(5x + 3y) - y(5x + 3y)$
$$= (4x - y)(5x + 3y)$$

(iii) $\qquad 6x^2 - 7x - 20 = 6x^2 - 15x + 8x - 20$

(*Note:* Split into four terms such that $6 \times -20 = -15 \times +8$.)
$$= 3x(2x - 5) + 4(2x - 5)$$
$$= (3x + 4)(2x - 5)$$

(iv) $\quad 14m^2 + 19mn - 3n^2 = 14m^2 + 21mn - 2mn - 3n^2$

(*Note:* Split $+19$ into numbers whose product is $-3 \times 14 = -42$, i.e. $19 = +21 - 2$.)
$$= 7m(2m + 3n) - n(2m + 3n)$$
$$= (7m - n)(2m + 3n)$$

(v) $$16a^2 - 9b^2 = (4a)^2 - (3b)^2$$
$$= (4a - 3b)(4a + 3b)$$

(using $X^2 - Y^2 = (X - Y)(X + Y)$)

(vi) $(2x + 3y)^2 - (x - y)^2$
$$= [(2x + 3y) - (x - y)][(2x + 3y) + (x - y)]$$
$$= (x + 4y)(3x + 2y)$$

3.1.3 Fractions

Addition and subtraction of fractions are illustrated as follows:

Examples:

(i) $$\frac{5}{3x} + \frac{7}{9x^2} - \frac{4}{xy} = \frac{5(3xy) + 7(y) - 4(9x)}{9x^2 y}$$
$$= \frac{15xy + 7y - 36x}{9x^2 y}$$

(ii) $$\frac{5}{2x + 1} - \frac{3}{2x - 1} = \frac{5(2x - 1) - 3(2x + 1)}{(2x + 1)(2x - 1)}$$
$$= \frac{10x - 5 - 6x - 3}{4x^2 - 1}$$
$$= \frac{4x - 8}{4x^2 - 1} = \frac{4(x - 2)}{4x^2 - 1}$$

(iii) $$\frac{x + 2}{x - 1} - \frac{3x}{x + 1} + \frac{2}{x^2 - 1}$$
$$= \frac{(x + 2)(x + 1) - 3x(x - 1) + 2}{(x - 1)(x + 1)}$$
$$= \frac{x^2 + 3x + 2 - 3x^2 + 3x + 2}{x^2 - 1}$$
$$= \frac{-2x^2 + 6x + 4}{x^2 - 1} = \frac{2(2 + 3x - x^2)}{x^2 - 1}$$

(*Note:* Such operations make use of bracket removal and factorization.)

3.2 Transposition of Formulae

This is one of the most important applications of algebra met with in *practical mathematics*. The reason is that formulae are usually *memorized in one form*, but it may be necessary to use them in *another form*.

Illustration:

The volume of a sphere is given by the formula $V = \frac{4}{3}\pi r^3$, where r is the radius of the sphere. (This is the usual formula memorized.)

Find the formula for the radius of a sphere of volume V. (This is done by transposing the formula.)

Proceed as follows:

Multiply by 3

$$3V = 4\pi r^3$$

Divide by 4π

$$\frac{3V}{4\pi} = r^3, \quad \text{or} \quad r^3 = \frac{3V}{4\pi}$$

Take the cube root of each side

$$r = \sqrt[3]{\frac{3V}{4\pi}}$$

(*Note:* Three steps are required to transpose the formula. Such steps are necessary to *transpose correctly*.)

3.2.1 Rules for the correct transposition of formulae

1. Add the same quantity to each side.
2. Subtract the same quantity from each side.
3. Multiply each side by the same quantity.
4. Divide each side by the same quantity.
5. Remove brackets or factorize as required.
6. Take the same power or root of each side.

(*Note:* Quantity—may often include letters and numbers. It is necessary to use *some* or all of these rules to transpose correctly.)

3.2.2 Harder examples in transposition

(i) Transpose the formula $V = \pi h[\sqrt{(r^2 + h^2)} - S]$ to obtain the formula for r.

(*Note:* So long as *correct rules* are applied at each stage in the transposition, there may be different orders used.)

A correct method would be as follows:
Divide each side by πh

$$\frac{V}{\pi h} = \sqrt{(r^2 + h^2)} - S$$

Add S to each side

$$\frac{V}{\pi h} + S = \sqrt{(r^2 + h^2)}$$

Square each side

$$\left(\frac{V}{\pi h} + S\right)^2 = r^2 + h^2$$

Subtract h^2 from each side

$$\left(\frac{V}{\pi h} + S\right)^2 - h^2 = r^2$$

Take the square root of each side and interchange sides; then

$$r = \sqrt{\left[\left(\frac{V}{\pi h} + S\right)^2 - h^2\right]}$$

or

$$r = \left[\left(\frac{V}{\pi h} + S\right)^2 - h^2\right]^{\frac{1}{2}}$$

(ii) Transpose the formula $v = V(1 - e^{-at})$ to find t. (The steps will not be stated in each case.)

$\dfrac{v}{V} = 1 - e^{-at}$. Add e^{-at} to each side and subtract $\dfrac{v}{V}$

$$e^{-at} = 1 - \frac{v}{V} = \frac{V - v}{V}$$

$$e^{at} = \frac{V}{V - v} \qquad \text{(note inversion here)}$$

Take logarithms to base e of each side:

$$at = \log_e \left(\frac{V}{V - v} \right)$$

$$\therefore \; t = \frac{1}{a} \log_e \left(\frac{V}{V - v} \right)$$

3.3 Surds (Quadratic)—Rationalization

3.3.1 Surds

A surd is a form like $\sqrt{3}$, $\sqrt{(ax + b)}$, etc.
Compound surds may be of the form $\sqrt{a} + \sqrt{b}$.
Conjugate surds are $\sqrt{a} + \sqrt{b}$, $\sqrt{a} - \sqrt{b}$.

Special notes:

(1) $$\sqrt{a} \times \sqrt{b} = \sqrt{(ab)}$$

(2) $$(\sqrt{a} - \sqrt{b})(\sqrt{a} + \sqrt{b}) = (\sqrt{a})^2 - (\sqrt{b})^2 = a - b$$

Examples:

(i) Simplify (by reducing to the lowest surd forms)

$$3\sqrt{125} + 7\sqrt{45} + \sqrt{27} - 4\sqrt{75}$$
$$= 3\sqrt{(25 \times 5)} + 7\sqrt{(9 \times 5)} + \sqrt{(9 \times 3)} - 4\sqrt{(25 \times 3)}$$
$$= 15\sqrt{5} + 21\sqrt{5} + 3\sqrt{3} - 20\sqrt{3}$$
$$= \underline{36\sqrt{5} - 17\sqrt{3}}$$

(ii) Simplify $(2\sqrt{5} - 3\sqrt{2})(7\sqrt{5} + 4\sqrt{2})$

$$= (2\sqrt{5}) \times (7\sqrt{5}) + (2\sqrt{5}) \times (4\sqrt{2}) - (3\sqrt{2}) \times (7\sqrt{5})$$
$$\quad - (3\sqrt{2}) \times (4\sqrt{2})$$
$$= 14(\sqrt{5})^2 + 8\sqrt{5} \times \sqrt{2} - 21\sqrt{2} \times \sqrt{5} - 12(\sqrt{2})^2$$
$$= 14 \times 5 + 8\sqrt{10} - 21\sqrt{10} - 12 \times 2$$
$$= \underline{46 - 13\sqrt{10}}$$

3.3.2 Rationalization

This is a process used with fractions in order to remove surds from the denominator.

Examples:

(i) Rationalize $\dfrac{1}{\sqrt{3}}$. Multiply numerator and denominator by $\sqrt{3}$.

$$\frac{1}{\sqrt{3}} = \frac{1}{\sqrt{3}} \times \frac{\sqrt{3}}{\sqrt{3}} = \frac{\sqrt{3}}{\sqrt{3} \times \sqrt{3}} = \frac{\sqrt{3}}{3} \qquad \text{or} \qquad \frac{1}{3}\sqrt{3}$$

(ii) Rationalize

$$\frac{5\sqrt{3} - 2\sqrt{2}}{3\sqrt{3} + \sqrt{2}}$$

Multiply numerator and denominator by $3\sqrt{3} - \sqrt{2}$.
(*Note:* Use is made of the *identity* $(X + Y)(X - Y) = X^2 - Y^2$.)

$$\frac{5\sqrt{3} - 2\sqrt{2}}{3\sqrt{3} + \sqrt{2}} = \frac{5\sqrt{3} - 2\sqrt{2}}{3\sqrt{3} + \sqrt{2}} \times \frac{3\sqrt{3} - \sqrt{2}}{3\sqrt{3} - \sqrt{2}}$$

$$= \frac{45 - 6\sqrt{6} - 5\sqrt{6} + 4}{(3\sqrt{3})^2 - (\sqrt{2})^2} = \frac{49 - 11\sqrt{6}}{27 - 2}$$

$$= \frac{49 - 11\sqrt{6}}{25} \qquad \text{or} \qquad \frac{1}{25}(49 - 11\sqrt{6})$$

WORKED EXAMPLES

(*a*) Simplify

$$\frac{x^2 - 2xy + y^2}{x^2 + 4xy + 3y^2} \times \frac{x^2 + xy - 6y^2}{x^2 - y^2}$$

$$= \frac{(x - y)^2 \times (x + 3y)(x - 2y)}{(x + y)(x + 3y) \times (x - y)(x + y)}$$

(Cancel out factors common to numerator and denominator.)

$$= \frac{(x - y)(x - 2y)}{(x + y)^2}$$

(b) Express $\dfrac{3a^2 + ab}{(a + b)^2} - \dfrac{a - b}{a + b} + \dfrac{b}{a - b}$ as a single fraction.

$$= \frac{(3a^2 + ab)(a - b) - (a - b)^2(a + b) + b(a + b)^2}{(a + b)^2(a - b)}$$

$$= \frac{(3a^3 - 2a^2b - b^2a) - (a + b)(a^2 - 2ab + b^2) + b(a^2 + 2ab + b^2)}{(a + b)^2(a - b)}$$

$$= \frac{\begin{aligned}(3a^3 - 2a^2b - b^2a) \\ - (a^3 - 2a^2b + ab^2 + ba^2 - 2ab^2 + b^3) + ba^2 + 2ab^2 + b^3)\end{aligned}}{(a + b)^2(a - b)}$$

$$= \frac{2a^3 + 2ab^2}{(a + b)^2(a - b)} = \frac{2a(a^2 + b^2)}{(a + b)^2(a - b)}$$

(c) Transpose the formula $\dfrac{a}{b} = \dfrac{e^x + e^{-x}}{e^x - e^{-x}}$ to find x.

$$a(e^x - e^{-x}) = b(e^x + e^{-x})$$
$$ae^x - ae^{-x} = be^x + be^{-x}$$
$$ae^x - be^x = be^{-x} + ae^{-x}$$
$$(a - b)e^x = (b + a)e^{-x} = (a + b)e^{-x}$$

Multiply each side by e^{+x}.

$$(a - b)e^x e^{+x} = (a + b)e^{-x}e^x = (a + b)e^0$$
$$(a - b)e^{2x} = (a + b)$$

$$e^{2x} = \frac{a + b}{a - b}$$

Take logs to base e of each side:

$$2x = \log_e\left(\frac{a + b}{a - b}\right)$$

$$\therefore \; x = \frac{1}{2}\log_e\left(\frac{a + b}{a - b}\right)$$

(d) Rationalize $\dfrac{3\sqrt{5} - 2\sqrt{3}}{\sqrt{5} + \sqrt{3}}$ and hence evaluate, given $\sqrt{15} = 3\cdot873$.

$$\frac{3\sqrt{5} - 2\sqrt{3}}{\sqrt{5} + \sqrt{3}} = \frac{3\sqrt{5} - 2\sqrt{3}}{\sqrt{5} + \sqrt{3}} \times \frac{\sqrt{5} - \sqrt{3}}{\sqrt{5} - \sqrt{3}}$$

$$= \frac{15 - 5\sqrt{15} + 6}{(\sqrt{5})^2 - (\sqrt{3})^2} = \frac{21 - 5\sqrt{15}}{5 - 3}$$

$$= \frac{21 - 19\cdot365}{2} = \frac{1}{2} \times 1\cdot635 = \underline{0\cdot8175}$$

Examples 3

1. Simplify $(A - B)(A^2 + AB + B^2)$ by removal of brackets.
2. Simplify $(A + B)(A^2 - AB + B^2)$ by removal of brackets.
3. Factorize $(3p + 2q)^2 - (p - q)^2$.
4. Factorize the expression $\frac{4}{3}\pi R^3 - \frac{4}{3}\pi r^3$.
5. Factorize $12m^2 + 13mn - 35n^2$.

6. Express $\dfrac{3}{x + 2} - \dfrac{5}{x^2 - 4} + \dfrac{7}{x - 2}$ as a single fraction.

7. Reduce $\dfrac{3a + 1}{2a^2 + 3a - 2} - \dfrac{a - 2}{2a^2 + 5a + 2}$ to a single fraction.

8. Express $\dfrac{5x^2 - 1}{(x + 1)^3} + \dfrac{2x}{(x + 1)^2} - \dfrac{3}{x + 1}$ as a single fraction.

9. By repeated multiplication express $(x + y)^3$ in powers of x and y.
10. By repeated multiplication express $(x - y)^4$ in powers of x and y.
11. Transpose the formula $S = \frac{1}{2}n[2a + (n - 1)d]$ to find d.

12. Rearrange the formula $S = \dfrac{a(1 - r^n)}{1 - r}$ to obtain n.

13. If $\dfrac{1}{f} = \dfrac{1}{v} + \dfrac{1}{u}$, transpose the formula to find u.

14. Transpose the formula $C = \dfrac{K(n - 1)A}{4\pi t}$ to find n.

15. The formula $T = 2\pi\sqrt{\left(\dfrac{K^2 + h^2}{hg}\right)}$ gives the period T of a compound pendulum. Transpose the formula to obtain g.

16. Rearrange $t = r\left[\sqrt{\left(\dfrac{f + r}{f - p}\right)} - 1\right]$ to find p.

17. The current I in an electrical circuit is given by $I = \dfrac{nE}{R + nr}$. Obtain the expression for n.

18. If $(1 - b)x = 1 + b$ and $(1 - c)y = 1 + c$, express $\dfrac{x - y}{1 + xy}$ in terms of b and c.

19. The formula $d = \sqrt{\left[\dfrac{2M}{xbc(1 - \frac{1}{3}x)} \right]}$ occurs in calculations relating to reinforced concrete. Transpose the formula to find M.

20. The resultant resistance R of three resistances r_1, r_2, r_3 connected in parallel is given by $\dfrac{1}{R} = \dfrac{1}{r_1} + \dfrac{1}{r_2} + \dfrac{1}{r_3}$. Rearrange the formula to express R in terms of r_1, r_2 and r_3.

21. In resisted motion, the velocity v at time t is given in terms of the initial velocity u by the formula $v = u(1 - e^{-kt})$. Obtain the expression for the time t.

22. The time t for a current to decrease from I to i is obtained from the formula $i = Ie^{-t/CR}$. Obtain the formula for t.

23. (i) Reduce $2\sqrt{63} + 5\sqrt{112} - 3\sqrt{20} + 6\sqrt{80}$ to lowest surd form.
    (ii) Reduce $\sqrt{48} - 11\sqrt{27} + 15\sqrt{18} - 3\sqrt{98}$ to lowest surd form.

24. Rationalize (i) $\dfrac{1}{\sqrt{2} - 1}$ (ii) $\dfrac{\sqrt{3} + 1}{\sqrt{3} - 1}$ (iii) $\dfrac{2\sqrt{5} - \sqrt{3}}{3\sqrt{5} + \sqrt{3}}$.

25. Rationalize $\dfrac{3\sqrt{7} - 2\sqrt{3}}{2\sqrt{7} + \sqrt{3}}$ and hence evaluate, given $\sqrt{21} = 4{\cdot}583$.

4

Simple, Simultaneous Linear and Quadratic Equations

Equations are statements of equality satisfied by one or a few values of the unknown quantities.

4.1 Simple Equations

4.1.1 Solution

When the equation has been simplified, the *one* unknown quantity only occurs to the power of 1. The operations required in order to solve equations are similar to those used in transposing formulae.

Examples:

(i) Solve the equation $3(4t - 1) - \frac{1}{4}(t + 2) = \frac{1}{3}(2t - 1) + \frac{1}{6}t$.
Multiply through by 12

$$36(4t - 1) - 3(t + 2) = 4(2t - 1) + 2t$$

Remove the brackets

$$144t - 36 - 3t - 6 = 8t - 4 + 2t$$
$$\therefore \ 131t = 38$$

Divide by 131

$$t = \tfrac{38}{131}$$

(ii) Solve the equation $\dfrac{2x + 3}{x - 4} = \dfrac{4x + 1}{2x - 5}$.

Multiply both sides by $(x - 4)(2x - 5)$

$$(2x + 3)(2x - 5) = (x - 4)(4x + 1)$$

Remove the brackets $\quad 4x^2 - 4x - 15 = 4x^2 - 15x - 4$

Simplify

$$\therefore \ 11x = 11$$
$$\therefore \quad x = 1$$

4.1.2 Simultaneous simple equations

Usually two or more unknown quantities are involved. Generally it is possible to arrive at the solutions by the following methods:
(i) *Substitution*   (ii) *Elimination*
or a combination of these two methods.

Example: Solve the equations

$$4(x + 3y) - x + 2y = 2(3x - y) + 5 \qquad \text{(i)}$$
$$2x - 3(x - 2y) = 4(x + y) - 7 \qquad \text{(ii)}$$

First simplify the two equations to the form $ax + by = c$

(i) becomes $\quad 4x + 12y - x + 2y = 6x - 2y + 5$

or $\quad\quad \underline{3x - 16y \quad\quad\quad = -5} \qquad \text{(iii)}$

(ii) becomes $\quad 2x - 3x + 6y \quad = 4x + 4y - 7$

or $\quad\quad \underline{5x - 2y \quad\quad\quad = 7} \qquad \text{(iv)}$

Multiply (iv) by 8 $\quad 40x - 16y = 56 \qquad \text{(v)}$

Subtract (iii) from (v) $\quad\quad 37x = 61$

$$\therefore \ x = \frac{61}{37}$$

y can now be found by substituting this value into (iii) or (iv). Substituting in (iv) $\quad 2y = 5x - 7 = \frac{46}{37}$

$$\therefore \ y = \frac{23}{37}$$

4.2 Quadratic Equations

These may be reduced to the *standard form* $ax^2 + bx + c = 0$, by simplification, where a, b and c do not contain x. a is called the *coefficient of x^2*, b is the *coefficient of x* and c is the *constant term*.

In general there will be two values of x which will satisfy the equation. (These may be referred to as the *solutions* or the *roots* of the equation.)

These roots may be (i) real and different, (ii) real and equal, or (iii) complex (i.e. involve $j = \sqrt{-1}$).

4.2.1 Methods for solving quadratic equations

Depending on the relationship between a, b and c, quadratic equations may be solved (i.e. their roots found) by one of the following methods:

 (i) Using *factors*.

 (ii) Using *completion of the square*.

(iii) Using a *formula*.

(iv) Using a *graph* (*or graphs*).

> Method (iv) will be illustrated in a later chapter.
> Methods (i), (ii) and (iii) are shown in the following examples.

(i) FACTORS

Example: Solve the equation $10x^2 - 29x - 21 = 0$, using *factors*.

 (*Note:* $10 \times (-21) = -210$, $-29 = -35 + 6$ and $-35 \times 6 = -210$.)

When the middle coefficient can be split in this way, the factors are found as follows:

$$10x^2 - 35x + 6x - 21 = 0$$
$$5x(2x - 7) + 3(2x - 7) = 0$$
$$\therefore (5x + 3)(2x - 7) = 0$$

Hence $\qquad 5x + 3 = 0 \qquad$ or $\qquad 2x - 7 = 0$

i.e. $\qquad\qquad x = -\dfrac{3}{5} \qquad$ or $\qquad x = \dfrac{7}{2}$

(ii) COMPLETING THE SQUARE

$X^2 + PX$ is made into a *complete square* by adding $(\tfrac{1}{2}P)^2$, i.e. $\tfrac{1}{4}P^2$; then the complete square is

$$X^2 + PX + \frac{1}{4}P^2 = \left(X + \frac{1}{2}P\right)^2$$

Example: Solve the equation $3x^2 + 4x - 5 = 0$.

$$3x^2 + 4x = 5$$

Divide through by 3, then

$$x^2 + \frac{4}{3}x = \frac{5}{3}$$

Add $\left(\dfrac{1}{2} \text{ of } \dfrac{4}{3}\right)^2$, i.e. $\dfrac{4}{9}$ to each side

$$x^2 + \frac{4}{3}x + \frac{4}{9} = \frac{5}{3} + \frac{4}{9}$$

$$= \frac{19}{9}$$

$$\therefore \left(x + \frac{2}{3}\right)^2 = \frac{19}{9}.$$

Take the square root of each side, then

$$x + \frac{2}{3} = \pm\sqrt{\frac{19}{9}} = \pm\frac{\sqrt{19}}{3}$$

$$\therefore x = -\frac{2}{3} \pm \frac{\sqrt{19}}{3} = \frac{-2 \pm \sqrt{19}}{3}$$

$$\therefore x = -2{\cdot}1196 \qquad \text{or} \qquad 0{\cdot}7863$$

(iii) METHOD USING THE FORMULA

The *formula* is obtained by *transposing* $ax^2 + bx + c = 0$.
The *completion of square* method is used as follows:
Divide by a

$$x^2 + \frac{b}{a} x + \frac{c}{a} = 0$$

$$\therefore\ x^2 + \frac{b}{a} x = -\frac{c}{a}$$

Add $\left(\frac{1}{2} \text{ of } \frac{b}{a}\right)^2 = \left(\frac{b}{2a}\right)^2 = \frac{b^2}{4a^2}$ to each side. Then

$$x^2 + \frac{b}{a} x + \frac{b^2}{4a^2} = -\frac{c}{a} + \frac{b^2}{4a^2} = \frac{b^2 - 4ac}{4a^2}$$

$$\therefore\ \left(x + \frac{b}{2a}\right)^2 = \frac{b^2 - 4ac}{4a^2}$$

Take the square root of each side

$$x + \frac{b}{2a} = \pm\sqrt{\frac{b^2 - 4ac}{4a^2}} = \frac{\pm\sqrt{(b^2 - 4ac)}}{2a}$$

Hence

$$x = -\frac{b}{2a} \pm \frac{\sqrt{(b^2 - 4ac)}}{2a}$$

$$\text{i.e. } x = \frac{-b \pm \sqrt{(b^2 - 4ac)}}{2a}$$

$b^2 - 4ac$ is called the *discriminant* of the quadratic equation. Its value allows a decision to be made about the *kind of roots*.

(i) If $b^2 - 4ac = 0$, the roots are *equal*.
(ii) If $b^2 - 4ac$ is a perfect square, the roots are *rational* (the equation can be solved using *factors*).
(iii) If $b^2 - 4ac$ is positive, but not a perfect square, the roots are *real and unequal*.

(iv) If $b^2 - 4ac$ is negative, the roots are *complex* and they will be of the form $X \pm jY$ where $j = \sqrt{-1}$.

Examples:

(i) Solve $4x^2 + x - 5 = 0$; $b^2 - 4ac = 1 + 80 = 81$
   $\therefore$ Roots rational and the equation *could* be solved by factors.
   Using the formula

$$x = \frac{-b \pm \sqrt{(b^2 - 4ac)}}{2a} = \frac{-1 \pm \sqrt{81}}{8}$$

$$x = \frac{-1 \pm 9}{8}$$

$$\therefore \ x = 1 \quad \text{or} \quad -1\tfrac{1}{4}$$

(ii) Solve $3p^2 + 2p - 4 = 0$; $b^2 - 4ac = 4 + 48 = 52$
   $\therefore$ Roots real and different:

$$p = \frac{-2 \pm \sqrt{52}}{6} = \frac{-2 \pm 7 \cdot 211}{6}$$

$$p = \frac{-9 \cdot 211}{6} \quad \text{or} \quad \frac{+5 \cdot 211}{6}$$

$$p = -1 \cdot 535 \quad \text{or} \quad 0 \cdot 868(5)$$

(iii) Solve $t^2 + 2t + 3 = 0$; $b^2 - 4ac = 4 - 12 = -8$
   $\therefore$ Roots *complex*

$$t = \frac{-2 \pm \sqrt{-8}}{2} = \frac{-2 \pm 2\sqrt{2}\sqrt{-1}}{2} = -1 \pm \sqrt{2}j$$

$$t = -1 \pm 1 \cdot 414j$$

4.3 Simultaneous Linear Equations (3 Unknowns)

The methods used to solve such equations are those of elimination and/or substitution. The techniques may be applied to 4 equations in 4 unknowns, etc. No additional theory is required.

Example: Solve the equations:

$$3a + 4b - 2c = 4 \tag{i}$$
$$5a + 2b + 3c = 10 \tag{ii}$$
$$4a - 3b + 4c = 15 \tag{iii}$$

Eliminate *one* of the unknowns.
Multiply (i) by 3 and (ii) by 2.

Then
$$9a + 12b - 6c = 12 \tag{iv}$$
$$10a + 4b + 6c = 20 \tag{v}$$

Add (iv) and (v), then $\quad \underline{19a + 16b = 32} \tag{A}$

Multiply (ii) by 4 and (iii) by 3. Then
$$20a + 8b + 12c = 40 \tag{vi}$$
$$12a - 9b + 12c = 45 \tag{vii}$$

Subtract (vii) from (vi), then $\quad \underline{8a + 17b = -5} \tag{B}$

(A) and (B) are solved for *a* and *b*, then *c* found by substitution.
Multiply (A) by 8 and (B) by 19. Then

$$\underline{152a + 128b = 256} \tag{C}$$
$$\underline{152a + 323b = -95} \tag{D}$$

Subtract (C) from (D); $195b = -351$

$$\therefore \ b = \frac{-351}{195} = -\frac{9}{5}$$

$$8a = -5 - 17b = -5 + \frac{153}{5} = \frac{128}{5}$$

$$\therefore \ a = \frac{16}{5}$$

From (i) $\quad 2c = 3a + 4b - 4 = \dfrac{48}{5} - \dfrac{36}{5} - 4 = -\dfrac{8}{5}$

$$\therefore \ c = -\frac{4}{5}$$

$\therefore$ Solutions are: $a = 3 \cdot 2, \ b = -1 \cdot 8, \ c = -0 \cdot 8$

Generally, in practical problems, solutions obtained would be put in fractional or decimal form. It is rare to obtain simple integral values as solutions in practical problems.

WORKED EXAMPLES

(a) Solve $2x(3x + 1) - 3(x - 2) = 4x^2 - 3(2x - 1)$.

Rearrange in '*standard*' form:

$$6x^2 + 2x - 3x + 6 = 4x^2 - 6x + 3$$

$$\therefore \underline{2x^2 + 5x + 3 = 0}$$

$$b^2 - 4ac = 5^2 - 4(2)(3) = 1$$

$\therefore$ Roots rational and the equation factorizes into

$$(2x + 3)(x + 1) = 0$$

i.e. $\qquad 2x + 3 = 0 \quad \text{or} \quad x + 1 = 0$

$$\underline{x = -1 \cdot 5} \quad \text{or} \quad \underline{x = -1}$$

(b) Solve the equation $5t^2 + 2t + 3 = 0$.

$b^2 - 4ac = 4 - 60 = -56$, roots complex

$$t = \frac{-2 \pm \sqrt{-56}}{10} = \frac{-2 \pm \sqrt{56}\sqrt{-1}}{10} = \frac{-2 \pm 7 \cdot 483\text{j}}{10}$$

$$\therefore \underline{t = -0 \cdot 2 \pm 0 \cdot 7483\text{j}}$$

(c) If $pL^2 + 2pL + p - q = 0$, express L in terms of p and q.

$$b^2 - 4ac = (2p)^2 - 4p(p - q) = 4p^2 - 4p^2 + 4pq = 4pq.$$

$$\therefore L = \frac{-2p \pm \sqrt{(4pq)}}{2p} = \frac{-2p \pm 2\sqrt{(pq)}}{2p}$$

$$L = -1 \pm \frac{1}{p}\sqrt{(pq)} = -1 \pm \sqrt{\frac{pq}{p^2}} = \underline{-1 \pm \sqrt{\frac{q}{p}}}$$

(d) Solve the following equations to find r, s and t.

$$4r + 2s - 3t = 5 \cdot 5 \qquad \text{(i)}$$

$$0 \cdot 5r - 1 \cdot 5s + 2t = 6 \cdot 0 \qquad \text{(ii)}$$

$$1 \cdot 5r - s + 6t = 14 \cdot 5 \qquad \text{(iii)}$$

Convert the coefficients into integers (whole numbers). Multiply (ii) by 2, (iii) by 2. The three equations may then be written as:

$$4r + 2s - 3t = 5 \cdot 5 \qquad \text{(iv)}$$

$$r - 3s + 4t = 12 \cdot 0 \qquad \text{(v)}$$

$$3r - 2s + 12t = 29 \cdot 0 \qquad \text{(vi)}$$

Add (iv) and (vi) $\qquad \underline{7r + 9t = 34 \cdot 5} \qquad$ (A)

Multiply (iv) by 3 and (v) by 2. Then

$$12r + 6s - 9t = 16 \cdot 5 \qquad \text{(vii)}$$

$$2r - 6s + 8t = 24 \cdot 0 \qquad \text{(viii)}$$

Add (vii) and (viii) $\qquad \underline{14r - t = 40 \cdot 5} \qquad$ (B)

Multiply (A) by 2 $\qquad \underline{14r + 18t = 69} \qquad$ (C)

Subtract (B) from (C) $\qquad 19t = 28 \cdot 5$

$$\therefore \ t = \frac{28 \cdot 5}{19} = 1 \cdot 5$$

From (A) $\qquad 7r = 34 \cdot 5 - 9t = 34 \cdot 5 - 13 \cdot 5 = 21$

$$\therefore \ r = \frac{21}{7} = 3 \cdot 0$$

Substitute in (iii) for r and t. Then

$$s = 1 \cdot 5r + 6t - 14 \cdot 5 = 4 \cdot 5 + 9 - 14 \cdot 5 = -1$$

$\therefore$ Solutions are $r = 3 \cdot 0$, $s = -1$, $t = 1 \cdot 5$.

Examples 4

1. Solve the equations $\dfrac{x}{3} - 2y = 4$; $2x + \dfrac{5}{6}y = -1\frac{2}{3}$.

2. Solve the equations $\frac{3}{4}a - 2(b + 1) = 3b + 5$; $2(a - 5) - 4(1 - b) = a - 3$.

3. Find x, y, z if: $x + 2y + 3z = 5$, $3x + y + 2z = 6$, $2x + 3y + z = 1$.

4. Find a, b, c if: $2a + b + 3c = -4$, $3a - 4b - 7c = -29$, $4a + 3b - 2c = -24$.

5. Solve for l, m and n, the equations
$l + m - n = 3$, $2l - 3m + 9n = 60$, $7l + 3m + 3n = 69$.

6. Find the values of P, Q, R which satisfy the equations
$3P + 2Q + 2R = 10$, $2P - Q - 3R = 4$, $4P + 3Q + R = 8$.

7. Obtain the solutions of the equations

$$3r + 2s + 2t - 10 = 0$$
$$2r - s - 3t + 4 = 0$$
$$4r + 3s + t - 8 = 0.$$

8. Determine the values of p_1, p_2, p_3 to satisfy the equations

$$3p_1 + 2p_2 - p_3 = -0.55$$
$$p_1 - 3p_2 + 4p_3 = 7.42$$
$$2p_1 + p_2 - 5p_3 = -6.53.$$

9. The currents, i_1, i_2 amp, in two branches of an electrical circuit are given by $0.5i_1 + 0.3i_2 = 5.2$; $1.2i_1 + 0.4i_2 = 8.7$. Calculate the currents correct to two decimal places.

10. Three currents, i_1, i_2, i_3, in an electrical network, are given by the equations

$$(R_1 + R_2)i_1 + R_1i_2 + R_1i_3 = E_1$$
$$R_1i_1 + (R_3 + R_1)i_2 + R_1i_3 = E_2$$
$$R_1i_1 + R_1i_2 + (R_4 + R_1)i_3 = E_3.$$

Calculate i_1, i_2, i_3 (to two decimal places) when
$R_1 = 5$, $R_2 = 6$, $R_3 = 2$, $R_4 = 9$, $E_1 = 5$, $E_2 = 0$, $E_3 = 2$.

11. Solve the equation $2x^2 + 3x = 4$ correct to 3 places of decimals.

12. Solve the equations (i) $3y^2 + 2y - 5 = 0$

(ii) $2a^2 + 5a - 4 = 0$

(iii) $2t^2 + 3t + 4 = 0.$

13. Solve the equations (i) $x^2 + x + 1 = 0$

(ii) $t^2 - 2t + 3 = 0$

(iii) $\dfrac{1}{p} = 2p - 3$ (to 3 decimal places).

14. Find the possible values of x if $\dfrac{3}{x^2} + \dfrac{2}{x} = -1$.

15. The height, h metres, risen by a body projected vertically with initial velocity u is given by $h = ut - \frac{1}{2}gt^2$. Calculate the possible values of t for $u = 100$, $g = 9.81$, $h = 154$.

16. The sum S of the first n terms of an arithmetic series is given by $S = \frac{1}{2}n[2a + (n - 1)d]$. Find the number of terms required to give a total of 341 when $a = 11$, $d = 4$.

17. The three sides, a, b, c of a triangle and the angle A are connected by the rule $a^2 = b^2 + c^2 - 2bc \cos A$. Calculate the possible values of b when $a = 9$, $c = 10$, angle $A = 60°$.

18. The sag d metres in a cable of length L metres when suspended between two points and subject to a tension T N is given by $d^2 - \dfrac{T}{w}d + \frac{1}{4}L^2 = 0$, where w is the weight in N per metre run. Calculate the sag in a cable when $T = 2500$ N, $L = 60$ metres and the total weight of the cable is 300 N.

19. The equation $Lx^2 + Rx + \dfrac{1}{C} = 0$ is obtained when considering an electrical circuit. Solve the equation for x and deduce that the condition for the two roots to be equal is $R^2 = \dfrac{4L}{C}$.

20. The volume, V cm^3 of a frustum of a cone is given by the formula $V = \frac{1}{3}\pi h \, (R^2 + Rr + r^2)$, where h is the height of the frustum in cm, R and r are the end radii in cm. Calculate the smaller of the radii r, when $V = 3850$ cm^3, $\pi = \dfrac{22}{7}$, $h = 21$ cm and $R = 10$ cm.

21. Solve the equation $9^x = 12(3^x) - 27$. (Hint: $9^x = (3^x)^2$.)

22. Calculate the two possible values of $\tan \theta$ if $\tan \theta$ satisfies the equation $4 \tan^2 \theta + 3 \tan \theta - 1 = 0$.

23. If $2 \sec^2 \theta - \tan \theta = 4$, calculate the two values of $\tan \theta$. (Hint: $\sec^2 \theta = 1 + \tan^2 \theta$.)

24. Solve the equation $2 \tan x - 5 \cot x = 7$ to obtain the values of $\tan x$. $\left(\text{Hint: } \cot x = \dfrac{1}{\tan x}.\right)$

25. Find the four solutions of the equation $u^2 + \dfrac{65}{u^2} = 18$. (Hint: Let $u^2 = x$.)

5

Simultaneous Quadratic Equations and Identities

5.1 Simultaneous Quadratic Equations

5.1.1 One linear, one quadratic

In general it will be found that *substitution techniques are preferable* to do the necessary elimination of one of the variables. *Geometrically* the solution of two such equations is equivalent to finding the coordinates of *two points of intersection* of a line with a quadratic curve.

Examples:
(i) Solve the equations (i) $2x + y = 5$; (ii) $x^2 + y^2 = 28$.
From equation (i), by transposition $y = 5 - 2x$.
Substitute this value for y in (ii).

Then
$$x^2 + (5 - 2x)^2 = 28$$

i.e. an equation for two values of x

$$x^2 + 4x^2 - 20x + 25 = 28$$
$$5x^2 - 20x - 3 = 0$$

Using the formula

$$x = \frac{20 \pm \sqrt{[(-20)^2 + 4(3)(5)]}}{10} = \frac{20 \pm \sqrt{460}}{10}$$

$$= \frac{20 \pm 21\cdot45}{10} = 4\cdot145 \quad \text{or} \quad -0\cdot145$$

The corresponding values of y are given by $y = 5 - 2x$,

i.e. $y = 5 - 2 \times 4 \cdot 145$, or $5 + 2 \times 0 \cdot 145$; $\underline{y = -3 \cdot 29 \text{ or } +5 \cdot 29}$

(ii) Solve the equations

$$y + x - 4 = 0 \qquad \text{(i)}$$
$$4x^2 + 3xy + y^2 + 3x - 3y + 7 = 0 \qquad \text{(ii)}$$

From equation (i) $y = 4 - x$.
Substitute this expression for y in (ii)

Then: $4x^2 + 3x(4 - x) + (4 - x)^2 + 3x - 3(4 - x) + 7 = 0$

$4x^2 + 12x - 3x^2 + 16 - 8x + x^2 + 3x - 12 + 3x + 7 = 0$

$\therefore \qquad\qquad 2x^2 + 10x + 11 = 0$

$$\therefore \; x = \frac{-10 \pm \sqrt{(100 - 88)}}{4} = \frac{-10 \pm \sqrt{12}}{4}$$

$$= \frac{-10 \pm 2\sqrt{3}}{4} = \frac{-5 \pm \sqrt{3}}{2} = \frac{-5 \pm 1 \cdot 732}{2}$$

$$= \frac{-6 \cdot 732}{2} \quad \text{or} \quad \frac{-3 \cdot 268}{2} = \underline{-3 \cdot 366 \quad \text{or} \quad -1 \cdot 634}$$

The corresponding values of y are given by $y = 4 - x$

i.e. $\qquad y = 4 - (-3 \cdot 366) \quad \text{or} \quad 4 - (-1 \cdot 634)$
$\qquad\qquad y = 7 \cdot 366 \quad \text{or} \quad 5 \cdot 634$

$\therefore$ Solutions are

x	$-3 \cdot 366$	$-1 \cdot 634$
y	$+7 \cdot 366$	$+5.634$

5.1.2 Two quadratic equations

Solving two equations of quadratic type is equivalent to finding *four possible points of intersection* of two quadratic curves. When the curves do not actually cut, *complex* roots are obtained.

Examples: (i) Solve the equations (i) $xy = 2$, (ii) $x^2 + y^2 = 5$.

From equation (i) $y = \dfrac{2}{x}$, substitute this value for y in (ii). Then

$$x^2 + \left(\frac{2}{x}\right)^2 = 5$$

$$x^2 + \frac{4}{x^2} = 5$$

$$\therefore \ x^4 + 4 = 5x^2$$
$$x^4 - 5x^2 + 4 = 0$$
$$(x^2 - 1)(x^2 - 4) = 0$$
$$x^2 - 1 = 0 \quad \text{or} \quad x^2 - 4 = 0$$
$$x = \pm 1 \quad \text{or} \qquad x = \pm 2$$

The corresponding values of y are given by $y = \dfrac{2}{x}$, i.e. ± 2 or ± 1

The four solutions may be listed as:

x	$+1$	-1	$+2$	-2
y	$+2$	-2	$+1$	-1

(ii) Solve the equations:

$$3x^2 + 2xy - 4y^2 = 6 \qquad \text{(i)}$$
$$x^2 + 3xy - 2y^2 = 4 \qquad \text{(ii)}$$

Eliminate the constants (6 and 4)
Multiplying (i) by 2 gives the equation:

$$6x^2 + 4xy - 8y^2 = 12 \qquad \text{(iii)}$$

Multiplying (ii) by 3 gives the equation:

$$3x^2 + 9xy - 6y^2 = 12 \qquad \text{(iv)}$$

Subtract equation (iv) from (iii):

$$3x^2 - 5xy - 2y^2 = 0$$

This factorizes because $b^2 - 4ac = 25 + 24 = 49$, i.e. perfect square

$$\therefore \ (3x + y)(x - 2y) = 0$$
$$\therefore \ \underline{x = 2y \ \text{ or } \ y = -3x}$$

Substitute $x = 2y$ in (ii): $4y^2 + 3(2y)y - 2y^2 = 4$

$$\therefore 8y^2 = 4; \quad y^2 = \frac{1}{2}; \quad y = \pm \frac{1}{\sqrt{2}}$$

This gives the solutions $x = \pm \frac{2}{\sqrt{2}}, y = \pm \frac{1}{\sqrt{2}}$

Substitute $y = -3x$ in (i): $3x^2 + 2x(-3x) - 4(9x^2) = 6$

$$\therefore -39x^2 = 6; \quad x^2 = -\frac{6}{39} = -\frac{2}{13}; \quad x = \pm\sqrt{\frac{2}{13}}\,j.$$

This gives the (imaginary) solutions $x = \pm\sqrt{\frac{2}{13}}\,j, y = \mp 3\sqrt{\frac{2}{13}}\,j$.

$\therefore$ Two real pairs of solutions, two imaginary pairs.
Solutions:

x	$+\sqrt{2}$	$-\sqrt{2}$	$+\sqrt{\dfrac{2}{13}}\,j$	$-\sqrt{\dfrac{2}{13}}\,j$
y	$+\dfrac{1}{\sqrt{2}}$	$-\dfrac{1}{\sqrt{2}}$	$-3\sqrt{\dfrac{2}{13}}\,j$	$+3\sqrt{\dfrac{2}{13}}\,j$

5.2 Algebraic Identities

An identity is a statement of equality *true for all values of the variable quantity or quantities.*

Examples:

$$(X + Y)^2 = X^2 + 2XY + Y^2; \quad 3x(x - 1) = 3x^2 - 3x$$
$$(X - Y)^2 = X^2 - 2XY + Y^2; \quad 9x^2 - 1 = (3x - 1)(3x + 1)$$
$$X^2 - Y^2 = (X + Y)(X - Y); \quad \frac{2}{x} + \frac{3}{x^2} = \frac{2x + 3}{x^2}$$
$$X^3 - Y^3 = (X - Y)(X^2 + XY + Y^2);$$
$$(a + b)(a + 2b) = a^2 + 3ab + 2b^2$$

are all *identities*.

5.2.1 Polynomials

A polynomial in x is an expression in x containing integral powers of x, e.g.

$x^2 + 2x + 3$; $2x^3 + 2x - 7$; $x^4 + x^2 + 1$ are polynomials.

IDENTITY OF POLYNOMIALS

If two polynomials are identically equal, then corresponding co-efficients *must* be equal, e.g. if

$$ax^3 + bx^2 + cx + d \equiv Ax^3 + Bx^2 + Cx + D$$

This is only possible if $a = A$, $b = B$, $c = C$, $d = D$.

5.2.2 Partial fractions

If $\dfrac{P(x)}{Q(x)}$ is a *proper* fraction where $P(x)$ and $Q(x)$ are polynomials in x with the degree of P lower than the degree of Q, then $\dfrac{P(x)}{Q(x)}$ may be broken up into *partial fractions*.

Examples: (i) Reduce $\dfrac{2x + 3}{(x - 1)(x + 2)}$ to partial fractions.

Let $\qquad \dfrac{2x + 3}{(x - 1)(x + 2)} = \dfrac{A}{x - 1} + \dfrac{B}{x + 2}$ (To be an identity)

Multiply by $(x - 1)(x + 2)$.

Then: $\qquad 2x + 3 = A(x + 2) + B(x - 1)$

Since this is an *identity*, i.e. true for *all* values of x, we may use *any* values of x, in particular $x = 1$, $x = -2$.

Let $x = 1$: then $5 = A(3)$

$$\therefore A = \frac{5}{3}$$

Let $x = -2$: then $-1 = B(-3)$

$$\therefore B = +\frac{1}{3}$$

$$\therefore \frac{2x + 3}{(x - 1)(x + 2)} = \frac{5}{3(x - 1)} + \frac{1}{3(x + 2)}$$

(*Note:* When allowing partial fractions, in general, highest proper fractions should be used.)

(ii) Reduce $\dfrac{5x - 1}{(x - 2)(x^2 + 1)}$ to partial fractions.

Since $x^2 + 1$ is quadratic, a linear numerator is necessary, as follows:

Let

$$\frac{5x - 1}{(x - 2)(x^2 + 1)} = \frac{A}{x - 2} + \frac{Bx + C}{x^2 + 1}$$

Multiply throughout by $(x - 2)(x^2 + 1)$.

Then $\underline{5x - 1 = A(x^2 + 1) + (Bx + C)(x - 2)}$ (Identity)

Let $x = 2$; $9 = A(4 + 1) = 5A$ $\therefore A = \dfrac{9}{5}$

Now since this is an identity of polynomials, the corresponding coefficients must be *equal*.

Equate some of the coefficients:

Coefficient of x^2 $\quad 0 = A + B$

$$\therefore B = -A = -\frac{9}{5}$$

Constant terms $\quad -1 = A - 2C$

$$\therefore 2C = A + 1 = \frac{14}{5}$$

$$\therefore C = \frac{7}{5}$$

$$\therefore \frac{5x - 1}{(x - 2)(x^2 + 1)} = \frac{+\dfrac{9}{5}}{x - 2} + \frac{-\dfrac{9}{5}x + \dfrac{7}{5}}{x^2 + 1}$$

$$= \frac{9}{5(x - 2)} + \frac{7 - 9x}{5(x^2 + 1)}$$

(iii) Reduce $\dfrac{3x^2 + x - 1}{(x - 1)^2(x + 2)}$ to partial fractions. (Because

$$\frac{A}{x - 1} + \frac{B}{(x - 1)^2} = \frac{A(x - 1) + B}{(x - 1)^2} = \frac{Fx + E}{(x - 1)^2}$$

it is possible to use fractions of simpler type when a factor is repeated.) Let

$$\frac{3x^2 + x - 1}{(x - 1)^2(x + 2)} = \frac{A}{x - 1} + \frac{B}{(x - 1)^2} + \frac{C}{x + 2}$$

Multiply throughout by $(x - 1)^2(x + 2)$.

Then $\underline{3x^2 + x - 1 = A(x - 1)(x + 2) + B(x + 2) + C(x - 1)^2}$

Let $x = 1$ $\qquad 3 = B(3)$

$\qquad\qquad \therefore \underline{B = 1}$

Let $x = -2$ $\qquad 9 = C(-3)^2 = C \times 9$

$\qquad\qquad \therefore \underline{C = 1}$

Equate coefficients of x^2

$$3 = A + C$$

$$\therefore \underline{A = 3 - C = 2}$$

$$\therefore \underline{\frac{3x^2 + x - 1}{(x - 1)^2(x + 2)} = \frac{2}{x - 1} + \frac{1}{(x - 1)^2} + \frac{1}{x + 2}}$$

WORKED EXAMPLES

(a) Solve the equations:

$$a - 2b = 3 \qquad\qquad\qquad (i)$$

$$a^2 + 4b^2 = 5 \qquad\qquad\qquad (ii)$$

From (i) $a = 2b + 3$

Substitute in (ii) $\qquad (2b + 3)^2 + 4b^2 = 5$

Simplify, then $\qquad 8b^2 + 12b + 4 = 0$

$$2b^2 + 3b + 1 = 0$$

$$(2b + 1)(b + 1) = 0$$

$$\therefore \underline{b = -\tfrac{1}{2} \quad \text{or} \quad -1}$$

$$\underline{a = +2 \quad \text{or} \quad +1}$$

(b) Solve the equations:

$$3l^2 + 4lm - m^2 = 5 \qquad\qquad\qquad (i)$$

$$17l^2 + 22lm - 17m^2 = 25 \qquad\qquad\qquad (ii)$$

Multiply (i) by 5 $\qquad 15l^2 + 20lm - 5m^2 = 25 \qquad\qquad (iii)$

Subtract (iii) from (ii)

$$2l^2 + 2lm - 12m^2 = 0$$
$$l^2 + lm - 6m^2 = 0$$
$$(l + 3m)(l - 2m) = 0$$
$$\therefore \underline{l = -3m \quad \text{or} \quad l = 2m}$$

Substitute $l = -3m$ in (i)

Then: $3(-3m)^2 + 4m(-3m) - m^2 = 5$, or $14m^2 = 5$, $m^2 = \dfrac{5}{14}$

$$\therefore \underline{m = \pm\sqrt{\frac{5}{14}} \qquad \text{Hence } l = \mp 3\sqrt{\frac{5}{14}}}$$

Substitute $l = 2m$ in (i)

$$3(2m)^2 + 4m(2m) - m^2 = 5, \text{ or } 19m^2 = 5, m^2 = \frac{5}{19}$$

$$\therefore \underline{m = \pm\sqrt{\frac{5}{19}} \qquad \text{Hence } l = \pm 2\sqrt{\frac{5}{19}}}$$

(c) Reduce $\dfrac{5x^2 + 2x - 1}{(x + 2)^2(x^2 + 4)}$ to partial fractions.

Let $\dfrac{5x^2 + 2x - 1}{(x + 2)^2(x^2 + 4)} = \dfrac{A}{x + 2} + \dfrac{B}{(x + 2)^2} + \dfrac{Cx + D}{x^2 + 4}$

Multiply throughout by $(x + 2)^2(x^2 + 4)$.

Then $5x^2 + 2x - 1 = A(x + 2)(x^2 + 4)$
$$+ B(x^2 + 4) + (Cx + D)(x + 2)^2$$

Let $x = -2$ $\qquad 20 - 4 - 1 = B(4 + 4)$

$$\therefore B = \frac{15}{8}$$

Equate coefficients

of x^3	$0 = A + C$	(i)
of x^2	$5 = 2A + B + D + 4C$	(ii)
constants	$-1 = 8A + 4B + 4D$	(iii)

From (i) $\qquad C = -A$

Substitute in (ii)

$$5 = -2A + \frac{15}{8} + D \qquad \text{(iv)}$$

Substitute in (iii)

$$-1 = 8A + \frac{15}{2} + 4D \qquad \text{(v)}$$

Multiply (iv) by 4

$$20 = -8A + \frac{15}{2} + 4D$$

$$\therefore \; 16A = -21 \qquad A = -\frac{21}{16}; \; C = +\frac{21}{16}; \; B = \frac{15}{8}; \; D = +\frac{1}{2}$$

$$\therefore \; \frac{5x^2 + 2x - 1}{(x + 2)^2(x^2 + 4)} = \frac{15}{8(x + 2)^2} - \frac{21}{16(x + 2)} + \frac{21x + 8}{16(x^2 + 4)}$$

Examples 5

1. Solve the equations $x^2 - 3xy + y^2 = -11$; $x + y = 7$.
2. Find the values of a and b if $a^2 + 3b^2 = 13$ and $2a + b = 4$.
3. Obtain the values of x and y to satisfy $x^2 + y^2 = 40$; $y = 3x$.
4. Solve the simultaneous equations: $y = 3x - 1$; $3x^2 - 7xy + 2y^2 + 8 = 0$.
5. Determine the values of l and m satisfying $3l^2 - 5m^2 = 7$; $3lm - 4m^2 = 2$.
6. Find the two pairs of solutions of the equations:

$$a^2 + ab + b^2 = 39; \qquad a - b = 3.$$

7. Solve the equations: $s^2 - 2st = 21$; $st + t^2 = 18$.
8. Obtain the four pairs of values satisfying:

$$x^2 + xy + 2y^2 = 44; \qquad 2x^2 - xy + y^2 = 16$$

9. Find the two pairs of real and two pairs of imaginary solutions of the equations: $3l^2 - 5lm = -2$; $4lm - 3m^2 = 1$.
10. Find the two pairs of real and two pairs of imaginary solutions of the equations: $x^2 - 2xy = 16$; $3xy - 2y^2 + 36 = 0$.
11. Solve the simultaneous equations: $4x^2 + xy + y^2 = 10$; $3x - 2y = 9$.
12. Determine L and M to satisfy $L^2 + M^2 = 10$; $2LM - M^2 = 6$.
13. Solve the equations: $a^2 + ab + 1 = 0$; $a^2 + 2b^2 = 9$.
14. Determine A and B to satisfy $A^2 - AB + B^2 = 3$; $A^2 + 3AB = 7$.

(Questions 15 onward are examples of partial fractions. Students are recommended to do as many as possible to acquire facility in the reduction of fractions to partial fractions.)

Reduce the following to *partial fractions*

15. (i) $\dfrac{x}{(x-1)(x-3)}$ (ii) $\dfrac{x+37}{x^2+4x-21}$ (iii) $\dfrac{5-x}{(x-2)(x+1)}$

16. (i) $\dfrac{x}{(1+x)(1-2x)}$ (ii) $\dfrac{5x+7}{x^2+x-20}$ (iii) $\dfrac{9x^2-11x+3}{x^2(1-2x)}$

17. (i) $\dfrac{3x+5}{1+2x-3x^2}$ (ii) $\dfrac{2x+1}{(x-1)(2x+3)}$ (iii) $\dfrac{x+7}{6x^2-x-1}$

18. (i) $\dfrac{2x^2-8x+2}{x(x-1)(x-2)}$ (ii) $\dfrac{2x^2+12x+1}{(x-1)(x-2)(x-3)}$

   (iii) $\dfrac{5x^2-7x+4}{(x+1)(x-2)(3x-1)}$

19. (i) $\dfrac{7x+5}{(x+2)(x+1)^2}$ (ii) $\dfrac{2x+1}{(x-1)^2(x+3)}$ (iii) $\dfrac{4x-5}{(2x-1)(x+1)^2}$

20. (i) $\dfrac{x^2+1}{(x-2)(x+1)^2}$ (ii) $\dfrac{5x+4}{(2x+1)(x-1)^2}$ (iii) $\dfrac{x^2-10x+12}{(x-1)^2(x-2)}$

21. (i) $\dfrac{2x^2+x-1}{(x+2)(x^2+x-3)}$ (ii) $\dfrac{x}{(x-1)(x^2+6)}$ (iii) $\dfrac{x-3}{(x+1)(x^2+x+1)}$

22. (i) $\dfrac{x^2-18x+9}{(x-3)(x^2+2x+3)}$ (ii) $\dfrac{3x+7}{(2x-1)(x^2+1)}$ (iii) $\dfrac{11x^2+6x+14}{(3x-1)(x^2+x+3)}$

23. $\dfrac{22x^2-11x+4}{(x-2)^2(x^2+3x+4)}$

24. $\dfrac{x^2+3x-1}{(x-1)^2(2x^2+x+1)}$

25. $\dfrac{6+3x-x^2}{(x+1)(2x^2+5x+3)}$

6

Arithmetic and Geometric Progressions and Series

6.1 Arithmetic Progressions and Series

6.1.1 Arithmetic progressions (A.P.)

These are sets of numbers (sequences) such that any of the numbers is obtained from the previous number by the addition of a constant amount (common difference).

Examples:

(i) 5, 9, 13, 17, 21, ... ; Common difference $= +4$

(ii) $\frac{1}{2}, \frac{3}{4}, 1, \frac{5}{4}, \frac{3}{2}, \ldots$;   Common difference $= +\frac{1}{4}$

(iii) 10, 8, 6, 4, 2, 0, $-2, \ldots$; Common difference $= -2$

6.1.2 Formula to represent all A.P.'s

Let $a =$ First term, $d =$ Common difference.
Then A.P. is $a, a + d, a + 2d, a + 3d, \ldots$
If T_n is the nth number, then $T_n = a + (n - 1)d$

6.1.3 Arithmetic series

Is obtained by adding the terms of an A.P. together. If $S_n =$ sum of the series, then

$$S_n = a + (a + d) + (a + 2d) + \ldots + [a + (n - 1)d] \ (n \text{ terms})$$

6.1.4 Formula for S_n

Consider the series $S = 1 + 2 + 3 + 4 + 5 + 6 + 7 + 8 + 9$

This may be rewritten as

$$S = 9 + 8 + 7 + 6 + 5 + 4 + 3 + 2 + 1$$

If these two expressions are added together

$$2S = 10 + 10 + 10 + 10 + 10 + 10 + 10 + 10 + 10$$
$$= 9 \times 10 = 90$$
$$\therefore \ S = 45$$

(*Note:* Sum of Series = Number of terms $\times \frac{1}{2}$(First + Last term).
This formula holds for all arithmetic series.)

6.1.5 General formula for S_n

$$S_n = a + (a + d) + (a + 2d) + (a + 3d) + \ldots + [a + (n - 1)d]$$

also

$$S_n = [a + (n - 1)d] + [a + (n - 2)d] + [a + (n - 3)d] + \ldots a$$

Adding together

$$2S_n = [a + a + (n - 1)d] + \ldots n \text{ times}$$
$$2S_n = n[2a + (n - 1)d]$$
$$\therefore \ S_n = \tfrac{1}{2}n[2a + (n - 1)d]$$

Also, if the last term is denoted by l, then $S_n = \frac{1}{2}n(a + l)$. These formulae are sufficient to deal with any arithmetic progression and series.

Examples on Arithmetic Progressions and Series:

(i) The fourth term of an A.P. is 11 and the fifteenth term is 33. Determine the progression.

Let the first term be a, common difference $= d$.

Then $\qquad T_n = a + (n - 1)d; \ T_4 = a + 3d = 11$
$$T_{15} = a + 14d = 33$$
$$\therefore \ 11d = 22, \ d = 2$$

hence $\qquad\qquad a = 11 - 3d = 5$

$\therefore$ The A.P. is 5, 7, 9, 11, 13, 15, ..., etc.

(ii) The fifth term of an A.P. is 8·6 and the twelfth term is 9·65. Find the progression and the sum of the first 30 terms of the progression.

Let the first term $= a$, common difference $= d$.

Then $\quad T_n = a + (n-1)d; \quad T_5 = a + 4d = 8·6$

$$T_{12} = a + 11d = 9·65$$

$$\therefore \ 7d = 1·05, \ \underline{d = 0·15}$$

hence $\qquad\qquad \underline{a = 8·6 - 4d = 8·0}$

$\therefore$ The A.P. is $\underline{8, \ 8·15, \ 8·30, \ 8·45, \ 8·60, \ldots}$

$$S_n = \tfrac{1}{2}n[2a + (n-1)d]$$

$$S_{30} = \tfrac{1}{2} \times 30[2 \times 8 + 29 \times 0·15] = 15[16 + 4·35]$$

$$\underline{S_{30} = 15 \times 20·35 = 305·25}$$

(iii) The first term of an A.P. is 2 and the common difference is 0·4. How many terms would be required to give a total of 170?

$$S_n = \tfrac{1}{2}n[2a + (n-1)d]; \quad \therefore \ 170 = \tfrac{1}{2}n[4 + (n-1) \times 0·4]$$

$$\therefore \ 170 = n[2 + 0·2(n-1)] = n[0·2n + 1·8]$$

$$\therefore \ 0·2n^2 + 1·8n - 170 = 0$$

$$\therefore \ n^2 + 9n - 850 = 0$$

$$(n - 25)(n + 34) = 0$$

$$\therefore \ \underline{n = 25 \quad \text{or} \quad -34}$$

Since n must be a positive integer, number of terms $= 25$

(iv) In a new production process, the number of parts produced in the first week of operation is 500. If the number of parts produced per week increases on an average by 15, find (a) how many might be produced in the 15th week, (b) the expected total production for the first 15 weeks.

Using the ideas of arithmetic progressions,

Let $a = 500$ be production during 1st week

$\quad d = 15$ is common difference.

$T_n = a + (n-1)d = $ Production during nth week

$T_{15} = 500 + 14 \times 15 = 500 + 210 = \underline{710}$ during 15th week

Total production during 15 weeks

$$= S_n = \tfrac{1}{2}n[2a + (n - 1)d]$$
$$= \tfrac{1}{2} \times 15[2 \times 500 + 14 \times 15]$$
$$= \tfrac{1}{2} \times 15 \times 1{,}210 = \underline{9075 \text{ parts}}$$

6.2 Geometric Progressions and Series

6.2.1 Geometric progressions (G.P.)

These are sets of numbers (sequences) such that any of the numbers is obtained from the previous number by multiplying by a constant number, i.e. *the ratio of any term to the previous term is a constant.*

Examples:

  (i) 5, 25, 125, 625, . . . ; common *ratio* 5
 (ii) 4, 2, 1, $\tfrac{1}{2}$, $\tfrac{1}{4}$, . . . ; common ratio $\tfrac{1}{2}$
(iii) 5, 0·5, 0·05, 0·005, . . . ; common ratio 0·1

Formula to represent all G.P.'s

Let $a =$ first term, $r =$ common ratio.
Then G.P. is $a, ar, ar^2, ar^3, \ldots$
 If T_n is the nth number (term)

$$T_n = ar^{n-1}$$

6.2.2 Geometric series

Is obtained by adding the terms of a G.P. together. If $S_n =$ sum of the series.
Then $S_n = a + ar + ar^2 + ar^3 + \ldots + ar^{n-1}$ (n terms)

6.2.3 Formula for S_n

Consider the series

$$S = 1 + 2 + 4 + 8 + 16 + 32 + 64 + 128 \qquad \text{(i)}$$

which is a geometric series, 1st term = 1, common ratio = 2.

Multiply by 2 (common ratio)

$$2S = 2 + 4 + 8 + 16 + 32 + 64 + 128 + 256 \qquad \text{(ii)}$$

Subtract (i) from (ii): $S = 256 - 1 = \underline{255}$

(*Note:* How the terms suffered a shift to the right after multiplication.)

6.2.4 General formula for S_n

$$S_n = a + ar + ar^2 + \ldots + ar^{n-1}$$
$$rS_n = \qquad ar + ar^2 + \ldots + ar^{n-1} + ar^n$$

By subtraction $S_n(1 - r) = a - ar^n$

$$\therefore S_n = \frac{a(1 - r^n)}{1 - r} \quad \text{or} \quad \frac{a(r^n - 1)}{r - 1}$$

Examples on Geometric Progressions and Series

(i) The third term of a G.P. is 12 and the sixth term is 96. Find the G.P. and the sum of the first 8 terms.

Let a = 1st term, r = common ratio

Then $\qquad T_3 = ar^2 = 12, \ T_6 = ar^5 = 96$

$$\frac{T_6}{T_3} = \frac{ar^5}{ar^2} = r^3 = \frac{96}{12} = 8$$

$$\therefore r = \sqrt[3]{8} = 2$$

$$\therefore a = \frac{12}{r^2} = 3$$

$\therefore$ G.P. is, $\underline{3, 6, 12, 24, 48, 96, \ldots}$

$$S_n = \frac{a(1 - r^n)}{1 - r} = \frac{3(1 - 2^8)}{1 - 2} = \frac{3(2^8 - 1)}{2 - 1}$$

$$S_8 = 3(256 - 1) = 3 \times 255 = \underline{765}$$

(ii) A sum of money of £100 invested at a *compound interest* rate of 3% is left for 8 years. Find the value at the end of 8 years.

3

Let R = Value of £1 after 1 year = $1 + \frac{3}{100}$ = £1·03.

∴ Sum increases at a rate such that the amount after 1 year = $100 \times R$, after 2 years = $100R^2$, etc. After 8 years = $100R^8$.

∴ Value at end of 8 years = £100$(1·03)^8$ = £100 × 1·267
$$= £126.70.$$

6.2.5 Sum to infinity of a geometric series

$$S_n = \frac{a(1 - r^n)}{1 - r} = \frac{a}{1 - r} - \frac{ar^n}{1 - r}$$

When r is less than 1 (numerically), i.e. $-1 < r < 1$ the numerical value of r^n, when *n is large*, is *very small*. Consequently, when r is between -1 and $+1$, it is possible to carry on writing down terms *to infinity*, but they soon become negligible.

It may be stated that, numerically, the value of r^n *tends to 0 as n tends to infinity* (∞). Hence $S_\infty = \frac{a}{1 - r}$

This is the sum which will not be exceeded, however many terms are written down.

It is called the *sum to infinity* (*only applicable* $-1 < r < +1$)

Examples:

(i) Find the sum to infinity of $5 + 0·5 + 0·05 + 0·005 + \ldots$
$$a = 5, \ r = 0·1$$

$$S_\infty = \frac{a}{1 - r} = \frac{5}{1 - 0·1} = \frac{5}{0·9} = 5.555\dot{5} \text{ or } 5\frac{5}{9}$$

(ii) The first term of a G.P. is 15 and $S_\infty = 22·5$; find r.

$$S_\infty = \frac{a}{1 - r}$$

$$\therefore \ 22·5 = \frac{15}{1 - r}$$

$$22·5 - 22·5r = 15$$

$$\therefore \ 22·5r = 7·5, \ r = \frac{7·5}{22·5} = \frac{1}{3}$$

WORKED EXAMPLES

(a) The sum of the first *five* terms of an A.P. is 40·5, and the sum of the first *eight* terms is 68·4. Find the sum of the first 13 terms.

Let $a = $ 1st term, $d = $ Common difference.

$$S_n = \tfrac{1}{2}n[2a + (n - 1)d]$$

$$\therefore S_5 = \tfrac{1}{2} \times 5(2a + 4d) = 40\cdot5$$

$$\therefore \underline{a + 2d = 8\cdot1} \qquad \text{(i)}$$

$$S_8 = \tfrac{1}{2} \times 8(2a + 7d) = 68\cdot4$$

$$\therefore \underline{2a + 7d = 17\cdot1} \qquad \text{(ii)}$$

Multiply (i) by 2: $2a + 4d = 16\cdot2$

$$\therefore 3d = 0\cdot9; \quad \therefore \underline{d = 0\cdot3}$$

Hence $\underline{a = 8\cdot1 - 2d = 8\cdot1 - 0\cdot6 = 7\cdot5}$

$$S_{13} = \tfrac{1}{2} \times 13(2a + 12d) = 13(a + 6d) = 13(7\cdot5 + 1\cdot8)$$
$$= 13 \times 9\cdot3 = \underline{120\cdot9}$$

(b) A body falls freely from rest. In successive seconds it travels distances which increase by a constant amount 9·81 m. If it falls 4·905 m during the first second, find (i) the total distance fallen in 15 seconds, (ii) the time required to fall 2100 m.

The distances in successive seconds form an A.P., first term 4·905, common difference 9·81 ($a = 4\cdot905$, $d = 9\cdot81$).
Total distance fallen in 15 seconds

$$= \tfrac{1}{2}n[2a + (n - 1)d] \text{ metres}$$
$$= \tfrac{1}{2} \times 15[9\cdot81 + 14 \times 9\cdot81] \text{ metres}$$
$$= \underline{1104 \text{ metres}}$$

Let $n = $ number of seconds required to fall 2100 metres.
Then

$$S_n = 2100 = \tfrac{1}{2}n[2a + (n - 1)d] = \tfrac{1}{2}n[9\cdot81 + (n - 1)9\cdot81]$$
$$= \tfrac{1}{2}n \times 9\cdot81n = 4\cdot905n^2$$
$$\therefore n^2 = 428\cdot2$$
$$n = \underline{20\cdot69 \text{ seconds}}$$

(c) Money is invested and accrues interest at a compound interest rate of $2\frac{1}{2}\%$. If an initial £50 is invested at the beginning of January, and subsequently £50 is added each January, find (i) total value of savings after 8 years, (ii) how many years before the value first exceeds £1000.

Let $R = 1 + 0.025 = 1.025 = $ value of £1 after 1 year, then at the end of n years

$$\text{amount } A = 50R^n + 50R^{n-1} + \ldots + 50R$$

$$= 50R(1 + R + \ldots + R^{n-1})$$

$$= \frac{50R(R^n - 1)}{R - 1} = \underline{2050(R^n - 1)}$$

$\therefore$ Amount after 8 years $= £2050(1.025^8 - 1)$

$$= £2050(1.218 - 1)$$

$$= £446.90$$

Let

$$2050(R^n - 1) = 1000; \quad R^n = 1 + \frac{1000}{2050} = \frac{61}{41}$$

$$n \log 1.025 = \log \frac{61}{41}$$

$$\therefore n = \frac{0.1725}{0.0107} = 16.12 \text{ years}$$

or $\underline{17}$ years before value exceeds £1000.

Examples 6

1. Write down the 8th, 15th and 20th terms of the progression 6, 10, 14, 18, ...
2. In an A.P., $T_5 = 4.8$, $T_{10} = 6.3$. Find the progression.
3. Find T_{13} and T_{30} for the A.P. in which $T_4 = 11.6$, $T_9 = 17.6$.
4. The third and eleventh terms of an A.P. are 8.7 and 12.3. Find S_{15} and S_{21}.
5. The sum of the first and fourth terms of an A.P. is 24 and the sum of the fifteenth and nineteenth terms is 82. Find the value of S_8.
6. In an A.P., $a = 8$, $d = 1.5$. How many terms are required for a sum $= 221$?
7. The sum of n terms of an A.P. is 876. If $a = 2$ and $d = 3$, find n.
8. Write down the 6th and 10th terms of the series, 3, 6, 12, 24, ...
9. In a G.P. $T_3 = 54$, $T_6 = 1,458$. Find the progression.

10. In a G.P. $T_2 = 10$, $T_4 = 40$. Find the two possible G.P.'s and write down the value of T_7 in each case.
11. In a G.P. $T_3 = 72$, $T_5 = 648$. Find the value of S_7 (two cases).
12. In a G.P. $a = 5$, $r = 2$. How many terms will give a sum of 635?
13. Insert three geometric means between 8 and 648. (The five numbers form a G.P.)
14. A G.P. has a common ratio of $\frac{1}{3}$ and the sum of the first two terms is 10. Find the value of the sum to infinity.
15. Write down S_∞ (of G.P.) in the cases: (i) $a = 8$, $r = \frac{1}{4}$, (ii) $a = 21$, $r = -\frac{1}{6}$.
16. From a piece of wire 4 m long exactly, 25 pieces are cut, each 5 mm longer than the previous piece. Find the longest and shortest lengths.
17. A car travels 2·5 m in the 1st second, 4 m in the 2nd second, 5·5 m in the 3rd second and so on. Find (i) how far it will travel in the 20th second, (ii) how far it will travel in the first 20 seconds, (iii) how many seconds it would take to travel 512·5 m.
18. A recording tape is 0·125 mm thick and is wound on a spool so that the inner and outer diameters of the spool are 5 cm and 15 cm. Treating the spool as composed of a large number of circular pieces with radius increasing in A.P., find the total length of tape on the spool, to the nearest centimetre (in metres and centimetres).
19. Battens (strips of wood) are cut to produce a decorative effect. The first cut gives a batten of 20 cm, and the lengths of the battens are increased by 6 mm at a time. How many battens will be obtained from a piece of timber of length 5·25 m, if 11 cm is wasted, and how long is the last batten?
20. The speeds of a cutting machine are to be six in number, ranging from 32 rev/min to 243 rev/min. If the speeds are in geometric progression, find the four intermediate speeds.
21. When a ball is allowed to fall, it rebounds to a height of $\frac{4}{5}$ of the distance fallen. If a ball is allowed to fall from a height of 3·5 m, find (i) how high it rises after the 4th impact, (ii) the total distance it travels up to the 5th impact, (iii) the total distance travelled before coming to rest.
22. A pendulum is set swinging. Its first oscillation is through 16° and each successive oscillation is $\frac{4}{5}$ of the previous oscillation. Find (i) the angle through which it oscillates during the 5th swing, (ii) the total angle it will travel through before coming to rest.
23. At the end of a certain year a tree was 6·5 m high. During the following year it grew 1·25 m and in each succeeding year the rate of growth was $\frac{3}{5}$ of that of the previous year. Find how high it was after 4 years, and show that it will never exceed a height of 9·625 m.
24. A sum of £100 is invested at the beginning of each year at a compound interest rate of 2%. (i) What will be the total, including interest, at the end of the 8th year? (ii) How long will it take for the sum to exceed £1250?
25. A firm pays £5000 for a machine. If depreciation is allowed for at a rate of 10% per annum, find (i) the value of the machine after 5 years, (ii) how long it will take for the value to depreciate to £2500. (Hint: Let $D = 1 - 0·10 = 0·9$ be the value of £1 after 1 year.)

7

Binomial Expansions

7.1 Binomial Expansions (Positive Integral Indices)

7.1.1 Meaning of a binomial

Basically, a binomial is a *two-term* expression. A 'trinomial' is a *three-term* expression, and so on. By rearrangements, all expressions containing more than two terms may be rearranged as binomials, e.g.

(i) *Binomials:* $1 + x$; $2x + 3y$; $x^2 + 1$; $a^3 + b^3$.

(ii) *Trinomials:* $1 + x + x^2$; $x^2 + y^2 + z^2$; $2s + 3t + 5m$

(iii) $1 + x + x^2 = 1 + x(1 + x)$, hence it can be treated as a binomial for expansion purposes.

7.1.2 Expansions

$$(x + y)^2 = x^2 + 2xy + y^2$$

$$(1 + x)^3 = (1 + x)(1 + 2x + x^2) = 1 + 3x + 3x^2 + x^3$$

$$(a - b)^3 = (a - b)(a^2 - 2ab + b^2) = a^3 - 3a^2b + 3ab^2 - b^3$$

All the expressions on the right-hand side of these identities may be regarded as *expansions* of the *binomials* on the left. It is possible to establish a general formula which can be used to write down the *expansions* of $(1 + x)^n$, $(a + b)^n$.

7.1.3 Binomial theorem (for expansions)

When n is any number (integral, positive, negative or fractional) it can be established that the expansion of $(1 + x)^n$ is as follows:

$$(1 + x)^n = 1 + \frac{n}{1} x + \frac{n(n - 1)}{1 \times 2} x^2 + \frac{n(n - 1)(n - 2)}{1 \times 2 \times 3} x^3 + \ldots$$

and so on

When n is a *positive integer*, there will be $n + 1$ terms.

When n is a *negative integer* or a *fraction* (positive or negative), it is possible to write down more and more terms, i.e. infinite expansions could be obtained. Usually for these to be *valid* (i.e. usable numerically), the numerical value of x should be less than 1, i.e. $-1 < x < 1$ or $|x| < 1$.

When n is a positive integer *only* an expansion like

$$(a + b)^n = a^n + \frac{n}{1} a^{n-1}b + \frac{n(n - 1)}{1 \times 2} a^{n-2}b^2 + \ldots$$

may be written down. (*There will be $n + 1$ terms only.*)

Note: $1 \times 2 \times 3 = 3!$ (Factorial 3)
$1 \times 2 \times 3 \times 4 \times 5 = 5!$ (Factorial 5).

Examples of expansions (n a positive integer)

(i) $(1 + x)^3 = 1 + \dfrac{3}{1} x + \dfrac{3 \times 2}{1 \times 2} x^2 + \dfrac{3 \times 2 \times 1}{1 \times 2 \times 3} x^3$

$\quad\quad = \underline{1 + 3x + 3x^2 + x^3}$

(ii) $(1 + x)^4 = 1 + \dfrac{4}{1} x + \dfrac{4 \times 3}{1 \times 2} x^2$

$$+ \frac{4 \times 3 \times 2}{1 \times 2 \times 3} x^3 + \frac{4 \times 3 \times 2 \times 1}{1 \times 2 \times 3 \times 4} x^4$$

$\quad\quad = \underline{1 + 4x + 6x^2 + 4x^3 + x^4}$

(*Note:* symmetry from either end.)

(iii) $(2a + b)^4 = (2a)^4 + \dfrac{4}{1}(2a)^3(b) + \dfrac{4 \times 3}{1 \times 2}(2a)^2(b)^2$

$$+ \dfrac{4 \times 3 \times 2}{1 \times 2 \times 3}(2a)(b)^3 + \dfrac{4 \times 3 \times 2 \times 1}{1 \times 2 \times 3 \times 4}(b)^4$$

$$= \underline{16a^4 + 32a^3b + 24a^2b^2 + 8ab^3 + b^4}$$

(iv) $(2x + 3y)^5 = (2x)^5 + \dfrac{5}{1}(2x)^4(3y) + \dfrac{5 \times 4}{1 \times 2}(2x)^3(3y)^2$

$$+ \dfrac{5 \times 4 \times 3}{1 \times 2 \times 3}(2x)^2(3y)^3 + \dfrac{5 \times 4 \times 3 \times 2}{1 \times 2 \times 3 \times 4}(2x)(3y)^4$$

$$+ \dfrac{5 \times 4 \times 3 \times 2 \times 1}{1 \times 2 \times 3 \times 4 \times 5}(3y)^5$$

$$= \underline{32x^5 + 240x^4y + 720x^3y^2 + 1080x^2y^3 + 810xy^4 + 243y^5}$$

Special Note: $(2x)^4 = (2^4) \times (x^4) = 16x^4$, etc.

7.2 Binomial Expansions (Negative and Fractional Indices)

7.2.1 Expansions when n is a negative integer

(i) $\dfrac{1}{1 + x} = (1 + x)^{-1} = 1 + \dfrac{(-1)}{1}x + \dfrac{(-1)(-2)}{1 \times 2}(x)^2$

$$+ \dfrac{(-1)(-2)(-3)}{1 \times 2 \times 3}(x)^3 + \ldots$$

$$= 1 - x + x^2 - x^3 + x^4 \ldots$$

(*Note:* a geometric series.)

(ii) $\dfrac{1}{(1 - 2x)^2} = (1 - 2x)^{-2} = [1 + (-2x)]^{-2}$

$$= 1 + \dfrac{(-2)}{1}(-2x) + \dfrac{(-2)(-3)}{1 \times 2}(-2x)^2$$

$$+ \dfrac{(-2)(-3)(-4)}{1 \times 2 \times 3}(-2x)^3 + \ldots$$

$$= \underline{1 + 4x + 12x^2 + 32x^3 + \ldots \text{ to infinity}}$$

7.2.2 Expansions when n is a fraction (positive or negative)

(i) $\quad (1 + x)^{\frac{3}{2}} = 1 + \left(\dfrac{3}{2}\right)(x) + \dfrac{\left(\dfrac{3}{2}\right)\left(\dfrac{1}{2}\right)}{1 \times 2}(x)^2$

$\qquad + \dfrac{\left(\dfrac{3}{2}\right)\left(\dfrac{1}{2}\right)\left(-\dfrac{1}{2}\right)}{1 \times 2 \times 3}(x)^3 + \dfrac{\left(\dfrac{3}{2}\right)\left(\dfrac{1}{2}\right)\left(-\dfrac{1}{2}\right)\left(-\dfrac{3}{2}\right)}{1 \times 2 \times 3 \times 4}(x)^4 + \ldots$

$\quad = 1 + \dfrac{3}{2}x + \dfrac{3}{8}x^2 - \dfrac{1}{16}x^3 + \dfrac{3}{128}x^4 + \ldots ad \infty \; (-1 < x < 1)$

(ii) $\quad \dfrac{1}{\sqrt{(1 - 2x)}} = (1 - 2x)^{-\frac{1}{2}} = [1 + (-2x)]^{-\frac{1}{2}}$

$\qquad\qquad = 1 + \left(-\dfrac{1}{2}\right)(-2x) + \dfrac{\left(-\dfrac{1}{2}\right)\left(-\dfrac{3}{2}\right)}{1 \times 2}(-2x)^2$

$\qquad\qquad + \dfrac{\left(-\dfrac{1}{2}\right)\left(-\dfrac{3}{2}\right)\left(-\dfrac{5}{2}\right)}{1 \times 2 \times 3}(-2x)^3 + \ldots ad \infty$

$= 1 + x + \dfrac{3}{2}x^2 + \dfrac{5}{2}x^3 + \ldots ad \infty \left(-1 < 2x < 1, \; -\dfrac{1}{2} < x < \dfrac{1}{2}\right)$

(iii) $\quad \dfrac{1}{\sqrt[3]{(1 + 4x)}} = \dfrac{1}{(1 + 4x)^{\frac{1}{3}}} = (1 + 4x)^{-\frac{1}{3}}$

$\qquad\qquad = 1 + \left(-\dfrac{1}{3}\right)(4x) + \dfrac{\left(-\dfrac{1}{3}\right)\left(-\dfrac{4}{3}\right)}{1 \times 2}(4x)^2$

$\qquad\qquad + \dfrac{\left(-\dfrac{1}{3}\right)\left(-\dfrac{4}{3}\right)\left(-\dfrac{7}{3}\right)}{1 \times 2 \times 3}(4x)^3 + \ldots$

$\qquad\qquad = 1 - \dfrac{4}{3}x + \dfrac{32}{9}x^2 - \dfrac{896}{81}x^3 + \ldots ad \infty$

$\qquad\qquad\qquad \left(-1 < 4x < 1, \; -\tfrac{1}{4} < x < \tfrac{1}{4}\right)$

7.3 Approximations

Consider

$$(1 + 0\cdot1)^5 = 1 + 5(0\cdot1) + \frac{5 \times 4}{1 \times 2}(0\cdot1)^2 + \frac{5 \times 4 \times 3}{1 \times 2 \times 3}(0\cdot1)^3$$

$$+ \frac{5 \times 4 \times 3 \times 2}{1 \times 2 \times 3 \times 4}(0\cdot1)^4 + \frac{5 \times 4 \times 3 \times 2 \times 1}{1 \times 2 \times 3 \times 4 \times 5}(0\cdot1)^5$$

i.e. $(1 + 0\cdot1)^5 = 1 + 5(0\cdot1) + 10(0\cdot01) + 10(0\cdot001)$

$$+ 5(0\cdot0001) + 1(0\cdot000\ 01)$$

$$= 1 + 0\cdot5 + 0\cdot10 + 0\cdot010 + 0\cdot000\ 5 + 0\cdot000\ 01$$

Taking the first two terms only $(1\cdot1)^5$ is approximately $1\cdot50$ (*1st order*)
Taking the first three terms only $(1\cdot1)^5$ is approximately $1\cdot60$ (*2nd order*)
Taking the first four terms only $(1\cdot1)^5$ is approximately $1\cdot61$ (*3rd order*)
Taking the first five terms only $(1\cdot1)^5$ is approximately $1\cdot6105$ (*4th order*)
Taking all six terms $(1\cdot1)^5 = 1\cdot610\ 51$

It is seen that the value (to 2 decimal places) is given by using the first four terms of the expansion. Naturally the accuracy obtained depends on the *order of the approximation*, i.e. how many terms are used.

When x is small

$$(1 + x)^n \simeq 1 + nx \qquad \text{(1st order)}$$

$$(1 + x)^n \simeq 1 + nx + \frac{n(n - 1)x^2}{1 \times 2} \text{ (2nd order)}$$

and so on.

Examples: (i) Neglecting powers of x greater than the second, find the approximate value of $\dfrac{\sqrt{(1 + x)}}{(1 - 2x)^2}$ up to the term in x^2.

$$\frac{\sqrt{(1+x)}}{(1-2x)^2} = (1+x)^{\frac{1}{2}} \times (1-2x)^{-2} \quad \text{(Expand each term)}$$

$$= \left[1 + \frac{1}{2}x + \frac{\frac{1}{2}\left(-\frac{1}{2}\right)}{1 \times 2}x^2 + \ldots \right]$$

$$\times \left[1 + (-2)(-2x) + \frac{(-2)(-3)}{1 \times 2}(-2x)^2 + \ldots \right]$$

$$= \left[1 + \frac{1}{2}x - \frac{1}{8}x^2 + \ldots \right]\left[1 + 4x + 12x^2 + \ldots \right]$$

$$= 1 + \left(\frac{1}{2}x + 4x \right) + \left(12x^2 + 4x\frac{1}{2}x - \frac{1}{8}x^2 \ldots \right)$$

$$= 1 + \frac{9}{2}x + 13\frac{7}{8}x^2 + \ldots = 1 + \frac{9}{2}x + \frac{111}{8}x^2 + \ldots$$

This expansion will be valid only if $-1 < x < 1$ and $-1 < 2x < 1$

$$\therefore \quad \underline{\text{Valid only if } -\tfrac{1}{2} < x < \tfrac{1}{2}}$$

(ii) Using first order binomial approximations, obtain the approximate value of $\dfrac{(1\cdot01)^3\sqrt{0\cdot96}}{\sqrt[3]{0\cdot94}}$.

$$\frac{(1\cdot01)^3 \times \sqrt{0\cdot96}}{\sqrt[3]{0\cdot94}} = (1 + 0\cdot01)^3 \times (1 - 0\cdot04)^{\frac{1}{2}} \times (1 - 0\cdot06)^{-\frac{1}{3}}$$

$$\simeq (1 + 3 \times 0\cdot01 + \ldots) \times \left(1 - \frac{1}{2} \times 0\cdot04 \ldots \right)$$

$$\times \left(1 + \frac{1}{3} \times 0\cdot06 \ldots \right)$$

$$\simeq 1 + 3 \times 0\cdot01 - \frac{1}{2} \times 0\cdot04 + \frac{1}{3} \times 0\cdot06 + \ldots$$

$$\simeq 1 + 0\cdot03 - 0\cdot02 + 0\cdot02 + \ldots$$

$$\simeq 1 + 0\cdot03 \simeq \underline{1\cdot03}$$

(iii) If l is small compared with d, using binomial approximations show that $F = \dfrac{M}{(d-l)^2} - \dfrac{M}{(d+l)^2} \simeq \dfrac{4Ml}{d^3}$.

$$F = \frac{M}{(d-l)^2} - \frac{M}{(d+l)^2} = \frac{M}{d^2\left(1 - \dfrac{l}{d}\right)^2} - \frac{M}{d^2\left(1 + \dfrac{l}{d}\right)^2}$$

$$= \frac{M}{d^2}\left[\frac{1}{\left(1 - \dfrac{l}{d}\right)^2} - \frac{1}{\left(1 + \dfrac{l}{d}\right)^2}\right] = \frac{M}{d^2}\left[\left(1 - \frac{l}{d}\right)^{-2} - \left(1 + \frac{l}{d}\right)^{-2}\right]$$

$$= \frac{M}{d^2}\left\{\left[1 + (-2)\left(-\frac{l}{d}\right) + \frac{(-2)(-3)}{1 \times 2}\left(-\frac{l}{d}\right)^2 \cdots\right]\right.$$

$$\left. - \left[1 + (-2)\left(\frac{l}{d}\right) + \frac{(-2)(-3)}{1 \times 2}\left(\frac{l}{d}\right)^2 + \cdots\right]\right\}$$

$$= \frac{M}{d^2}\left\{\left[1 + \frac{2l}{d} + \frac{3l^2}{d^2} + \cdots\right] - \left[1 - \frac{2l}{d} + \frac{3l^2}{d^2} + \cdots\right]\right\}$$

$$= \frac{M}{d^2}\left(\frac{4l}{d} + \cdots\right) \simeq \underline{\frac{4Ml}{d^3}}$$

[*Note:* $(d + l)^2 = d^2\left(1 + \dfrac{l}{d}\right)^2$ *so that* $(1 + x)^n$ *can be used for* x *numerically less than* 1.]

WORKED EXAMPLES

(*a*) Write down the full expansion of $(1 + 2x)^6$.

$$(1 + 2x)^6 = 1 + \frac{6}{1}(2x) + \frac{6 \times 5}{1 \times 2}(2x)^2 + \frac{6 \times 5 \times 4}{1 \times 2 \times 3}(2x)^3$$

$$+ \frac{6 \times 5 \times 4 \times 3}{1 \times 2 \times 3 \times 4}(2x)^4 + \frac{6 \times 5 \times 4 \times 3 \times 2}{1 \times 2 \times 3 \times 4 \times 5}(2x)^5$$

$$+ \frac{6 \times 5 \times 4 \times 3 \times 2 \times 1}{1 \times 2 \times 3 \times 4 \times 5 \times 6}(2x)^6$$

$$= \underline{1 + 12x + 60x^2 + 160x^3 + 240x^4 + 192x^5 + 64x^6}$$

(b) Expand $(2a + b)^5$ in ascending powers of b.

$$(2a + b)^5 = (2a)^5 + \frac{5}{1}(2a)^4(b) + \frac{5 \times 4}{1 \times 2}(2a)^3(b)^2$$

$$+ \frac{5 \times 4 \times 3}{1 \times 2 \times 3}(2a)^2(b)^3 + \frac{5 \times 4 \times 3 \times 2}{1 \times 2 \times 3 \times 4}(2a)(b)^4$$

$$+ \frac{5 \times 4 \times 3 \times 2 \times 1}{1 \times 2 \times 3 \times 4 \times 5}(b)^5$$

$$= 32a^5 + 80a^4b + 80a^3b^2 + 40a^2b^3 + 10ab^4 + b^5$$

(c) Neglecting second and higher powers of x, find the approximate value of $\dfrac{(1 - 2x)^5(1 + 3x)^{\frac{1}{2}}}{\sqrt[3]{(8 - 2x)}} = E$.

$$E = \frac{(1 - 2x)^5 \times (1 + 3x)^{\frac{1}{2}}}{\sqrt[3]{\left[8\left(1 - \frac{1}{4}x \right) \right]}}$$

(Note: $8 - 2x = 8(1 - \frac{1}{4}x)$, $\sqrt[3]{8} = 2$.)

$$= \frac{(1 - 2x)^5 \times (1 + 3x)^{\frac{1}{2}}}{2\left(1 - \frac{1}{4}x \right)^{\frac{1}{3}}}$$

$$= \frac{1}{2}(1 - 2x)^5 \times (1 + 3x)^{\frac{1}{2}} \times \left(1 - \frac{1}{4}x \right)^{-\frac{1}{3}}$$

$$\simeq \frac{1}{2}\left[1 + 5(-2x) + \frac{1}{2}(3x) + \left(-\frac{1}{3} \right)\left(-\frac{1}{4}x \right) + \dots \right];$$

neglecting x^2, etc.

$$\simeq \frac{1}{2}\left(1 - 10x + \frac{3}{2}x + \frac{1}{12}x \right) \simeq \frac{1}{2}\left(1 - \frac{101}{12}x \right)$$

$$\therefore \underline{E \simeq \frac{1}{2} - \frac{101}{24}x}$$

(d) Find the approximate change in $P = \dfrac{x^3\sqrt{y}}{z^4}$ when x increases by 1%, y decreases by 1·5%, z increases by 0·8%.

Let increased value of x be $X = x + \frac{1}{100}x = x(1 + \frac{1}{100}) = x(1 + 0.01)$

Let decreased value of y be $Y = y - \frac{1.5}{100}y = y(1 - 0.015)$

Let increased value of z be $Z = z + \frac{0.8}{100}z = z(1 + 0.008)$

Let the new value of P be P_1.
Then

$$P_1 = \frac{X^3 Y^{\frac{1}{2}}}{Z^4} = \frac{x^3(1 + 0.01)^3 \times \sqrt{y} \times (1 - 0.015)^{\frac{1}{2}}}{z^4(1 + 0.008)^4}$$

$$= \frac{x^3 \sqrt{y}}{z^4}(1 + 0.01)^3 \times (1 - 0.015)^{\frac{1}{2}} \times (1 + 0.008)^{-4}$$

$$\simeq \frac{x^3 \sqrt{y}}{z^4}\left[1 + 3 \times 0.01 - \frac{1}{2} \times 0.015 + (-4) \times (0.008)\right]$$

$$\simeq P(1 + 0.03 - 0.0075 - 0.032) = P(1 - 0.0095)$$

$\therefore P$ decreases by $0.0095 \times 100\% = \underline{0.95\%}$ approximately.

Examples 7

1. Write down the full expansion of $(1 + 2x)^4$.
2. Write down the full expansion of $(2a - b)^5$.
3. Expand $(2x - 3y)^4$ in ascending powers of y.
4. Expand $(1 + 4x)^{3/2}$ as far as the term in x^3.
5. Expand $(1 - 3x)^{-4}$ as far as the term in x^3.
6. Expand the function $\frac{1}{(1 + 3x)^2}$ as far as the x^3 term. What values must x lie between for the expansion to be valid?
7. Write down the expansion of $(1 + x)^6 - (1 - x)^6$.
8. If x is very small, so that powers of x greater than the first may be neglected, find the approximate value of $\frac{\sqrt{(1 + 4x)}}{(1 - x)^5}$.
9. Using a binomial expansion, evaluate $\sqrt{1.1}$ to 3 decimal places.
10. Find the cube root of 8.16 to 3 decimal places (without logarithms).
11. Expand $\frac{1}{1 + 3x} + \frac{1}{1 - 3x}$ as far as the term in x^4.
12. Use a 1st order binomial approximation to evaluate $\frac{(0.95)^4 \times \sqrt[3]{7.92}}{\sqrt{9.09}}$.

13. Express $\dfrac{3x}{(1 + 2x)(1 - x)}$ in partial fractions and hence expand the function as far as the term in x^3.

14. Express $\dfrac{5x + 3}{(1 + 3x)(1 + x)}$ in partial fractions and hence expand the function as far as the term in x^3. For what values of x is the expansion valid?

15. If $M = \dfrac{a^4 b^{3/2}}{\sqrt{c}}$ find the approximate percentage change in M when a increases by 1.8%, b decreases by 0.6%, c increases by 1.2%.

16. Using the expression $E = \dfrac{MV^2}{2g}$ find, using a binomial approximation, the increase in E if V increases by 0.5% and g decreases by 0.8%.

17. Using a binomial approximation, if a is large compared with x, find the approximate value of $E = \dfrac{Px}{(a + x)^{3/2}} - \dfrac{Px}{(a - x)^{3/2}}$.

18. Expand $\dfrac{1}{\sqrt{(1 - x^2)}}$ as far as the term in x^6.

19. If h is small compared with x and powers of h greater than the first are neglected, show that $\dfrac{(x + h)^n - x^n}{h} = nx^{n-1}$.

20. Evaluate $\sqrt[3]{998.5}$ to 3 decimal places without using logarithms.

8

Trigonometry

8.1 Angles of Any Size

8.1.1 Right-angled triangle

θ (theta) and ϕ (phi) are complementary angles, i.e. $\theta + \phi = 90°$. From previous trigonometry as done in the General Course, the

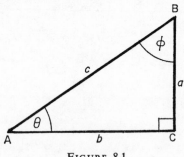

FIGURE 8.1

trigonometric ratios for the *acute angle* θ are as follows:

$$\sin \theta = \frac{a}{c} \, ; \ \cos \theta = \frac{b}{c} \, ; \ \tan \theta = \frac{a}{b} \, ;$$

$$\text{cosec } \theta = \frac{1}{\sin \theta} = \frac{c}{a} \, ; \ \sec \theta = \frac{1}{\cos \theta} = \frac{c}{b} \, ; \ \cot \theta = \frac{1}{\tan \theta} = \frac{b}{a}$$

It should also be noted that:

$$\underline{\sin \theta = \cos \phi}; \quad \underline{\tan \theta = \cot \phi}; \quad \underline{\sec \theta = \operatorname{cosec} \phi}$$

e.g. $\sin 80° = \cos 10°$; $\tan 57° = \cot 33°$; $\sec 37° = \operatorname{cosec} 53°$.

8.1.2 Angles of any magnitude

Consider a point, whose position is defined in the x–y plane by two coordinates x and y. Using ordinary graphical notation, x or y may be *positive or negative*.

If $OP = r$, this will be treated as *positive only*.

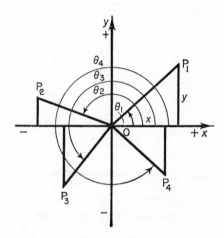

FIGURE 8.2

Angles $0°$–$90°$. Sin θ_1, cos θ_1, tan θ_1, all positive and values are read directly from the tables.

Angles $90°$–$180°$. Sin θ_2 positive, cos θ_2, tan θ_2 negative.
    Sin $\theta_2 = \sin (180 - \theta_2)$; cos $\theta_2 = -\cos (180 - \theta_2)$;
    tan $\theta_2 = -\tan (180 - \theta_2)$.

Angles $180°$–$270°$. Sin θ_3, cos θ_3 negative, tan θ_3 positive.
    Sin $\theta_3 = -\sin (\theta_3 - 180°)$; cos $\theta_3 = -\cos (\theta_3 - 180°)$;
    tan $\theta_3 = +\tan (\theta_3 - 180°)$.

Angles 270°–360°. Sin θ_4, tan θ_4 negative, cos θ_4 positive.
    Sin $\theta_4 = -\sin(360° - \theta_4)$; cos $\theta_4 = +\cos(360° - \theta_4)$;
    tan $\theta_4 = -\tan(360° - \theta_4)$.

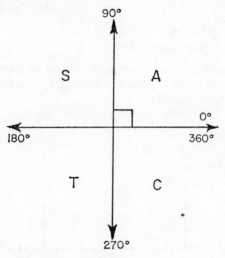

FIGURE 8.3

Special Notes (1) Signs for the ratios memorized with the A.S.T.C
                   rule.
                (2) Magnitudes used to *read tables* are always
                   acute angles relative to the horizontal axis.

Examples:

  (i) sin 150° $= +\sin(180° - 150°) = +\sin 30° = 0\cdot5000$

 (ii) cos 224° $= -\cos(224° - 180°) = -\cos 44° = -0\cdot7193$

(iii) tan 316° $= -\tan(360° - 316°) = -\tan 44° = -0\cdot9657$

 (iv) sin 512° $= \sin(512° - 360°) = \sin 152°$
                $= +\sin(180° - 152°) = +\sin 28° = +0\cdot4695$

  (v) cos 830° $= \cos(830° - 720°) = \cos(110°)$
                $= -\cos(180° - 110°) = -\cos 70° = -0\cdot3420$

Special Notes (*to write down the correct trigonometric ratio*)
(1) Reduce the angle to one between 0°–360°, by subtracting multiples of 360°.
(2) Decide on the quadrant and apply the A.S.T.C. rule.
(3) Fix the sign, then reduce to 0°–90° angle to read the tables.

8.2 Periodic Functions

All the trigonometric functions are periodic of period 360° (or 2π radians). This means that the values repeat exactly after an interval of 360° (or 2π radians). If, therefore, sketch graphs are drawn of the functions $\sin\theta$, $\cos\theta$, $\tan\theta$, they are seen to be as follows:

(*Note.* (1) $\sin\theta$ and $\cos\theta$ never exceed 1 numerically, (2) $\tan\theta$ may assume any value between $+\infty$ and $-\infty$.)

Sin θ

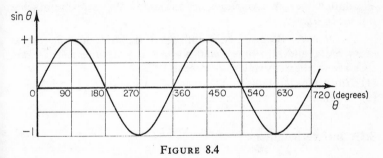

FIGURE 8.4

Cos θ as above, but 90° out of phase (or out of step)

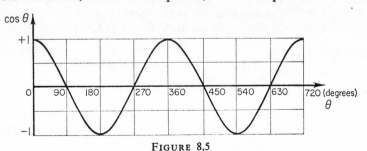

FIGURE 8.5

Tan θ

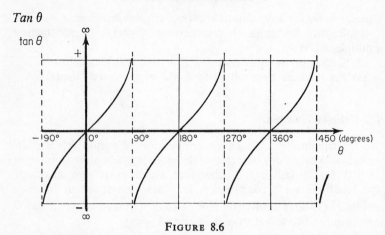

FIGURE 8.6

The dotted lines are *asymptotes*, i.e. lines which the graph approaches but *never crosses*.

Special note. Because sin θ and cos θ are *periodic*, and repeat every *cycle*, and also have *equal positive and negative peak values*, they are used extensively to represent
(1) *Harmonic vibrations (oscillations).*
(2) *Alternating currents and voltages.*

8.2.1 Inverse notation

This is a notation widely used in trigonometry.
e.g.   (i) $\sin^{-1}(x)$ stands for the *angle* whose sine is x.
     (ii) $\tan^{-1}(x)$ stands for the *angle* whose tangent is x.
     (iii) $\cos^{-1}(x)$ stands for the *angle* whose cosine is x, and so on.

Examples:
 (i) If sin θ = 0·5
         θ = $\sin^{-1}(0·5)$ = 30°, 150°, 390°, etc.
(ii) If cos θ = 0·75
         θ = $\cos^{-1}(0·75)$ = 41°24′, 318°36′, 401°24′, etc.
     When finding solutions to trigonometric equations, it is possible to write down many angles because the functions are *periodic*.

8.3 Identities

8.3.1 Trigonometric identities

These are *statements of equality true for all values of the variable angle*. (Compare with the definition of an algebraic identity.)

The *definitions* of cosecant, secant and cotangent give simple *identities*, e.g.

$$\operatorname{cosec} \theta = \frac{1}{\sin \theta} \; ; \qquad \sec \theta = \frac{1}{\cos \theta}$$

$$\cot \theta = \frac{1}{\tan \theta} \quad \text{are all } \textit{identities.}$$

Consider the triangle ABC (Figure 8.7):

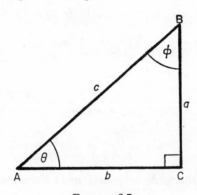

FIGURE 8.7

$$\sin \theta = \frac{a}{c} \; ; \qquad \cos \theta = \frac{b}{c} \; ; \qquad \tan \theta = \frac{\sin \theta}{\cos \theta}$$

$$(\cos \theta)^2 + (\sin \theta)^2 = \frac{a^2}{c^2} + \frac{b^2}{c^2} = \frac{a^2 + b^2}{c^2} = \frac{c^2}{c^2} = 1$$

$$\therefore \quad \underline{\sin^2 \theta + \cos^2 \theta = 1} \quad \text{(True for \textit{all} values of } \theta.)$$

These are *very important* identities.

8.3.2 Deduction of further identities (using simple known ones)

Examples:

(i) Show that $1 + \tan^2 \theta = \sec^2 \theta$.

Now

$$1 + \tan^2 \theta = 1 + \left(\frac{\sin \theta}{\cos \theta}\right)^2 = 1 + \frac{\sin^2 \theta}{\cos^2 \theta}$$

$$= \frac{\cos^2 \theta + \sin^2 \theta}{\cos^2 \theta} = \frac{1}{\cos^2 \theta}$$

$$\therefore \ 1 + \tan^2 \theta = \left(\frac{1}{\cos \theta}\right)^2 = \sec^2 \theta$$

(ii) Prove that

$$\frac{1}{1 + \cos \theta} + \frac{1}{1 - \cos \theta} = 2 \operatorname{cosec}^2 \theta.$$

Now

$$\frac{1}{1 + \cos \theta} + \frac{1}{1 - \cos \theta} = \frac{1 - \cos \theta + 1 + \cos \theta}{(1 + \cos \theta)(1 - \cos \theta)} = \frac{2}{1 - \cos^2 \theta}$$

$$= \frac{2}{\sin^2 \theta} = 2 \left(\frac{1}{\sin \theta}\right)^2 = 2 \operatorname{cosec}^2 \theta$$

Many other identities may be proved in similar ways.

8.3.3 Trigonometric equations

These are statements of equality true for only certain values of the angle (the solutions).

Examples:

(i) Solve the equation $\cos \theta = 0{\cdot}7$.

$$\theta = \cos^{-1} 0{\cdot}7$$

$$\theta = 45°34', \ 314°26', \ 405°34', \ \text{etc.}$$

(ii) Solve the equation $\sin \theta \cos \theta = \frac{1}{2} \sin \theta$.

$\sin \theta \cos \theta - \frac{1}{2} \sin \theta = 0$; $\therefore \sin \theta (\cos \theta - \frac{1}{2}) = 0$

Hence $\sin \theta = 0$

$$\theta = \sin^{-1} 0 = 0°, 180°, 360°, 540°, \ldots$$

or $\cos \theta = \frac{1}{2} = 0.5$

$$\theta = \cos^{-1}(0.5) = 60°, 300°, 420°, \text{etc.}$$

(iii) Solve the equation $8 \sin^2 \theta = 7 - 2 \cos \theta$.

Replace $\sin^2 \theta$ by $1 - \cos^2 \theta$ using the identity $\cos^2 \theta + \sin^2 \theta = 1$.

$$\therefore 8(1 - \cos^2 \theta) = 7 - 2 \cos \theta$$
$$\therefore 8 \cos^2 \theta - 2 \cos \theta - 1 = 0$$
$$(4 \cos \theta + 1)(2 \cos \theta - 1) = 0$$
$$\therefore 2 \cos \theta - 1 = 0; \quad \cos \theta = 0.5$$
$$\theta = \cos^{-1}(0.5) = 60°, 300°, \text{etc.}$$

or $4 \cos \theta + 1 = 0$; $\cos \theta = -0.25$;

$$\theta = \cos^{-1}(-0.25) = (180° - 75°31') \text{ or } 180° + 75°31'$$
$$= 104°29' \text{ or } 255°31'$$

(*Notes:* (1) Never *cancel out* ratios as they can be *zero*. (2) Many solutions can usually be found.)

WORKED EXAMPLES

(*a*) Prove the identity $1 + \cot^2 \theta = \operatorname{cosec}^2 \theta$.

$$\cot \theta = \frac{1}{\tan \theta} = \frac{\cos \theta}{\sin \theta}$$

$$\therefore 1 + \cot^2 \theta = 1 + \left(\frac{\cos \theta}{\sin \theta}\right)^2 = 1 + \frac{\cos^2 \theta}{\sin^2 \theta}$$

$$= \frac{\sin^2 \theta + \cos^2 \theta}{\sin^2 \theta} = \frac{1}{\sin^2 \theta}$$

$$\therefore 1 + \cot^2 \theta = \left(\frac{1}{\sin \theta}\right)^2 = (\operatorname{cosec} \theta)^2 = \operatorname{cosec}^2 \theta$$

(b) Prove the identity $\dfrac{\cos \theta}{1 - \sin \theta} + \dfrac{\cos \theta}{1 + \sin \theta} = 2 \sec \theta$.

$$\frac{\cos \theta}{1 - \sin \theta} + \frac{\cos \theta}{1 + \sin \theta} = \frac{\cos \theta\,(1 + \sin \theta) + \cos \theta\,(1 - \sin \theta)}{(1 - \sin \theta)(1 + \sin \theta)}$$

$$= \frac{2 \cos \theta}{1 - \sin^2 \theta}$$

$$= \frac{2 \cos \theta}{\cos^2 \theta} = \frac{2}{\cos \theta} = 2\left(\frac{1}{\cos \theta}\right) = 2 \sec \theta$$

(c) Solve the equation $2 \sec^2 \theta = 3(2 - \tan \theta)$.

It was previously shown that $\sec^2 \theta = 1 + \tan^2 \theta$.

∴ Substituting for $\sec^2 \theta$ in the equation

$$2(1 + \tan^2 \theta) = 6 - 3 \tan \theta$$

$$\therefore\ \ 2 \tan^2 \theta + 3 \tan \theta - 4 = 0$$

This is a *quadratic equation* from which *two values of tan θ* can be found

$$\tan \theta = \frac{-3 \pm \sqrt{(9 + 32)}}{2 \times 2} = \frac{-3 \pm \sqrt{41}}{4}$$

$$\therefore\ \ \tan \theta = \frac{-3 \pm 6\cdot403}{4} = \frac{-9\cdot403}{4} \ \ \text{or} \ \ \frac{+3\cdot403}{4}$$

∴ $\tan \theta = 0\cdot8507(5)$

∴ $\theta = \tan^{-1}(0\cdot8507) = \underline{40°23'\ \text{or}\ 220°23'}$

or $\tan \theta = -2\cdot3507(5)$

∴ $\theta = \tan^{-1}(-2\cdot3507) = 180° - 66°58'\ \text{or}\ 360° - 66°58'$

∴ $\underline{\theta = 113°2'\ \text{or}\ 293°2'}$

∴ $\theta = 40°23',\ 113°2',\ 220°23',\ 293°2'$ are solutions of the equation lying between $0°$ and $360°$.

(d) Solve $\sin 2\theta = 0\cdot5$.

$$2\theta = \sin^{-1}(0\cdot5) = 30°,\ 150°,\ 390°,\ 510°$$

$$\therefore\ \ \underline{\theta = 15°,\ 75°,\ 195°,\ 255°}$$

(e) Find possible values of t to satisfy the equation

sin ωt = 0·5 (t, seconds; angles in <u>radians</u>).

$$\omega t = \sin^{-1}(0.5) = \frac{\pi}{6}, \quad \pi - \frac{\pi}{6}, \quad 2\pi + \frac{\pi}{6}, \quad 3\pi - \frac{\pi}{6}$$

$$\therefore \omega t = \frac{\pi}{6}, \quad \frac{5\pi}{6}, \quad \frac{13\pi}{6}, \quad \frac{17\pi}{6}$$

$$\therefore t = \frac{\pi}{6\omega}, \quad \frac{5\pi}{6\omega}, \quad \frac{13\pi}{6\omega}, \quad \frac{17\pi}{6\omega}, \quad \text{etc.}$$

(*Note:* ω is usually angular velocity in radians per second.)

Examples 8

1. Given $\sin A = \frac{3}{5}$ and $\cos B = \frac{12}{13}$ (A and B acute angles) without using trigonometric tables, calculate the value of $\sin A \cos B + \cos A \sin B$.

2. If $\tan \theta = -\frac{3}{4}$ and θ is obtuse (90° < θ < 180°), without using trigonometric tables evaluate $\dfrac{6 \sin \theta + 3 \cos \theta}{\sec \theta + \csc \theta}$.

3. If $\cos \phi = 0.734$, calculate possible values of $\sin \phi$ (without trigonometric tables).

4. Given $\sin A = 0.563$, calculate the value of $2\cos^2 A - 1$ (without trigonometric tables).

5. If $y = \sin \theta$, set up a table showing the values of y for values of θ from 0° to 360° in steps of 15°. Hence draw the graph of y against θ.

6. If $E = 10 \cos \theta$, set up a table showing the values of E for values of θ between 0° and 360° in steps of 15°. Hence draw the (E, θ) graph.

7. Write down the possible values of θ (0° < θ < 360°) when (i) $\theta = \sin^{-1}(0.6)$, (ii) $\theta = \cos^{-1}(-0.78)$, (iii) $\theta = \tan^{-1}(1.345)$.

8. Using suitable right-angled triangles (not drawn to scale) write down the values of $\sin \theta$, $\cos \theta$, $\tan \theta$ when (i) θ = 45°, (ii) θ = 30°, (iii) θ = 60°.

9. Calculate (in radians) the angles A, B and C between 0 and $\frac{1}{2}\pi$ when (i) $A = \sin^{-1}(0.72)$, (ii) $B = \cos^{-1}(0.385)$, (iii) $C = \tan^{-1}(0.596)$.
Establish (prove) the following identities (10–17).

10. $(\sin \theta + \cos \theta)^2 + (\sin \theta - \cos \theta)^2 = 2$.

11. $\cot \theta + \tan \theta = \sec \theta \csc \theta$.

12. $\dfrac{\sin \theta}{\sec \theta - 1} + \dfrac{\sin \theta}{\sec \theta + 1} = 2 \cot \theta$.   13. $\dfrac{2 \tan \theta}{1 + \tan^2 \theta} = 2 \sin \theta \cos \theta$.

14. $\dfrac{1}{1 + \tan^2 \theta} + \dfrac{1}{1 + \cot^2 \theta} = 1$.

15. $\dfrac{\cos\theta}{1-\cos\theta} + \dfrac{\cos\theta}{1+\cos\theta} = 2\cot\theta\operatorname{cosec}\theta$.

16. $(\sin A + \sin B)^2 + (\cos A - \cos B)^2 = 2(1 + \sin A \sin B - \cos A \cos B)$.

17. $\cos^2 A - \cos^2 B = \sin^2 B - \sin^2 A$.

Solve the equations 18–28, in each case giving solutions between 0° and 360°.

18. $4\sin\theta = 5\cos\theta$.

19. $3\cos\theta = 1\cdot8\cot\theta$.

20. $3\cos\theta = 4\tan\theta$.

21. $10\sin^2\theta = 3(\cos\theta + 3)$.

22. $4\sec^2\theta = 6 - 3\tan\theta$.

23. $\cot\theta + 2\tan\theta = 3$.

24. $4\cos\theta + \sec\theta = 5$.

25. $5\sin\theta + 2\operatorname{cosec}\theta = 7$.

26. $\sin 2\theta = 0\cdot7848$.

27. $\cos 3\theta = 0\cdot4415$.

28. $\sin(\theta - 30°) = 0\cdot5687$.

29. If the angle is in radians, find a positive value of t to satisfy the equation $\cos 5t = 0\cdot3821$.

30. Find a positive value of t to satisfy the equation $\sin(100\pi t) = 0\cdot5242$ (angle in radians).

9

Solution of Triangles

The solution of a triangle means the determination of *all* the *angles* and the *sides* of a triangle. In order to *solve* any triangle, sufficient information must be given. The information given is usually enough *for the triangle to be constructed to scale*. Almost all trigonometrical problems, involving the solution of triangles, can be done by breaking the figure up into *suitable right-angled triangles*.

9.1 Right-Angled Triangle

Solutions of right-angled triangles can be obtained by *stating correctly the definitions of sine, cosine, tangent, etc.*

Examples:

(i) Solve the right-angled triangle XYZ in which angle $X = 37°24'$, angle $Y = 90°$, $XZ = 11·7$ cm (Figure 9.1).

$$\text{Angle } Z = 180° - (90° + 37°24')$$
$$= 180° - 127°24' = \underline{52°36'}$$

$$\frac{ZY}{11·7} = \sin 37°24'$$

$$\therefore \ ZY = 11·7 \times \sin 37°24' = \underline{7·108 \text{ cm}}$$

$$\frac{XY}{11·7} = \cos 37°24'$$

$$\therefore \ XY = 11·7 \times \cos 37°24' = \underline{9·294 \text{ cm}}$$

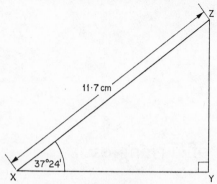

FIGURE 9.1

(ii) Solve the triangle in which angle P = 90°, PQ = 6·78 cm, PR = 9·52 cm. (Figure 9.2)

$$\tan \angle PQR = \frac{9·52}{6·78} = 1·4040 \text{ (using logs)}$$

$$\therefore \quad \underline{\angle PQR = 54°33'}$$

$$\tan \angle PRQ = \frac{6·78}{9·52} = 0·7122$$

$$\therefore \quad \underline{\angle PRQ = 35°27'}$$

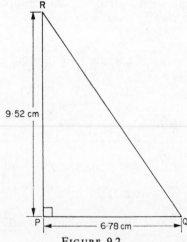

FIGURE 9.2

The hypotenuse may be found using the theorem of Pythagoras or as follows:

$$\frac{9 \cdot 52}{QR} = \sin PQR = \sin 54°33'$$

$$\therefore \; QR = \frac{9 \cdot 52}{\sin 54°33'} = \underline{11 \cdot 69 \, cm}$$

Special Notes: (i) 3 elements of the triangle *must* be given for a solution to be found. (ii) It is more methodical to do a separate calculation for the second angle rather than deduct the total from 180°.

9.1.1 Example to illustrate the solution of a general triangle by forming right-angled triangles

Solve the triangle ABC in which AB = 5·9 cm, BC = 8·4 cm, angle ABC = 51°17′. (Figure 9.3).

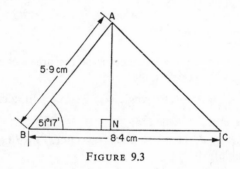

FIGURE 9.3

Draw the altitude AN. This produces two right-angled triangles.

$$\frac{AN}{5 \cdot 9} = \sin 51°17';$$

$$\therefore \; AN = 5 \cdot 9 \times \sin 51°17' = \underline{4 \cdot 604 \, cm}$$

$$\frac{BN}{5 \cdot 9} = \cos 51°17'$$

$$\therefore \; BN = 5 \cdot 9 \cos 51°17' = \underline{3 \cdot 691 \, cm}$$

Angle BAN = $90° - 51°17' = \underline{38°43'}$

$\qquad$ NC = $8·4 - 3·691 = \underline{4·709 \text{ cm}}$

$\qquad$ AC = $\sqrt{(AN^2 + NC^2)} = \sqrt{\{(4·604)^2 + (4·709)^2\}}$

$\qquad\qquad = \sqrt{(21·20 + 22·18)} = \sqrt{43·38} = \underline{6·586 \text{ cm}}$

$\qquad$ tan $\angle ACN = \dfrac{4·604}{4·709} = 0·9779$

$\qquad \therefore \quad \underline{\angle ACN = 44°21'}$

If this is correct, $\angle NAC = 45°39'$,

$\therefore$ Angle BAC = $38°43' + 45°39' = \underline{84°22'}$

$\therefore$ Using the given *three* elements, the other elements are

$\qquad$ AC = 6·586 cm, $\angle$BCA = 44°21', $\angle$BAC = 84°22'

It will be seen later that the use of the *cosine law* and *sine law* may reduce the amount of calculation required.

9.2 Areas of Triangles

All the formulae for the calculation of the areas of triangles are derived from the basic formula.

$\qquad \triangle$ = Area of triangle = $\frac{1}{2}$ Base $\times$ Altitude

9.2.1 Two useful formulae are:

(i) $\triangle = \frac{1}{2}bc \sin A$; [$\frac{1}{2} \times$ (Product two sides) $\times$ (Sine included angle)].

(*Note: A, B, C* for *angles; a, b, c* for lengths of *opposite* sides.)

$$\triangle = \frac{1}{2} bh = \frac{1}{2} b \times c \sin A \quad \text{(Figure 9.4)}$$

$$\therefore \; \triangle = \frac{1}{2} bc \sin A$$

$$\left(= \frac{1}{2} ac \sin B = \frac{1}{2} ab \sin C \right)$$

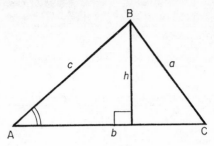

FIGURE 9.4

(ii) $\triangle = \sqrt{[s(s-a)(s-b)(s-c)]}$ where s = semi-perimeter = $\frac{1}{2}(a+b+c)$.

Using the right-angled triangles:

$$h^2 = c^2 - x^2 = a^2 - (b-x)^2 \quad \text{(Figure 9.5)}$$
$$\therefore \ c^2 - x^2 = a^2 - (b^2 - 2bx + x^2)$$

$$\therefore \ x = \frac{b^2 + c^2 - a^2}{2b}$$

$$\therefore \ h^2 = c^2 - \left[\frac{b^2 + c^2 - a^2}{2b}\right]^2 \qquad (A^2 - B^2)$$

$$= \left[c + \frac{b^2 + c^2 - a^2}{2b}\right]\left[c - \frac{b^2 + c^2 - a^2}{2b}\right]$$

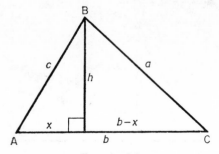

FIGURE 9.5

$$\therefore \ h^2 = \left[\frac{2bc + b^2 + c^2 - a^2}{2b}\right] \times \left[\frac{a^2 - (b^2 + c^2 - 2bc)}{2b}\right]$$

$$= \frac{[(b + c)^2 - a^2] \times [a^2 - (b - c)^2]}{4b^2}$$

$$= \frac{(b + c + a)(b + c - a)(a + c - b)(a + b - c)}{4b^2}.$$

But $$2s = a + b + c$$

$$\therefore \ b + c - a = 2(s - a)$$

Similarly $$a + c - b = 2(s - b), \quad a + b - c = 2(s - c)$$

$$\therefore \ h^2 = \frac{1}{4b^2} 2^4 s(s - a)(s - b)(s - c)$$

$$\therefore \ h = \frac{2}{b} \sqrt{[s(s - a)(s - b)(s - c)]}$$

$$\therefore \ \Delta = \frac{1}{2} bh = \sqrt{[s(s - a)(s - b)(s - c)]}$$

9.3 Sine Rule for the Solution of a Triangle

The use of this rule may avoid the process of dividing the triangle into right-angled triangles.

Consider a general triangle ABC [Figure 9.6]. Divide into two right-angled triangles as shown.

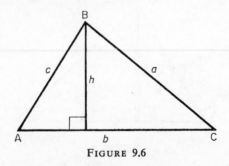

FIGURE 9.6

Then
$$\sin A = \frac{h}{c} \quad \therefore \ h = c \sin A$$

$$\sin C = \frac{h}{a} \quad \therefore \ h = a \sin C$$

$\therefore$ It follows that $c \sin A = a \sin C$

or
$$\frac{\sin A}{a} = \frac{\sin C}{c}$$

Similarly, by drawing the altitude from A to BC we find

$$b \sin C = c \sin B \quad \text{or} \quad \frac{\sin C}{c} = \frac{\sin B}{b}$$

Hence
$$\frac{\sin A}{a} = \frac{\sin B}{b} = \frac{\sin C}{c}$$

or
$$\frac{a}{\sin A} = \frac{b}{\sin B} = \frac{c}{\sin C}$$

9.3.1 The sine rule

This may be stated in words as follows: *The sides of a triangle are proportional to the sines of the opposite angles.*

In order to apply the *sine rule*, one side and the opposite angle must be known and one other element given.

9.3.2 The 'ambiguous' case of solution

Two possible triangles may result when given certain data. This data would allow *two* triangles to be constructed. The *sine rule*, giving rise to the ambiguous case is illustrated as follows:

Example: Solve the triangle ABC, in which AB = 19·7 cm, BC = 16·2 cm, angle $A = 42°27'$ [Figure 9.7].

$$\text{BN} = 19\cdot7 \times \sin 42°27' = 13\cdot3 \text{ cm.}$$

Since the side opposite the given angle has a length greater than

4

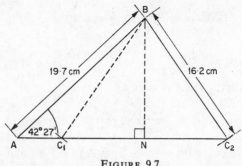

FIGURE 9.7

BN, but less than AB, if the triangle were *constructed*, it can be seen that the *construction arc* to locate C would cut the side opposite B in two points C_1 and C_2. Hence there will be two solutions when the sine rule is used.

Using the sine rule $\dfrac{\sin C}{19\cdot 7} = \dfrac{\sin 42°27'}{16\cdot 2}$

$$\therefore \sin C = \frac{19\cdot 7 \times \sin 42°27'}{16\cdot 2}$$

$$\therefore \quad \underline{C = 55°11' \text{ or } 124°49'}$$

No.	Log
19·7	1·2945
sin 42°27'	$\bar{1}$·8293
	1·1238
16·2	1·2095
sin C	$\bar{1}$·9143

$$\therefore \text{ Angle } ABC_2 = 180° - (42°27' + 55°11')$$

$$= \underline{82°22'}$$

$$\text{Angle } ABC_1 = 180° - (42°27' + 124°49') = \underline{12°44'}$$

To find the third side in each case:

$$\frac{AC_1}{\sin 12°44'} = \frac{16\cdot 2}{\sin 42°27'}$$

$$\frac{AC_2}{\sin 82°22'} = \frac{16\cdot 2}{\sin 42°27'}$$

$$\therefore \ AC_1 = \frac{16 \cdot 2 \times \sin 12°44'}{\sin 42°27'} = \underline{5 \cdot 289 \text{ cm}}$$

$$AC_2 = \frac{16 \cdot 2 \times \sin 82°22'}{\sin 42°27'} = \underline{23 \cdot 79 \text{ cm}}$$

$\therefore$ *Solutions are:*

    (i) $b = 5 \cdot 289$ cm; $C = 124°49'$; $B = 12°44'$

    (ii) $b = 23 \cdot 79$ cm; $C = 55°11'$; $B = 82°22'$

WORKED EXAMPLES

(*a*) The sides of a triangle are 22·3 cm, 16·9 cm and 12·5 cm. Calculate the area of the triangle and hence find the angles. Let the triangle be ABC, $a = 22 \cdot 3$ cm, $b = 16 \cdot 9$ cm, $c = 12 \cdot 5$ cm.

$$s = \frac{1}{2}(a + b + c) = \frac{51 \cdot 7}{2} = 25 \cdot 85 \text{ cm}$$

$$s - a = 3 \cdot 55 \text{ cm}; \quad s - b = 8 \cdot 95 \text{ cm}; \quad s - c = 13 \cdot 35 \text{ cm}$$

$$\triangle = \sqrt{[s(s-a)(s-b)(s-c)]}$$
$$= \sqrt{(25 \cdot 85 \times 3 \cdot 55 \times 8 \cdot 95 \times 13 \cdot 35)} = \underline{104 \cdot 7 \text{ cm}^2}$$

$$\therefore \tfrac{1}{2}bc \sin A = 104 \cdot 7;$$

$$\sin A = \frac{209 \cdot 4}{16 \cdot 9 \times 12 \cdot 5}$$

$$\therefore \ \underline{A = 82°26' \text{ or } A = 97°34'}$$

and $\dfrac{1}{2} ac \sin B = 104 \cdot 7$; $\sin B = \dfrac{209 \cdot 4}{22 \cdot 3 \times 12 \cdot 5}$; $\underline{B = 48°41'}$

and $\dfrac{1}{2} ab \sin C = 104 \cdot 7$; $\sin C = \dfrac{209 \cdot 4}{22 \cdot 3 \times 16 \cdot 9}$; $\underline{C = 33°45'}$

(*Note: A is the largest angle and can be obtuse. Using the obtuse angle* $A + B + C = 180°0'$.)

(*b*) Solve the triangle XYZ in which $x = 58 \cdot 9$ cm, $Y = 52°7'$, $Z = 28°11'$. Calculate also the area of the triangle [Figure 9.8]

$$X = 180° - (52°7' + 28°11')$$
$$= 180° - 80°18' = \underline{99°42'}$$

Using the sine rule

$$\frac{XZ}{\sin 52°7'} = \frac{XY}{\sin 28°11'} = \frac{58·9}{\sin 99°42'}$$

Angle X is obtuse, but $\sin 99°42' = +\sin 80°18'$

$$\therefore XZ = \frac{58·9 \times \sin 52°7'}{\sin 80°18'} = \underline{47·17\,\text{cm}}$$

and $$XY = \frac{58·9 \times \sin 28°11'}{\sin 80°18'} = \underline{28·22\,\text{cm}}$$

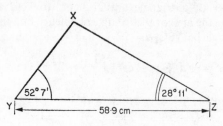

FIGURE 9.8

$$\text{Area of triangle} = \frac{1}{2}\,xz \sin Y$$

$$= \frac{1}{2} \times 58·9 \times 28·22 \sin 52°7'$$

$$= 29·45 \times 28·22 \times \sin 52°7'$$

$$= \underline{655·7\,\text{cm}^2}$$

(*Note: It is usually advisable to make a fair sketch when doing any trigonometrical problem. This is particularly important when solving practical problems.*)

Examples 9

1. A triangle PQR has PQ = 5·9 metres, QR = 9·2 metres and angle Q = 107°15′. Calculate the area of the triangle.
2. The three sides of a triangle are 15·65 m, 11·74 m and 8·93 m. Calculate the area of the triangle and the smallest angle.
3. The area of a triangle is 160 cm². Two sides include an angle of 46°19′ and one of these sides is 25·6 cm. Find the other side.

4. Two tangents from a point P to a circle include an angle of 67°. Each tangent is 11·5 cm long. Find the area of the circle.

5. In the quadrilateral ABCD, AB = 11 cm, BC = 14 cm, CD = 19 cm, DA = 15 cm, and diagonal BD = 12 cm. Calculate its area and the angles A and C.

6. To calculate the angle of a V notch, a cylindrical bar of radius 30·2 mm is placed in with its axis parallel to the base of the Vee. If the top of the cylinder is 118·6 mm above the base of the Vee, calculate the Vee angle.

7. Two points A and B are on a sloping hillside with B above A. The hill slopes at 28°15′ to the horizontal along AB. A 2 metre pole placed vertically at B subtends an angle of 7°12′ at A. Calculate the distance AB and the height of B above A.

8. From two points A and B on one side of a river, 100 metres apart, observations made to a point P on the opposite side are as follows: angle PAB = 53°17′, angle PBA = 67°9′. Calculate the distances of P from A and B, and the shortest distance from P to AB.

9. In order to estimate the height of a tower at a point C, two elevations are taken to the top of the tower from points A and B, which are 60 metres apart. A bears S 50° E of C and B bears S 40° W of C. The elevation at A is 12°17′ and at B 15°6′. Calculate the height of the tower.

10. ABC is a triangle of forces. AB is 3·5 cm and represents a force of 17·5 N. Angle BAC = 47°30′, angle ABC = 72°15′. Calculate the forces represented by the sides AC and BC.

11. The base of a minor segment of a circle (of radius 7·5 cm) is 9·8 cm. Calculate the area of the segment of the circle.

12. The angle PQR of a triangle is 65°, PQ = 17·6 cm, QR = 29·5 cm. Calculate the area of the triangle PQR. If the bisector of angle Q meets PR in T, calculate the ratio of the areas of triangles QPT and QRT.

10

Cosine Rule and Radius of Circumcircle

10.1 Cosine Rule

This rule (to be established) may be used to begin the solution of any triangles in two cases:

> (i) Given two sides and the included angle.
>
> (ii) Given the three sides.

In case (i) the rule allows the third side to be calculated.

In case (ii) the rule allows one angle (or all the angles) to be calculated.

Again, in order to establish the rule, use is made of the *trigonometry of the right-angled triangle* and the theorem of Pythagoras.

10.1.1 Proof of the rule

The results for acute angles and obtuse angles will be established side by side as follows:

(i) *Acute case*   (ii) *Obtuse case*

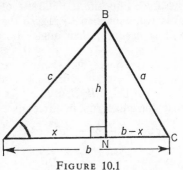   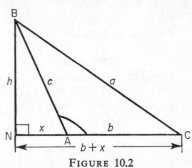

FIGURE 10.1   FIGURE 10.2

Two right-angled triangles are formed in each case.

$c^2 = h^2 + x^2$	$c^2 = h^2 + x^2$
$a^2 = h^2 + (b - x)^2$	$a^2 = h^2 + (b + x)^2$
$a^2 = h^2 + x^2 + b^2 - 2bx$	$a^2 = h^2 + x^2 + b^2 + 2bx$
$a^2 = c^2 + b^2 - 2bx$	$a^2 = c^2 + b^2 + 2bx$
but $x = c \cos A$	but $x = c \cos (180° - A)$
	$\qquad = -c \cos A$
$\therefore\ a^2 = b^2 + c^2 - 2bc \cos A :$	$a^2 = b^2 + c^2 - 2bc \cos A$

Therefore it is established that, for acute and obtuse angles:

$$a^2 = b^2 + c^2 - 2bc \cos A$$

Special Note: When using the formula, it is important to remember

 (i) When A is *acute, cos A* is *positive.*

 (ii) When A is *obtuse, cos A* is *negative.*

10.1.2 Transposition of the cosine rule

The form established in 10.1.1 is mainly used to calculate the *third* side when two sides and the included angle are given. When three sides are given, the formula is transposed as follows:

$$2bc \cos A = b^2 + c^2 - a^2$$
$$\therefore\ \cos A = \frac{b^2 + c^2 - a^2}{2bc}$$

and in this form, direct substitution in this formula of the three sides a, b, c, gives the cosine of the angle opposite a. The use of tables of squares (or square roots) is recommended to reduce the amount of calculation. If cosine A is *negative*, then angle A is *obtuse*.

The formula should be memorized as above, but it must be borne in mind that b and c enclose A, and a is the third side. In many problems the letters involved will *not* be A, B, C, a, b, c. As, in a number of cases, trigonometric formulae run in threes, so:

$$b^2 = a^2 + c^2 - 2ac \cos B; \qquad c^2 = a^2 + b^2 - 2ab \cos C$$

$$\cos B = \frac{a^2 + c^2 - b^2}{2ac}; \qquad \cos C = \frac{a^2 + b^2 - c^2}{2ab}$$

Illustrations

(i) Calculate side a of triangle ABC if $b = 7\cdot8$ cm, $c = 9\cdot7$ cm, $A = 57°33'$.

$$\begin{aligned}
a^2 &= b^2 + c^2 - 2bc \cos A \\
&= (7\cdot8)^2 + (9\cdot7)^2 - 2 \times 7\cdot8 \times 9\cdot7 \cos 57°33' \\
&= 60\cdot84 + 94\cdot09 - 15\cdot6 \times 9\cdot7 \times 0\cdot5366 \qquad &1\cdot1931 \\
&= 154\cdot93 - 81\cdot21 = \underline{73\cdot72} \qquad &0\cdot9868 \\
\therefore \quad a &= \sqrt{73\cdot72} = \underline{8\cdot586 \text{ cm}} \qquad &\overline{1\cdot7297} \\
& &\overline{1\cdot9096}
\end{aligned}$$

(Square root tables used for the squares and square root.)

(ii) Calculate x in triangle XYZ if $y = 19\cdot3$ cm, $z = 25\cdot6$ cm, and $X = 107°12'$.

$$\begin{aligned}
x^2 &= y^2 + z^2 - 2yz \cos X \\
&= (19\cdot3)^2 + (25\cdot6)^2 - 2 \times 19\cdot3 \times 25\cdot6 \cos 107°12' \\
&= 372\cdot6 + 655\cdot2 - 38\cdot6 \times 25\cdot6 \times (-\cos 72°48') \\
&= 1{,}027\cdot8 + 38\cdot6 \times 25\cdot6 \times 0\cdot2957 \qquad &1\cdot5866 \\
&= 1{,}027\cdot8 + 292\cdot1 = \underline{1{,}319\cdot9} \qquad &1\cdot4082 \\
\therefore \quad x &= \sqrt{1{,}320} = \underline{36\cdot33 \text{ cm}} \qquad &\overline{1\cdot4708} \\
& &\overline{2\cdot4656}
\end{aligned}$$

(*Note:* Cosine *negative* when the angle is obtuse.)

(iii) Find, using the cosine rule, the three angles of the triangle whose sides are 9, 13, 17 centimetres.

Let $a = 9$ cm, $b = 13$ cm, $c = 17$ cm.

$$\cos A = \frac{b^2 + c^2 - a^2}{2bc} = \frac{13^2 + 17^2 - 9^2}{2 \times 13 \times 17} = \frac{169 + 289 - 81}{442} = \frac{377}{442}$$

$$\therefore \cos A = 0{\cdot}8529$$

$$\therefore \underline{A = \cos^{-1}(0{\cdot}8529) = 31°29'}$$

$$\cos B = \frac{a^2 + c^2 - b^2}{2ac} = \frac{9^2 + 17^2 - 13^2}{2 \times 9 \times 17} = \frac{81 + 289 - 169}{306} = \frac{201}{306}$$

$$\therefore \cos B = 0{\cdot}6569$$

$$\therefore \underline{B = \cos^{-1}(0{\cdot}6569) = 48°56'}$$

$$\cos C = \frac{a^2 + b^2 - c^2}{2ab} = \frac{9^2 + 13^2 - 17^2}{2 \times 9 \times 13} = \frac{81 + 169 - 289}{234}$$

$$= -\frac{39}{234}$$

$$\therefore \cos C = -0{\cdot}1666 \ (C \text{ obtuse})$$

$$\therefore \underline{C = 180° - 80°25' = 99°35'}$$

Check: $\underline{A + B + C = 180°0'}$

10.2 Circumcircle of a Triangle

This is the circle which can be drawn to pass through the three vertices. Its radius (or diameter) is directly connected with the *sine rule*. If R is the radius of the circle, it will be proved that

$$\underline{R = \frac{a}{2 \sin A} = \frac{b}{2 \sin B} = \frac{c}{2 \sin C}}$$

or

$$\underline{D = \frac{a}{\sin A} = \frac{b}{\sin B} = \frac{c}{\sin C}}$$

(D is the diameter)

10.2.1 Radius of the circle

Each side of the triangle is a chord of the circle. The centre O can be found by finding the intersection of the perpendicular bisectors of the sides. [Figure 10.3].

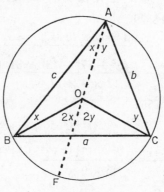

FIGURE 10.3

Since triangles BOA, COA are isosceles, if their base angles are x and y as shown.

Then
$$\angle BOF = x + x = 2x$$
$$\angle COF = y + y = 2y$$
$$\angle BOC = 2x + 2y = 2(x + y) = 2 \times \text{angle } A$$

(A useful geometrical theorem.)

Bisect angle BOC [Figure 10.4]. Then since BOC is isosceles, it follows that $\dfrac{a/2}{R} = \sin A$ or $R = \dfrac{a}{2 \sin A}$

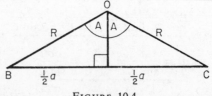

FIGURE 10.4

and because of the sine rule it follows that

$$R = \frac{a}{2 \sin A} = \frac{b}{2 \sin B} = \frac{c}{2 \sin C}$$

or

$$D = \frac{a}{\sin A} = \frac{b}{\sin B} = \frac{c}{\sin C}$$

$(D$ is the diameter)

Example: Calculate the radius of the circle to pass through the vertices of a triangle whose sides are 11·5 cm, 13·6 cm, 7·9 cm. Let $a = 11·5$ cm, $b = 13·6$ cm, $c = 7·9$ cm.
Then

$$\cos A = \frac{b^2 + c^2 - a^2}{2bc} = \frac{13·6^2 + 7·9^2 - 11·5^2}{2 \times 13·6 \times 7·9}$$

$$= \frac{184·9 + 62·4 - 132·2}{27·2 \times 7·9} = \frac{115·1}{214·9} = 0·5357$$

$$\therefore A = \cos^{-1}(0·5357) = 57°36'$$

$$\sin A = 0·8443$$

Radius of circumcircle

$$R = \frac{a}{2 \sin A} = \frac{11·5}{2 \times 0·8443} = \frac{5·75}{0·8443} \text{ cm}$$

$$\therefore R = 6·811 \text{ cm.}$$

10.3 The Ambiguous Case of Solution of a Triangle

When the cosine rule is used (when the data is of correct form) no ambiguity arises, since, if the cosine is negative, the angle is obtuse. However, when the sine rule is used, as explained in 9.3.2, two triangles are possible on occasions. This is because the sine of an obtuse angle is positive. The general case of ambiguity may be explained as follows:

Given two sides and one opposite angle:

Given A, a, c, (Figure 10.5) if $a > c \sin A$ but $a < c$, when the triangle is solved, there are two possible angles BC_1A (obtuse),

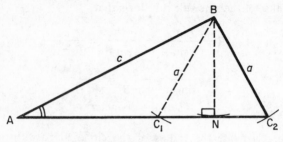

FIGURE 10.5

BC_2A (acute). These two angles have the same sine. If the figure is *constructed* to scale, the arc, centre B and radius a, will cut the side opposite B in two points.

Note: (i) For example see 9.3.2.

(ii) If $c \sin A = a$ (exactly), the triangle will be right angled at N.

(iii) If $c \sin A > a$, the triangle is not real, i.e. cannot be constructed.

Special Note: When a right-angled triangle is given, it should *not* be solved using the general sine and cosine rules.

WORKED EXAMPLES

(a) Two forces of magnitudes 3·9 and 5·7 N act at a point O. The angle between the forces is 67°15′. Calculate the magnitude of the resultant force and the angle its line of action makes with the larger force (Figure 10.6).

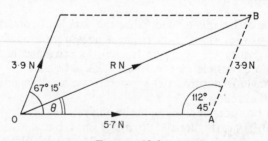

FIGURE 10.6

The resultant, to scale, is represented by R N, the diagonal of the parallelogram. Using the triangle OAB ($\angle$OAB $= 180° - 67°15' = 112°45'$),

$$R^2 = (5\cdot7)^2 + (3\cdot9)^2 - 2 \times 5\cdot7 \times 3\cdot9 \times \cos 112°45'$$

$$\therefore\ R^2 = 32\cdot49 + 15\cdot21 + 5\cdot7 \times 7\cdot8 \times 0\cdot3867$$

$$(\cos 112°45' = -\cos 67°15')$$

$$= 47\cdot70 + 17\cdot20 = 64\cdot90$$

$$\therefore\ \underline{R = \sqrt{64\cdot90} = 8\cdot056\ \text{N}.}$$

If θ is the angle made by the resultant with the 5·7 N force,

$$\frac{\sin \theta}{3\cdot9} = \frac{\sin 112°45'}{8\cdot056} = \frac{\sin 67°15'}{8\cdot056}$$

$$\therefore\ \sin \theta = \frac{3\cdot9 \times \sin 67°15'}{8\cdot056} = 0\cdot4466$$

$$\underline{\theta = 26°32'}$$

$\therefore$ The resultant force is 8·056 N at 26°32' to 5·7 N force.

(b) A surveyor is to lay out the centre line of a circular track, to pass through three points A, B and C. Observations recorded in his notebook are as follows: AB = 100 m, BC = 140 m, angle ABC = 146°. Calculate the radius of the circular centre line (Figure 10.7).

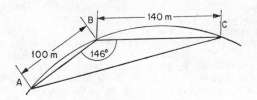

FIGURE 10.7

$$AC^2 = 100^2 + 140^2 - 2 \times 100 \times 140 \times \cos 146°$$

$$= 10\,000 + 19\,600 + 28\,000 \cos 34°$$

$$= 29\,600 + 28\,000 \times 0\cdot8290$$

$$\therefore \ AC^2 = 29\,600 + 23\,212 = 52\,812$$

$$\therefore \ AC = \sqrt{52\,812} = 229 \cdot 8 \text{ metres}$$

Radius of curve

$$R = \frac{AC}{2 \sin 146°} = \frac{229 \cdot 8}{2 \sin 34°} = \frac{114 \cdot 9}{\cdot 5592} \text{ metres}$$

$$= 205 \cdot 6 \text{ metres}$$

$$\simeq \underline{206 \text{ metres}}$$

Examples 10

1. Calculate the area and angles of the triangle with sides of lengths 8, 15 and 20 centimetres.

2. Solve the triangle ABC, given AB = 9·2 cm, AC = 12·5 cm and angle BAC = 47°25′. Calculate the area of the triangle and radius of the circumcircle.

3. Calculate the third side and radius of the circumcircle of the triangle XYZ given XY = 5·72 cm, XZ = 8·93 cm, angle YXZ = 121°17′.

4. In the quadrilateral PQRS (taken in order), QP = 7·6 cm, QR = 6·9 cm, QS = 9·5 cm, angle PQS = 51°23′, angle SQR = 32°17′. Calculate the area of the figure, the lengths of PS and RS and the diagonal PR.

5. In the quadrilateral ABCD (taken in order), AB = 9 cm, BC = 11 cm, CD = 14 cm, DA = 17 cm and AC = 13 cm. Find the area of the figure and the sum of the angles ABC and ADC.

6. Forces of 17·5 N and 22·4 N act through a point O. The angle between the forces is 61°28′. Find the magnitude of the resultant force and the angle which it makes with the larger force.

7. Find the magnitude and direction of the resultant of two forces of magnitudes 55 and 75 N, if the forces include an angle of 120°.

8. A roadway is to be cut so that its centre line is an arc of a circle and passes through A, B and C. Find the radius of the arc, in metres to the nearest metre, when AB = 160 m, BC = 180 m and AC = 280 m.

9. A, B, C and D are stations in a survey forming a quadrilateral such that AB = 148·5 m, AD = 126·6 m, angle ABC = 70°33′, angle BAC = 41°19′ and angle BAD = 79°41′. Calculate the length of CD.

10. A quadrilateral ABCD is the plan of a survey. The distance AB is 200 m, and the following angles are observed: angle BAC = 35°, angle ABC = 65°, angle ABD = 30° and angle DAC = 45°. Calculate the length of CD and the area of ABCD.

11. In part of a mechanism shown in Figure 10.8, a link AB 81 cm long, has a block pivoted to each end. These blocks can slide in grooves as indicated. The point of intersection of the line of centres is at C. Initially BC = 55·5 cm, AC = 41·1 cm. Calculate the angle between the line of centres (BCA) and the inclination of AB to AC. If the block B moves 15 cm towards C from the given position, find how far A moves.

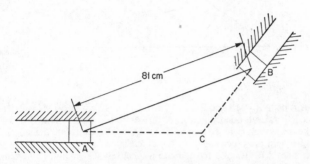

81 cm

B

C

A

FIGURE 10.8

12. The angles of elevation of a hilltop are 30° from P_1 and 40° from P_2, both P_1 and P_2 being at sea-level. The bearings of the hilltop, which is 120 metres high, are N25°E from P_1 and N30°W from P_2. Find the distance P_1P_2 and the bearing of P_2 from P_1.

13. In the triangle ABC, AB = 8·9 cm, BC = 11·5 cm and angle ABC = 117°13′. Solve the triangle, calculate its area and the radius of the circumcircle.

14. A man finds that the line from a point on one bank of a straight canal to the foot of a tree on the opposite bank makes an angle of 19°18′ with the bank on which he is standing. He then walks 25 metres along the bank, without passing the tree and finds that the line to the tree makes an angle of 34°39′ with the banks. Find the breadth of the canal.

15. To move from island T to island N, which is 18 Km due South of T, a ship follows the course S62°W for 10 Km, then changes its course to S23°E, and sometime later changes its course to N45°E, now heading straight for N. Find how long it takes the ship, assuming that it travels at a uniform speed of 15 Km/hour.

16. In a quadrilateral ABCD, AB = CD, BC = 30 m, AD = 20 m, angle BAD = 50° and angle BCD = 40°. Calculate the lengths of AB, BD, angle DBC and the area of the quadrilateral.

17. To find the distance of a landmark P from a point A (P is not visible from A), a surveyor takes readings from two points B and C in line with A from which P is visible. The measurements are recorded as shown in the sketch (Figure 10.9). Calculate the distance of P from A, and the shortest distance

of P from AB. Calculate also the radius of the circle to pass through A, P and B.

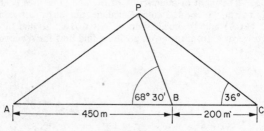

FIGURE 10.9

18. Four rods, AB = 18 cm, BC = 24 cm, CD = 16 cm and DA = 21 cm, are joined to form a quadrilateral. A further rod is used to join B and D and make the system rigid, so that angle BCD = 80°. Calculate the length of the rod BD and the other angles of the quadrilateral.

19. Two sides AB, BC of a triangle are respectively 9·8 cm and 12·7 cm and the area is 53·5 cm². Calculate the included acute angle and the third side.

20. The diameter of the circumcircle of a triangle is 65 cm. One of the sides is 45 cm. Find the size of the opposite angle.

11

Compound Angle Formulae

11.1 Sin $(A + B)$ and cos $(A + B)$

11.1.1 Compound angles

These normally consist of the sum and/or difference of two or more angles. The formulae to be established express the trigonometric ratios of compound angles in terms of the trigonometric ratios of the separate angles. The formulae may be established in at least two ways. One method only will be used.

11.1.2 Sin $(A + B)$

Consider the area of the triangle PQR (Figure 11.1):

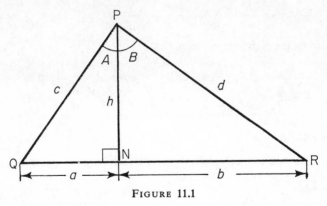

FIGURE 11.1

$$\triangle PQR = \triangle PNQ + \triangle PNR$$

$$\tfrac{1}{2} cd \sin (A + B) = \tfrac{1}{2} hc \sin A + \tfrac{1}{2} hd \sin B$$

Multiply throughout by $\dfrac{2}{cd}$.

Then

$$\sin (A + B) = \frac{h}{d} \sin A + \frac{h}{c} \sin B$$

but

$$\frac{h}{d} = \cos B; \qquad \frac{h}{c} = \cos A$$

$$\therefore \; \sin (A + B) = \cos B \sin A + \cos A \sin B$$

$$\text{or} \; \underline{\sin (A + B) = \sin A \cos B + \cos A \sin B}$$

11.1.3 Cos $(A + B)$

Referring to Figure 11.1, and applying the cosine rule to find the angle $(A + B)$:

$$\cos (A + B) = \frac{c^2 + d^2 - (a + b)^2}{2cd} = \frac{c^2 + d^2 - (a^2 + b^2 + 2ab)}{2cd}$$

$$= \frac{(c^2 - a^2) + (d^2 - b^2) - 2ab}{2cd} = \frac{h^2 + h^2 - 2ab}{2cd}$$

$$= \frac{2h^2}{2cd} - \frac{2ab}{2cd} = \frac{h}{c} \frac{h}{d} - \frac{a}{c} \frac{b}{d}$$

But from the right-angled triangles:

$$\frac{h}{c} = \cos A; \quad \frac{h}{d} = \cos B; \quad \frac{a}{c} = \sin A; \quad \frac{b}{d} = \sin B$$

$$\therefore \; \underline{\cos (A + B) = \cos A \cos B - \sin A \sin B}$$

11.1.4

It is essential to memorize the above results and to realize that, since the sine of an angle increases with increase of angle, the *expansion* of $\sin (A + B)$ involves a *plus* sign, whereas, since the cosine decreases with increase of angle, the *expansion* of cos $(A + B)$ involves a *negative* sign (acute angles).

11.2 Sin $(A - B)$ and cos $(A - B)$

11.2.1 Sin $(A - B)$

Consider the area of the triangle PQR (Figure 11.2):

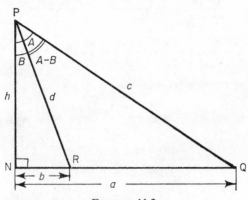

FIGURE 11.2

$$\triangle PQR = \triangle PNQ - \triangle PNR$$

$$\therefore \ \tfrac{1}{2} cd \sin (A - B) = \tfrac{1}{2} hc \sin A - \tfrac{1}{2} hd \sin B$$

Multiply throughout by $\dfrac{2}{cd}$.

Then

$$\sin (A - B) = \frac{h}{d} \sin A - \frac{h}{c} \sin B$$

but

$$\frac{h}{d} = \cos B; \qquad \frac{h}{c} = \cos A$$

$$\sin (A - B) = \cos B \sin A - \cos A \sin B$$

or

$$\underline{\sin (A - B) = \sin A \cos B - \cos A \sin B}$$

11.2.2 Cos $(A - B)$

Referring to (Figure 11.2), and applying the cosine rule to find the angle $(A - B)$:

$$\cos(A - B) = \frac{c^2 + d^2 - (a - b)^2}{2cd} = \frac{c^2 + d^2 - (a^2 + b^2 - 2ab)}{2cd}$$

$$= \frac{(c^2 - a^2) + (d^2 - b^2) + 2ab}{2cd} = \frac{h^2 + h^2 + 2ab}{2cd}$$

$$= \frac{2h^2}{2cd} + \frac{2ab}{2cd} = \frac{h}{c}\frac{h}{d} + \frac{a}{c}\frac{b}{d}$$

But from the right-angled triangles:

$$\frac{h}{c} = \cos A; \quad \frac{h}{d} = \cos B; \quad \frac{a}{c} = \sin A; \quad \frac{b}{d} = \sin B$$

$$\therefore \quad \underline{\cos(A - B) = \cos A \cos B + \sin A \sin B}$$

11.2.3

It is essential to memorize the above results and appreciate that, since the sine of an angle decreases with decrease of angle, the expansion of $\sin(A - B)$ involves a *negative* sign, whereas, since the cosine increases with decrease in angle, the expansion of $\cos(A - B)$ involves a *positive* sign (acute angles).

Although the above expansions have been established for acute angles they hold for angles of any magnitude.

11.3 Expansions for tan $(A + B)$, tan $(A - B)$

These may be established geometrically in terms of the tangents of the separate angles A and B but the proofs are much more complicated than the above proofs. The results will be established by means of the identity $\tan\theta = \dfrac{\sin\theta}{\cos\theta}$.

11.3.1 Tan $(A + B)$

Use is made of the expansions for $\sin (A + B)$ and $\cos (A + B)$ as follows:

$$\tan (A + B) = \frac{\sin (A + B)}{\cos (A + B)} = \frac{\sin A \cos B + \cos A \sin B}{\cos A \cos B - \sin A \sin B}$$

divide the numerator and denominator by $\cos A \cos B$: then

$$\tan (A + B) = \frac{\dfrac{\sin A}{\cos A} + \dfrac{\sin B}{\cos B}}{1 - \dfrac{\sin A}{\cos A}\dfrac{\sin B}{\cos B}}$$

(*Note:* All four terms are divided by $\cos A \cos B$.)

$$\therefore \quad \tan (A + B) = \frac{\tan A + \tan B}{1 - \tan A \tan B}$$

11.3.2 Tan $(A - B)$

Use is made of the expansions for $\sin (A - B)$ and $\cos (A - B)$ as follows:

$$\tan (A - B) = \frac{\sin (A - B)}{\cos (A - B)} = \frac{\sin A \cos B - \cos A \sin B}{\cos A \cos B + \sin A \sin B};$$

divide the numerator and denominator by $\cos A \cos B$ as above: then

$$\tan (A - B) = \frac{\dfrac{\sin A}{\cos A} - \dfrac{\sin B}{\cos B}}{1 + \dfrac{\sin A}{\cos A}\dfrac{\sin B}{\cos B}}$$

(*Note:* All four terms are divided by $\cos A \cos B$.)

$$\therefore \quad \tan (A - B) = \frac{\tan A - \tan B}{1 + \tan A \tan B}$$

WORKED EXAMPLES

(a) If $\cos A = \frac{3}{5}$, $\tan B = \frac{5}{12}$, A and B being acute, find the values of $\sin(A + B)$, $\cos(A + B)$, $\tan(A + B)$ without using trigonometric tables.

In order to write down the required ratios for A and B, separate sketches are used as shown (Figure 11.3). The third

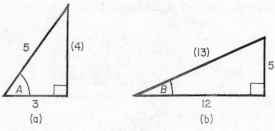

FIGURE 11.3

side of the two triangles can be calculated using *Pythagoras' theorem*.

$$\sin(A + B) = \sin A \cos B + \cos A \sin B$$

$$= \frac{4}{5} \times \frac{12}{13} + \frac{3}{5} \times \frac{5}{13} = \underline{\frac{63}{65}}$$

$$\cos(A + B) = \cos A \cos B - \sin A \sin B$$

$$= \frac{3}{5} \times \frac{12}{13} - \frac{4}{5} \times \frac{5}{13} = \underline{\frac{16}{65}}$$

$$\tan(A + B) = \frac{\sin(A + B)}{\cos(A + B)} = \frac{63}{65} \div \frac{16}{65} = \frac{63}{16} = 3\underline{\frac{15}{16}}$$

(b) Without using trigonometric tables, evaluate, using appropriate compound angle formulae, $\sin 15°$, $\cos 75°$, $\tan 15°$ (to 4 decimal places).

$15°$ can be formed by compounding $45°$ and $30°$ or $45°$ and $60°$. The ratios for these angles can be written down using the sketches (Figure 11.4).

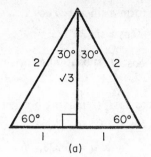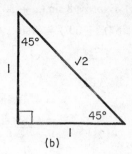

FIGURE 11.4

$\sin 15° = \sin(45° - 30°)$ [form $\sin(A - B)$]

$\quad = \sin 45° \cos 30° - \cos 45° \sin 30° = \dfrac{1}{\sqrt{2}} \times \dfrac{\sqrt{3}}{2} - \dfrac{1}{\sqrt{2}} \times \dfrac{1}{2}$

$\quad = \dfrac{\sqrt{3} - 1}{2\sqrt{2}} = \dfrac{\sqrt{6} - \sqrt{2}}{4}$

$\quad = \dfrac{2 \cdot 449 - 1 \cdot 414}{4} = \dfrac{1 \cdot 035}{4} = \underline{0 \cdot 2587(5)}$

$\qquad\qquad\qquad\qquad = \underline{0 \cdot 2588}$

$\cos 75° = \cos(45° + 30°) = \cos 45° \cos 30° - \sin 45° \sin 30°$

$\quad = \dfrac{1}{\sqrt{2}} \dfrac{\sqrt{3}}{2} - \dfrac{1}{\sqrt{2}} \dfrac{1}{2} = \dfrac{\sqrt{3} - 1}{2\sqrt{2}} = 0 \cdot 2588$ (as above)

$\tan 15° = \tan(45° - 30°)$ [form $\tan(A - B)$]

$\quad = \dfrac{\tan 45° - \tan 30°}{1 + \tan 45° \tan 30°} = \dfrac{1 - \dfrac{1}{\sqrt{3}}}{1 + 1 \times \dfrac{1}{\sqrt{3}}} = \dfrac{\sqrt{3} - 1}{\sqrt{3} + 1}$

$\quad = \dfrac{(\sqrt{3} - 1)(\sqrt{3} - 1)}{(\sqrt{3} + 1)(\sqrt{3} - 1)} = \dfrac{4 - 2\sqrt{3}}{2} = 2 - \sqrt{3}$

$\quad = 2 - 1 \cdot 7321$

$\quad = \underline{0 \cdot 2679}$

(*Note:* $\sin 15° = \cos 75°$ since the angles are complementary.)

(c) Express $8 \sin(x + 30°)$ in the form $a \sin x + b \cos x$.

$$8 \sin(x + 30°) = 8(\sin x \cos 30° + \cos x \sin 30°)$$

$$= 8\left(\frac{\sqrt{3}}{2} \sin x + \frac{1}{2} \cos x\right) \text{ (substituting for } \sin 30°$$

and $\cos 30°$)

$$= 4\sqrt{3} \sin x + 4 \cos x \quad \text{(removing brackets)}$$

$$= \underline{6 \cdot 928 \sin x + 4 \cos x}$$

(note $a = 6 \cdot 928$, $b = 4$)

(d) If $\tan(A + B) = 1 \cdot 8$ and $\tan A = 0 \cdot 6$, calculate $\tan B$.

$$\tan(A + B) = \frac{\tan A + \tan B}{1 - \tan A \tan B}$$

$$\therefore \ 1 \cdot 8 = \frac{0 \cdot 6 + \tan B}{1 - 0 \cdot 6 \times \tan B}$$

$$\therefore \ 1 \cdot 8(1 - 0 \cdot 6 \tan B) = 0 \cdot 6 + \tan B$$

$$\therefore \ 1 \cdot 2 = 2 \cdot 08 \tan B$$

$$\therefore \ \tan B = \frac{1 \cdot 2}{2 \cdot 08} = \underline{0 \cdot 5769}$$

(e) Given $\cos 24° = 0 \cdot 9135$, calculate $\cos 12°$.

$$\cos 24° = \cos(12° + 12°) = \cos 12° \cos 12° - \sin 12° \sin 12°$$

$$= \cos^2 12° - \sin^2 12° = \cos^2 12° - (1 - \cos^2 12°)$$

$$\cos 24° = 2 \cos^2 12° - 1$$

$$\therefore \ 2 \cos^2 12° = 1 + \cos 24°$$

$$\therefore \ \cos^2 12° = \frac{1 + \cos 24°}{2} = \frac{1 + 0 \cdot 9135}{2} = \frac{1 \cdot 9135}{2} = 0 \cdot 9568$$

$$\therefore \ \cos 12° = \sqrt{0 \cdot 9568} = \underline{0 \cdot 9782}$$

(f) By expansion, find possible values of R and α in order that $3 \cos x + 4 \sin x$ may be expressed as $R \cos(x - \alpha)$.

Let $R \cos(x - \alpha) = 3 \cos x + 4 \sin x$ (to be an *identity*)

$$\therefore \ R(\cos x \cos \alpha + \sin x \sin \alpha) = 3 \cos x + 4 \sin x \text{ (Remove brackets)}$$

$$\therefore \ \underline{\underline{(R \cos \alpha)}} \cos x + \underline{\underline{(R \sin \alpha)}} \sin x = \underline{\underline{3}} \cos x + \underline{4} \sin x$$

For this identity to be true:

$$R \cos \alpha = 3 \qquad \text{(i)}$$
$$R \sin \alpha = 4 \qquad \text{(ii)}$$

Squaring and adding $R^2 \cos^2 \alpha + R^2 \sin^2 \alpha = 3^2 + 4^2 = 25$

$$R^2(\cos^2 \alpha + \sin^2 \alpha) = 25$$

but $\qquad \cos^2 \alpha + \sin^2 \alpha = 1$

$\therefore \; R^2 = 25 \qquad \therefore \; R = \sqrt{25} = \underline{5}$

Divide (ii) by (i)

$$\frac{R \sin \alpha}{R \cos \alpha} = \frac{4}{3}$$

$$\therefore \; \tan \alpha = \frac{4}{3}$$

$$\therefore \qquad \underline{\alpha = 53°8'}$$

$\therefore \; \underline{3 \cos x + 4 \sin x = 5 \cos (x - 53°8')}$

(g) Reduce $10 \sin (x + 35°) + 20 \cos (x - 47°)$ to the form $p \sin x + q \cos x$, stating the values of p and q to 3 decimal places.

$10 \sin (x + 35°) + 20 \cos (x - 47°)$

$\quad = 10(\sin x \cos 35° + \cos x \sin 35°)$
$\qquad + 20(\cos x \cos 47° + \sin x \sin 47°)$

$\quad = 10[\sin x(0{\cdot}8192) + \cos x(0{\cdot}5736)]$
$\qquad + 20[\cos x(0{\cdot}6820) + \sin x(0{\cdot}7314)]$

$\quad = 8{\cdot}192 \sin x + 5{\cdot}736 \cos x + 13{\cdot}640 \cos x + 14{\cdot}628 \sin x$

$\quad = (8{\cdot}192 + 14{\cdot}628) \sin x + (5{\cdot}736 + 13{\cdot}640) \cos x$

$\quad = \underline{22{\cdot}820 \sin x + 19{\cdot}376 \cos x}$

Hence $p = 22{\cdot}820, \; q = 19{\cdot}376$

(*Note: Repeated application to numerical problems is necessary to appreciate fully the significance of compound angle formulae.*)

Examples 11

1. Given $\tan A = \frac{4}{3}$, $\cos B = \frac{5}{13}$ (A and B acute angles), without using trigonometric tables, evaluate $\sin (A + B)$, $\cos (A - B)$, $\tan (A - B)$.

2. Given $\sin P = \frac{24}{25}$ (P acute), $\tan Q = -\frac{12}{5}$ (Q obtuse), without using trigonometric tables, evaluate $\sin (Q - P)$, $\cos (P + Q)$, $\tan (P + Q)$.

3. If $\tan X = \frac{3}{7}$, $\tan Y = \frac{5}{3}$, without using trigonometric tables evaluate $\tan (X + Y)$, $\tan (Y - X)$, $\cot (X + Y)$, $\cot (Y - X)$.

4. If $\tan (A - B) = 0.78$, $\tan B = 0.5$, calculate $\tan A$ without using trigonometric tables.

5. Using suitable diagrams, write down the trigonometric ratios for 45° and 30°. Hence evaluate $\cos 15°$ and $\cos 7\frac{1}{2}°$ without using trigonometric tables.

6. Given $\sin A = 0.7832$, $\cos B = 0.5341$ (A and B acute), calculate the values of $\cos A$ and $\sin B$. Hence obtain $\sin (A + B)$, $\cos (A - B)$ to four significant figures.

7. If $\tan x = 0.38$, calculate the value of $\tan 2x$ without using trigonometric tables.

8. Find, without using trigonometric tables, the values of $\cos 2\theta$ and $\sin 2\theta$, given $\tan \theta = \frac{3}{4}$.

9. If $\sin A = +\frac{3}{5}$ ($90° < A < 180°$) and $\tan B = +\frac{5}{12}$ ($180° < B < 270°$), calculate the values of $\sin (A + B)$ and $\cos (B - A)$.

10. Given $\cos 20° = 0.9397$, without using trigonometric tables calculate the values of $\cos 10°$ and $\sin 10°$.

11. Express $20 \cos (\theta - 30°)$ in the form $a \cos \theta + b \sin \theta$.

12. Express $15 \sin (\theta + 20°)$ in the form $a \sin \theta + b \cos \theta$.

13. Reduce $20 \sin (x + 24°) + 30 \sin (x - 53°)$ to the form $p \sin x + q \cos x$, stating the values of p and q to 3 significant figures.

14. Express $10 \cos (x - 37°) - 5 \cos (x + 43°)$ in the form $A \cos x + B \sin x$, stating the values of A and B to 3 significant figures.

15. By expansion find possible values of R and α in order that $5 \sin x + 12 \cos x$ may be expressed as $R \sin (x + \alpha)$.

16. By expansion find possible values of R and α in order that $4 \cos \theta - 3 \sin \theta$ may be expressed as $R \cos (\theta + \alpha)$.

17. Determine possible values of R and α (α acute) when $6.8 \sin x + 3.5 \cos x = R \sin (x + \alpha)$.

18. Prove the identity $\tan A + \tan B = \dfrac{\sin (A + B)}{\cos A \cos B}$.

19. Prove the identity $\sin (A + B) + \sin (A - B) = 2 \sin A \cos B$.

20. Prove the identity $\cos (A - B) - \cos (A + B) = 2 \sin A \sin B$.

12

Double Angle Formulae and Compound Waves

12.1 Double Angle Formulae

These formulae express $\sin 2\theta$, $\cos 2\theta$, $\tan 2\theta$, etc. in terms of the trigonometric ratios of the angle θ. The formulae may be established by using the compound angle formulae of Chapter 11 for $A + B$ by putting $A = B = \theta$.

12.1.1 Sin 2θ

$$\sin (A + B) = \sin A \cos B + \cos A \sin B, \text{ put } A = B = \theta$$

Then $\sin (\theta + \theta) = \sin \theta \cos \theta + \cos \theta \sin \theta$

$$\therefore \underline{\sin 2\theta = 2 \sin \theta \cos \theta}$$

12.1.2 Cos 2θ

$$\cos (A + B) = \cos A \cos B - \sin A \sin B$$
$$\cos (\theta + \theta) = \cos \theta \cos \theta - \sin \theta \sin \theta$$
$$\therefore \underline{\cos 2\theta = \cos^2 \theta - \sin^2 \theta} \qquad \text{(i)}$$

Two alternative forms for the expansion of $\cos 2\theta$ may be obtained as follows:

$$\cos^2 \theta + \sin^2 \theta = 1$$

111

$$\therefore \; \sin^2 \theta = 1 - \cos^2 \theta \text{ or } \cos^2 \theta = 1 - \sin^2 \theta$$

$$\therefore \; \cos 2\theta = \cos^2 \theta - (1 - \cos^2 \theta) = \cos^2 \theta - 1 + \cos^2 \theta$$

$$\therefore \; \underline{\cos 2\theta = 2 \cos^2 \theta - 1} \qquad \text{(ii)}$$

Also: $\cos 2\theta = 2(1 - \sin^2 \theta) - 1 = 2 - 2 \sin^2 \theta - 1$

$$\therefore \; \underline{\cos 2\theta = 1 - 2 \sin^2 \theta} \qquad \text{(iii)}$$

12.1.3 Tan 2θ

$$\tan (A + B) = \frac{\tan A + \tan B}{1 - \tan A \tan B}$$

$$\tan (\theta + \theta) = \frac{\tan \theta + \tan \theta}{1 - \tan \theta \tan \theta}$$

Then

$$\underline{\tan 2\theta = \frac{2 \tan \theta}{1 - \tan^2 \theta}}$$

12.1.4 Tan 2θ (alternative proof)

$$\tan 2\theta = \frac{\sin 2\theta}{\cos 2\theta} = \frac{2 \sin \theta \cos \theta}{\cos^2 \theta - \sin^2 \theta}$$

Divide numerator and denominator by $\cos^2 \theta$

$$= \frac{\dfrac{2 \sin \theta \cos \theta}{\cos^2 \theta}}{1 - \dfrac{\sin^2 \theta}{\cos^2 \theta}} = \frac{2 \tan \theta}{1 - \tan^2 \theta}$$

12.1.5 Cot 2θ

$$\cot 2\theta = \frac{1}{\tan 2\theta} = \frac{1 - \tan^2 \theta}{2 \tan \theta}$$

Divide numerator and denominator by $\tan^2 \theta$

$$= \frac{\cot^2 \theta - 1}{2 \cot \theta}$$

12.2 Addition of Periodic Waves

$$a \sin \theta \pm b \cos \theta; \quad a \cos \theta \pm b \sin \theta$$

These may be expressed in forms like $R \sin (\theta \pm \alpha)$, $R \cos (\theta \pm \alpha)$, where R is the amplitude of the resultant waveform. By choosing a suitable form, α will be an acute angle in each case.

12.2.1 $a \sin \theta + b \cos \theta$

Let $a \sin \theta + b \cos \theta = R \sin (\theta + \alpha) = R(\sin \theta \cos \alpha + \cos \theta \sin \alpha)$
or $a \sin \theta + b \cos \theta = (R \cos \alpha) \sin \theta + (R \sin \alpha) \cos \theta$.
This must be an identity, i.e. true for *all* values of θ. Hence:

$$R \cos \alpha = a \qquad \text{(i)}$$
$$R \sin \alpha = b \qquad \text{(ii)}$$

Divide (ii) by (i):

$$\frac{R \sin \alpha}{R \cos \alpha} = \frac{b}{a}; \quad \frac{\sin \alpha}{\cos \alpha} = \frac{b}{a}$$

$$\therefore \ \tan \alpha = \frac{b}{a}$$

$$\therefore \quad \alpha = \tan^{-1}\left(\frac{b}{a}\right)$$

Square and add (i) and (ii):

$$R^2 \cos^2 \alpha + R^2 \sin^2 \alpha = a^2 + b^2$$
$$R^2(\cos^2 \alpha + \sin^2 \alpha) = a^2 + b^2$$

but $\cos^2 \alpha + \sin^2 \alpha = 1$

$$\therefore \ R^2 = a^2 + b^2; \ R = \sqrt{(a^2 + b^2)}$$

Hence $\quad a \sin \theta + b \cos \theta = \sqrt{(a^2 + b^2)} \sin \left(\theta + \tan^{-1}\frac{b}{a}\right)$

where α is the smallest positive angle (acute) such that $\tan \alpha = \dfrac{b}{a}$.

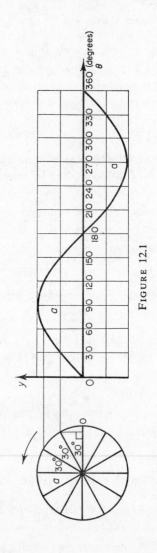

FIGURE 12.1

Using similar reasoning, it can be shown that

$$a \sin \theta - b \cos \theta = \sqrt{(a^2 + b^2)} \sin \left(\theta - \tan^{-1} \frac{b}{a} \right)$$

$$a \cos \theta - b \sin \theta = \sqrt{(a^2 + b^2)} \cos \left(\theta + \tan^{-1} \frac{b}{a} \right)$$

$$a \cos \theta + b \sin \theta = \sqrt{(a^2 + b^2)} \cos \left(\theta - \tan^{-1} \frac{b}{a} \right)$$

When making use of the above results, it is preferable to choose the compound angle form beginning with the same form as the sum or difference, and choose $\pm \alpha$ so that expansion of the compound angle form gives the same signs as the left-hand side, e.g.

$$8 \underline{\cos} \theta + 5 \sin \theta = R \underline{\cos} (\theta - \alpha)$$

$$R = \sqrt{(8^2 + 5^2)}; \quad \tan \alpha = \frac{5}{8}, \text{ etc.}$$

12.3 Vector Method of Addition of $a \cos \theta \pm b \sin \theta$, etc.

The periodic curves $\sin \theta$ and $\cos \theta$ can be constructed by projection from circles whose radii are the amplitudes of the curves (see Figure 12.1).

The diagram explains how the curve $y = a \sin \theta$ may be plotted using a 'rotating vector'. Similarly, $y = b \cos \theta$ may be plotted, but θ is measured anti-clockwise from the vertical position. The resultant curve obtained by adding $a \sin \theta$ to $b \cos \theta$ may be plotted by finding the resultant vector as follows (see Figure 12.2):

The rotation of AB is used to plot $y = a \sin \theta$.

The rotation of AC is used to plot $y = b \cos \theta$.

AD is the resultant vector and its rotation is used to plot $y = a \sin \theta + b \cos \theta$

$$R = \sqrt{(a^2 + b^2)}, \quad \tan \alpha = \frac{b}{a}$$

If AF represents the resultant vector after a displacement θ as shown, the height of F above the initial line is $y = a \sin \theta + b \cos \theta$.

Similar constructions may be used to obtain the resultant for any combination $a \cos \theta \pm b \sin \theta$; $a \sin \theta \pm b \cos \theta$.

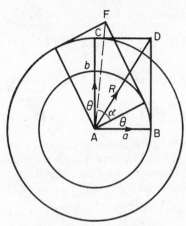

FIGURE 12.2

The method outlined above may be extended to the addition of waveforms which are not 90° out of phase, e.g. to find the resultant wave form when two wave forms like $y = a \cos(\theta + \alpha)$, $y = b \sin(\theta + \beta)$ are added. This method is particularly useful for obtaining the resultant of two wave forms like $e_1 \sin(\omega t + \alpha)$ and $e_2 \cos(\omega t + \beta)$, where ω is an angular velocity in radians per second and t is time in seconds. Vector methods are particularly useful in engineering problems.

WORKED EXAMPLES

(a) If angle θ is acute and $\tan \theta = \frac{3}{4}$, without using trigonometric tables, evaluate $\sin 2\theta$, $\cos 2\theta$, $\tan 2\theta$.

From sketch (Figure 12.3),

$$\sin \theta = \frac{3}{5}, \quad \cos \theta = \frac{4}{5}$$

$$\sin 2\theta = 2 \sin \theta \cos \theta = 2 \times \frac{3}{5} \times \frac{4}{5} = \frac{24}{25} = \underline{0 \cdot 9600}$$

$$\cos 2\theta = \cos^2 \theta - \sin^2 \theta = \left(\frac{4}{5}\right)^2 - \left(\frac{3}{5}\right)^2 = \frac{7}{25} = \underline{0 \cdot 2800}$$

$$\tan 2\theta = \frac{\sin 2\theta}{\cos 2\theta} = \frac{24}{25} \div \frac{7}{25} = \frac{24}{7} = \underline{3 \cdot 4286}$$

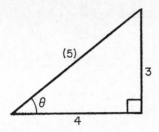

FIGURE 12.3

or $\quad \tan 2\theta = \dfrac{2 \tan \theta}{1 - \tan^2 \theta} = \dfrac{2 \times \dfrac{3}{4}}{1 - \left(\dfrac{3}{4}\right)^2} = \dfrac{3/2}{7/16} = \underline{\dfrac{24}{7}}$

(b) Given $\cos 30° = 0·8660$, calculate $\cos 15°$ and $\cos 7\frac{1}{2}°$.

$$\cos 2\theta = 2 \cos^2 \theta - 1$$

Let $\theta = 15°$

$$\cos 30° = 2 \cos^2 15° - 1$$
$$\therefore \ 2 \cos^2 15° = 1 + \cos 30°$$
$$\therefore \ \cos^2 15° = \tfrac{1}{2}(1 + \cos 30°) = \tfrac{1}{2}(1 + 0·8660)$$
$$= 0·9330$$
$$\therefore \ \cos 15° = \sqrt{0·9330} = \underline{0·9659}$$

Let $\theta = 7\frac{1}{2}°$ in the $\cos 2\theta$ identity then

$$\cos 15° = 2 \cos^2 7\tfrac{1}{2}° - 1$$
$$2 \cos^2 7\tfrac{1}{2}° = 1 + \cos 15°$$
$$\cos^2 7\tfrac{1}{2}° = \tfrac{1}{2}(1 + \cos 15°) = \tfrac{1}{2}(1 + 0·9659)$$
$$= 0·9829(5)$$
$$\therefore \ \cos 7\tfrac{1}{2}° = \sqrt{0·9829(5)} = \underline{0·9914}$$

(c) If $\tan 2\theta = 1·8$, calculate two possible values of $\tan \theta$

$$\tan 2\theta = \frac{2 \tan \theta}{1 - \tan^2 \theta} = 1·8$$

5

$$\therefore \; 2\tan\theta = 1{\cdot}8 - 1{\cdot}8\tan^2\theta$$

$$1{\cdot}8\tan^2\theta + 2\tan\theta - 1{\cdot}8 = 0$$

$$\tan\theta = \frac{-2 \pm \sqrt{[4 + 4(1{\cdot}8)(1{\cdot}8)]}}{2 \times 1{\cdot}8} = \frac{-2 \pm \sqrt{16{\cdot}96}}{3{\cdot}6}$$

$$= \frac{-2 \pm 4{\cdot}118}{3{\cdot}6} = \frac{2{\cdot}118}{3{\cdot}6} \quad \text{or} \quad \frac{-6{\cdot}118}{3{\cdot}6}$$

$$= \underline{0{\cdot}5883 \quad \text{or} \quad -1{\cdot}699}$$

(d) Prove the identity

$$\frac{\cos\theta}{\cos\theta + \sin\theta} + \frac{\sin\theta}{\cos\theta - \sin\theta} = \sec 2\theta.$$

Left-hand side

$$= \frac{\cos\theta(\cos\theta - \sin\theta) + \sin\theta(\cos\theta + \sin\theta)}{(\cos\theta + \sin\theta)(\cos\theta - \sin\theta)} = \frac{\cos^2\theta + \sin^2\theta}{\cos^2\theta - \sin^2\theta}$$

$$= \frac{1}{\cos 2\theta} = \sec 2\theta$$

(e) If A is the angle of a triangle, show that

$$\cos\frac{A}{2} = \sqrt{\left[\frac{s(s-a)}{bc}\right]}$$

where s is the semi-perimeter of the triangle.

$$\cos A = 2\cos^2\frac{A}{2} - 1 = \frac{b^2 + c^2 - a^2}{2bc}$$

$$\left(\text{using } \cos 2\theta \text{ formula, } \theta = \frac{A}{2}\right)$$

$$\therefore \; 2\cos^2\frac{A}{2} = 1 + \frac{b^2 + c^2 - a^2}{2bc} = \frac{2bc + b^2 + c^2 - a^2}{2bc}$$

$$= \frac{(b+c)^2 - a^2}{2bc}$$

$$= \frac{(b+c+a)(b+c-a)}{2bc}; \quad a + b + c = 2s$$

$$b + c - a = 2s - 2a$$

$$\therefore \cos^2 \frac{A}{2} = \frac{2s(2s - 2a)}{4bc} = \frac{s(s - a)}{bc}$$

$$\therefore \cos \frac{A}{2} = \sqrt{\left[\frac{s(s - a)}{bc}\right]}$$

(*Note:* This formula can be used to calculate A, given a, b, c.)

(*f*) Express $7 \cdot 8 \cos \theta + 12 \cdot 5 \sin \theta$ in the form $R \cos (\theta - \alpha)$.

Let $7 \cdot 8 \cos \theta + 12 \cdot 5 \sin \theta = R \cos (\theta - \alpha)$

$$= R(\cos \theta \cos \alpha + \sin \theta \sin \alpha)$$

$7 \cdot 8 \cos \theta + 12 \cdot 5 \sin \theta = (R \cos \alpha) \cos \theta + (R \sin \alpha) \sin \theta$

$$\therefore R \cos \alpha = 7 \cdot 8 \qquad \text{(i)}$$

$$R \sin \alpha = 12 \cdot 5 \qquad \text{(ii)}$$

Divide (ii) by (i):

$$\tan \alpha = \frac{12 \cdot 5}{7 \cdot 8} = 1 \cdot 6030$$

$$\therefore \alpha = 58°3'$$

Square and add (i) and (ii):

$$R^2(\cos^2 \alpha + \sin^2 \alpha) = 7 \cdot 8^2 + 12 \cdot 5^2 = 60 \cdot 84 + 156 \cdot 3$$

$$\therefore R^2 = 217 \cdot 14$$

$$\therefore \underline{R = \sqrt{217 \cdot 14} = 14 \cdot 73}$$

$$\therefore \underline{7 \cdot 8 \cos \theta + 12 \cdot 5 \sin \theta = 14 \cdot 73 \cos (\theta - 58°3')}$$

(*g*) Express $20 \sin (\theta + 20°) + 10 \cos (\theta + 50°)$ in the form $R \sin (\theta + \alpha)$.

$20 \sin (\theta + 20°) + 10 \cos (\theta + 50°)$

$= 20(\sin \theta \cos 20° + \cos \theta \sin 20°)$
$$+ 10(\cos \theta \cos 50° - \sin \theta \sin 50°)$$

$= 20(0 \cdot 9397 \sin \theta + 0 \cdot 3420 \cos \theta)$
$$+ 10(0 \cdot 6428 \cos \theta - 0 \cdot 7660 \sin \theta)$$

$= (18 \cdot 794 - 7 \cdot 660) \sin \theta + (6 \cdot 840 + 6 \cdot 428) \cos \theta$

$= 11 \cdot 134 \sin \theta + 13 \cdot 268 \cos \theta$

Using the method of reduction

let $11 \cdot 134 \sin \theta + 13 \cdot 268 \cos \theta = R \sin (\theta + \alpha)$

$$= R(\sin \theta \cos \alpha + \cos \theta \sin \alpha)$$

$\therefore \quad R \cos \alpha = 11 \cdot 134 \qquad \qquad \text{(i)}$

$\qquad R \sin \alpha = 13 \cdot 268 \qquad \qquad \text{(ii)}$

$\therefore \quad \tan \alpha = \dfrac{13 \cdot 268}{11 \cdot 134} = 1 \cdot 1920; \qquad \alpha = 50°$

$R^2(\cos^2 \alpha + \sin^2 \alpha) = 11 \cdot 134^2 + 13 \cdot 268^2; \quad R = 17 \cdot 31$

$\therefore \quad \underline{20 \sin (\theta + 20°) + 10 \cos (\theta + 50°) = 17 \cdot 31 \sin (\theta + 50°)}$

Examples 12

1. Given $\tan \theta = \frac{9}{40}$, calculate the values of $\sin 2\theta$, $\cos 2\theta$, $\tan 2\theta$ without using trigonometric tables.
2. If $180° < A < 270°$ and $\sin A = -\frac{12}{13}$; $90° < B < 180°$ and $\tan B = -\frac{4}{3}$, calculate $\sin (A - B)$, $\cos (A + B)$, $\cos 2A$, $\sin 2B$.
3. A is an acute angle and $\tan A = \frac{3}{4}$, B is an obtuse angle and $\sin B = \frac{5}{13}$. Calculate $\sin 2A + \sin 2B$, $\cos 2A - \cos 2B$.
4. Given $\cos A = 0 \cdot 66$ (A acute), without using trigonometric tables, calculate the values of $\sin 2A$, $\cos 2A$, $\tan 2A$.
5. Calculate the possible values of $\cos \theta$ if $4 \cos 2\theta + 2 \cos \theta + 3 = 0$.
6. Calculate the values of $\sin \theta$ when $9 \cos 2\theta = 13 - 18 \sin \theta$.
7. Prove the identity $\sin 2\theta = \dfrac{2 \tan \theta}{1 + \tan^2 \theta}$.
8. Prove the identity $\cos 2\theta = \dfrac{1 - \tan^2 \theta}{1 + \tan^2 \theta}$.
9. Prove the identity $\cot \theta + \tan \theta = 2 \operatorname{cosec} 2\theta$.
10. Prove the identity $\cot \theta - \cot 2\theta = \operatorname{cosec} 2\theta$.
11. Show that $\dfrac{\sin^2 2A}{2 \cos^2 A} = 1 - \cos 2A$.
12. Show that $(\cos \theta + \sin \theta)^2 = 1 + \sin 2\theta$, and hence prove the identity $\sec 2\theta + \tan 2\theta = \dfrac{\cos \theta + \sin \theta}{\cos \theta - \sin \theta}$.
13. By writing $3\theta = (2\theta + \theta)$, prove $\sin 3\theta = 3 \sin \theta - 4 \sin^3 \theta$.
14. Using the method suggested in 13, prove $\cos 3\theta = 4 \cos^3 \theta - 3 \cos \theta$.
15. If $\tan 2x = 3 \cdot 2$, find the values of $\tan x$.
16. For a triangle ABC, using a method similar to that used in the worked examples, prove that $\sin \dfrac{A}{2} = \sqrt{\left[\dfrac{(s - b)(s - c)}{bc} \right]}$. Use the formula to calculate A given $a = 13$, $b = 8$, $c = 9$.
17. Express $7 \cos \theta - 5 \sin \theta$ in the form $R \cos (\theta + \alpha)$.

18. Find R and α in order that $5 \sin \theta + 12 \cos \theta = R \sin (\theta + \alpha)$.
19. Determine R and α if $8 \cos (\theta - 30°) + 9 \sin (\theta + 20°) = R \sin (\theta + \alpha)$.
20. Express $3 \sin x - \sqrt{3} \cos x = E$ as $R \sin (x - \alpha)$. What is the maximum value of E?
21. Find the maximum and minimum values of $\cos \theta - 2 \sin \theta$.
22. Express $E = 100 \cos \theta - 50 \sin \theta$ in the form $R \cos (\theta + \alpha)$.
23. Express $5 \sin \omega t + 10 \cos \omega t$ in the form $E \sin (\omega t + \alpha)$.   [$\alpha$ in radians]
24. Write $20 \cos (x + 30°) + 40 \sin (x + 45°)$ as $R \cos (x - \alpha)$.
25. Express $4 \sin 2x + 9 \cos 2x$ in the form $R \sin (2x + \alpha)$.

13

Further Trigonometric Identities

13.1 Sum and Product Formulae (Identities)

Consider

$$\sin (A + B) = \sin A \cos B + \cos A \sin B \qquad (1)$$
$$\sin (A - B) = \sin A \cos B - \cos A \sin B \qquad (2)$$

Add (1) and (2) together, then,

$$\sin (A + B) + \sin (A - B) = 2 \sin A \cos B \qquad (3)$$

Subtract (2) from (1), then,

$$\sin (A + B) - \sin (A - B) = 2 \cos A \sin B \qquad (4)$$

From (3) and (4) it follows that the sum or difference of two sines may be expressed as a product of a sine and cosine. Conversely, a product of a sine and cosine may be expressed as a sum or difference of two sines.

If the sum $A + B = S$ and the difference $A - B = T$ then

$$2A = S + T, \text{ i.e. } A = \tfrac{1}{2}(S + T)$$
$$2B = S - T, \text{ i.e. } B = \tfrac{1}{2}(S - T)$$

$\therefore$ (3) may be written as:

$$\underline{\sin S + \sin T = 2 \sin \tfrac{1}{2}(S + T) \cos \tfrac{1}{2}(S - T)} \qquad (5)$$

and (4) may be written as

$$\underline{\sin S - \sin T = 2 \cos \tfrac{1}{2}(S + T) \sin \tfrac{1}{2}(S - T)} \qquad (6)$$

also
$$\sin A \cos B = \tfrac{1}{2}[\sin (A + B) + \sin (A - B)] \qquad (7)$$

$$\cos A \sin B = \tfrac{1}{2}[\sin (A + B) - \sin (A - B)] \qquad (8)$$

Similar formulae may be derived involving cosines of sums and differences.

$$\cos (A + B) = \cos A \cos B - \sin A \sin B \qquad (9)$$

$$\cos (A - B) = \cos A \cos B + \sin A \sin B \qquad (10)$$

Hence
$$\cos (A + B) + \cos (A - B) = 2 \cos A \cos B \qquad (11)$$

$$\cos (A - B) - \cos (A + B) = 2 \sin A \sin B \qquad (12)$$

and rearrangements of these produce:

$$\cos S + \cos T = 2 \cos \tfrac{1}{2}(S + T) \cos \tfrac{1}{2}(S - T) \qquad (13)$$

$$\cos T - \cos S = 2 \sin \tfrac{1}{2}(S + T) \sin \tfrac{1}{2}(S - T) \qquad (14)$$

and:
$$\cos A \cos B = \tfrac{1}{2}[\cos (A + B) + \cos (A - B)] \qquad (15)$$

$$\sin A \sin B = \tfrac{1}{2}[\cos (A - B) - \cos (A + B)] \qquad (16)$$

Numerical Illustrations of the Product and Sum Formulae:

(i) $\sin 80° + \sin 40° = 2 \sin \tfrac{1}{2}(80° + 40°) \cos \tfrac{1}{2}(80° - 40°)$
$$= 2 \sin 60° \cos 20°$$

(ii) $\sin 120° - \sin 70° = 2 \cos \tfrac{1}{2}(120° + 70°) \sin \tfrac{1}{2}(120° - 70°)$
$$= 2 \cos 95° \sin 25°$$

(iii) $\cos 70° + \cos 50° = 2 \cos \tfrac{1}{2}(70° + 50°) \cos \tfrac{1}{2}(70° - 50°)$
$$= 2 \cos 60° \cos 10°$$

(iv) $\cos 60° - \cos 80° = 2 \sin \tfrac{1}{2}(60° + 80°) \sin \tfrac{1}{2}(80° - 60°)$
$$= 2 \sin 70° \sin 10°$$

(v) $\sin 5\theta + \sin 3\theta = 2 \sin \tfrac{1}{2}(5\theta + 3\theta) \cos \tfrac{1}{2}(5\theta - 3\theta)$
$$= 2 \sin 4\theta \cos \theta$$

(vi) $\sin 4\theta - \sin 2\theta = 2 \cos \tfrac{1}{2}(4\theta + 2\theta) \sin \tfrac{1}{2}(4\theta - 2\theta)$
$$= 2 \cos 3\theta \sin \theta$$

(vii) $\cos 4x + \cos 6x = 2 \cos \tfrac{1}{2}(4x + 6x) \cos \tfrac{1}{2}(6x - 4x)$
$$= 2 \cos 5x \cos x$$

(viii) $\cos 2\theta - \cos 6\theta = 2 \sin \frac{1}{2}(2\theta + 6\theta) \sin \frac{1}{2}(6\theta - 2\theta)$
$$= 2 \sin 4\theta \sin 2\theta$$

(ix) $2 \sin 80° \cos 50° = \sin 130° + \sin 30°$

(x) $2 \cos 70° \sin 30° = \sin 100° - \sin 40°$

(xi) $\cos 5\theta \cos 3\theta = \frac{1}{2}(\cos 8\theta + \cos 2\theta)$

(xii) $\sin 5x \sin x = \frac{1}{2}(\cos 4x - \cos 6x)$

13.2 Trigonometric Equations

Some equations were dealt with in Chapter 8. In general, it is necessary to use identities of some kind to simplify the equations before attempting solutions. Solution of trigonometric equations involves the calculation of trigonometric ratios and hence the angles satisfying the equation.

13.2.1 Equations of types $a \sin^2 \theta + b \cos \theta = c$ and $a \cos^2 \theta + b \cos \theta = c$

These may be reduced by using $\sin^2 \theta = 1 - \cos^2 \theta$ or $\cos^2 \theta = 1 - \sin^2 \theta$.

Example: Solve the equation $2 \cos^2 \theta + \sin \theta = 1$.
 Substitute $1 - \sin^2 \theta$ for $\cos^2 \theta$, then:

$$2(1 - \sin^2 \theta) + \sin \theta = 1; \quad 2 \sin^2 \theta - \sin \theta - 1 = 0$$
$$(2 \sin \theta + 1)(\sin \theta - 1) = 0$$
$$\therefore \underline{\sin \theta = 1 \quad \text{or} \quad -\tfrac{1}{2}}$$

$\therefore \theta = \sin^{-1}(1) = 90°$
and $\theta = \sin^{-1}(-\tfrac{1}{2}) = 210°, 330°$ $\Big\}$ between 0° and 360°

$$\therefore \underline{\text{Solutions are } \theta = 90°, 210°, 330°}$$

13.2.2 Equations of types $a \sec^2 \theta + b \tan \theta = c$ and $a \tan^2 \theta + b \sec \theta = c$

These may be reduced by using $\sec^2 \theta = 1 + \tan^2 \theta$.

Example: Solve the equation $3 \sec^2 \theta + 2 \tan \theta = 5$.

$$3(1 + \tan^2 \theta) + 2 \tan \theta = 5; \quad 3 \tan^2 \theta + 2 \tan \theta - 2 = 0$$

$$\tan \theta = \frac{-2 \pm \sqrt{(4 + 24)}}{6} = \frac{-2 \pm 2\sqrt{7}}{6} = \frac{-1 \pm \sqrt{7}}{3}$$

$$= -1 \cdot 2153 \quad \text{or} \quad +0 \cdot 5487$$

$$\therefore \ \theta = \tan^{-1} 0 \cdot 5487 = 28°45', \ 208°45'$$

$$\text{or} \ \ \underline{\theta = \tan^{-1}(-1 \cdot 2153) = 129°27', \ 309°27'}$$

13.2.3 Equations of types $a \cos 2\theta + b \sin \theta = c$ and $a \cos 2\theta + b \cos \theta = c$

These may be reduced by using $\cos 2\theta = 2 \cos^2 \theta - 1$ or $\cos 2\theta = 1 - 2 \sin^2 \theta$.

Example: Solve the equation $6 \cos 2\theta = \cos \theta - 5$.
Substitute $2 \cos^2 \theta - 1 = \cos 2\theta$

$$\therefore \ 6(2 \cos^2 \theta - 1) = \cos \theta - 5; \quad 12\cos^2 \theta - \cos \theta - 1 = 0$$

$$\therefore \ (4 \cos \theta + 1)(3 \cos \theta - 1) = 0$$

$$\therefore \ \cos \theta = \tfrac{1}{3} \quad \text{or} \quad -\tfrac{1}{4}$$

$$\cos \theta = 0 \cdot 3333 \quad \text{or} \quad -0 \cdot 2500$$

$$\therefore \ \theta = 70°32' \quad \text{or} \quad 289°28' \\ \text{or} \ \theta = \underline{104°29'} \quad \text{or} \quad 255°31'$$ Solutions between 0° and 360°

13.2.4 Equations of types $a \cos \theta \pm b \sin \theta = c$ and $a \sin \theta \pm b \cos \theta = c$

All equations like these may be solved by first expressing the left-hand side in compound angle form, i.e. $R \cos (\theta \pm \alpha)$ or $R \sin(\theta \pm \alpha)$ as shown in Chapter 12.

Example: Find values of θ, between 0° and 360°, satisfying the equation $3 \cos \theta - 4 \sin \theta = 3 \cdot 825$.

$$\text{Let} \qquad 3 \cos \theta - 4 \sin \theta = R \cos (\theta + \alpha)$$

$$= R(\cos \theta \cos \alpha - \sin \theta \sin \alpha)$$

Then $\qquad R \cos \alpha = 3; \; R \sin \alpha = 4$

$$R^2(\cos^2 \alpha + \sin^2 \alpha) = 3^2 + 4^2$$

$$R^2 = 25$$

$$\therefore \; R = 5$$

$$\tan \alpha = \frac{4}{3} = 1 \cdot 3333; \qquad \alpha = 53°8'$$

$\therefore$ The equation reduces to the form

$$5 \cos (\theta + 53°8') = 3 \cdot 825$$

Divide by 5 $\qquad \cos (\theta + 53°8') = 0 \cdot 7650$

$$\therefore \; (\theta + 53°8') = 40°6', \; 319°54', \; 400°6'$$

$\therefore \; \theta = 40°6' - 53°8', \; 319°54' - 53°8', \; 400°6' - 53°8'$

$\qquad \theta = -13°2'; \; 266°46'; \; 346°58'$

$\therefore$ Solutions between $0°$ and $360°$ are

$$\underline{\theta = 266°46' \qquad \text{or} \qquad 346°58'}$$

WORKED EXAMPLES

(a) Prove the identity $(\sin 50° + \sin 10°)/(\cos 50° + \cos 10°) =$ tan 30°.

Using sums expressed as products:

Left-hand side $= \dfrac{2 \sin \frac{1}{2}(50° + 10°) \cos \frac{1}{2}(50° - 10°)}{2 \cos \frac{1}{2}(50° + 10°) \cos \frac{1}{2}(50° - 10°)}$

$\qquad\qquad\qquad = (2 \sin 30° \cos 20°)/(2 \cos 30° \cos 20°)$

$\qquad\qquad\qquad = (\sin 30°)/(\cos 30°) = \underline{\tan 30°}$

(b) Prove the identity $(\sin 5\theta - \sin \theta)/(\cos 5\theta + \cos \theta) = \tan 2\theta$.

Left-hand side $= (2 \cos 3\theta \sin 2\theta)/(2 \cos 3\theta \cos 2\theta)$

$\qquad\qquad\qquad = (\sin 2\theta)/(\cos 2\theta) = \underline{\tan 2\theta}$

(c) By using the sine rule for a triangle, and sum and product formulae, show, that for a triangle ABC

$$\tan \frac{1}{2}(B - C) = \frac{b - c}{b + c} \cot \frac{A}{2}.$$

From the sine rule for a triangle ABC

$$\frac{a}{\sin A} = \frac{b}{\sin B} = \frac{c}{\sin C} = 2R$$

$\therefore\ a = 2R \sin A,\ b = 2R \sin B,\ c = 2R \sin C$

$$\therefore\ \frac{b - c}{b + c} = \frac{2R(\sin B - \sin C)}{2R(\sin B + \sin C)} = \frac{\sin B - \sin C}{\sin B + \sin C}$$

$$= \frac{2 \cos \tfrac{1}{2}(B + C) \sin \tfrac{1}{2}(B - C)}{2 \sin \tfrac{1}{2}(B + C) \cos \tfrac{1}{2}(B - C)}$$

$$= \frac{\tan \tfrac{1}{2}(B - C)}{\tan \tfrac{1}{2}(B + C)}$$

but $A + B + C = 180°$

$$\therefore\ \tfrac{1}{2}(B + C) = 90° - \tfrac{1}{2}A$$

$$\therefore\ \tan \tfrac{1}{2}(B + C) = \cot (\tfrac{1}{2}A)$$

$$\therefore\ \frac{b - c}{b + c} = \frac{\tan \tfrac{1}{2}(B - C)}{\cot \tfrac{1}{2}A}$$

or $\quad \tan \tfrac{1}{2}(B - C) = \dfrac{b - c}{b + c} \cot \dfrac{A}{2}$

This formula may be used to solve a triangle given two sides and included angle, e.g. if $b = 13\cdot7$, $c = 8\cdot9$ and angle $A = 75°$, find angles B and C.

$$\tan \tfrac{1}{2}(B - C) = \frac{13\cdot7 - 8\cdot9}{13\cdot7 + 8\cdot9} \cot 37\tfrac{1}{2}° = \frac{4\cdot8}{22\cdot6} \cot 37°30'$$

$$= 0\cdot2768$$

$$\therefore\ \tfrac{1}{2}(B - C) = 15°28'$$

$\therefore\ B - C = 30°56'$, but $B + C = 180° - A = 105°$

Hence $B = 67°58'$; $C = 37°2'$

(d) Solve the equation $2 \sec x - 3 \cos x = 5$ for $0 < x < 360°$.
$\sec x = 1/\cos x$

$$\therefore\ 2/(\cos x) - 3 \cos x = 5$$

Multiply by $\cos x$

$$2 - 3\cos^2 x = 5\cos x \qquad \text{or} \qquad 3\cos^2 x + 5\cos x - 2 = 0$$
$$\therefore \ (3\cos x - 1)(\cos x + 2) = 0$$
$$\therefore \ \underline{\cos x = 0 \cdot 3333} \qquad \text{or} \qquad \underline{-2}$$

Since $\cos x$ must lie between -1 and $+1$

$$\therefore \ x = \cos^{-1}(0 \cdot 3333) = \underline{70°32'} \qquad \text{or} \qquad \underline{289°28'}$$

(e) Solve the equation $\cot 2\theta + \tan \theta = 4$ for $0 < \theta < 360°$.

$$\tan 2\theta = (2 \tan \theta)/(1 - \tan^2 \theta)$$
$$\therefore \ \cot 2\theta = (1 - \tan^2 \theta)/(2 \tan \theta)$$

$\therefore$ Equation reduces to $(1 - \tan^2 \theta)/(2 \tan \theta) + \tan \theta = 4$

Multiply by $2 \tan \theta$

$$1 - \tan^2 \theta + 2 \tan^2 \theta = 8 \tan \theta$$
$$\tan^2 \theta - 8 \tan \theta + 1 = 0$$
$$\tan \theta = \tfrac{1}{2}[8 \pm \sqrt{(64 - 4)}] = \tfrac{1}{2}(8 \pm \sqrt{60})$$
$$= 4 \pm \sqrt{15} = 4 \pm 3 \cdot 8730 = 7 \cdot 8730 \quad \text{or} \quad 0 \cdot 1270$$
$$\therefore \ \theta = \tan^{-1}(7 \cdot 8730) = 82°48' \qquad \text{or} \qquad 262°48'$$
$$\text{and} \ \theta = \tan^{-1}(0 \cdot 1270) = \underline{7°14'} \qquad \text{or} \qquad \underline{187°14'}$$

(f) Solve the equation

$$\cos 2\theta + 5 \sin \theta = 1 \cdot 8.$$
$$\cos 2\theta = 1 - 2 \sin^2 \theta$$
$$\therefore \ 1 - 2 \sin^2 \theta + 5 \sin \theta = 1 \cdot 8$$
$$2 \sin^2 \theta - 5 \sin \theta + 0 \cdot 8 = 0$$
$$\sin \theta = \tfrac{1}{4}[5 \pm \sqrt{(25 - 6 \cdot 4)}] = \tfrac{1}{4}(5 \pm 4 \cdot 3130)$$
$$= \tfrac{1}{4} \times 9 \cdot 313 \quad \text{or} \quad \tfrac{1}{4} \times 0 \cdot 6870$$
$$= 2 \cdot 3282 \quad \text{or} \quad 0 \cdot 171\ 75$$

Since $\sin \theta$ must lie between -1 and $+1$

$$\therefore \ \underline{\theta = \sin^{-1}(0 \cdot 171\ 75) = 9°54'} \qquad \text{or} \qquad \underline{170°6'}$$

(g) Solve the equation $\sin 2\theta + \sin 3\theta = 0$.

Express the left-hand side as a product:

$$2 \sin \tfrac{5}{2}\theta \cos \tfrac{1}{2}\theta = 0$$

$\therefore \cos \tfrac{1}{2}\theta = 0$

$\qquad \therefore \tfrac{1}{2}\theta = 90°, 270°$

$\qquad \therefore \theta = 180° (540°)$

or $\sin \tfrac{5}{2}\theta = 0$

$\qquad \therefore \tfrac{5}{2}\theta = 0°, 180°, 360°, 540°, 720°, 900°$

$\qquad \therefore \theta = 0°, 72°, 144°, 216°, 288°, 360°$

(h) Find the least positive value of t to satisfy

$$5 \sin (20t) + 12 \cos (20t) = 9 \cdot 1.$$

Left-hand side $= R \sin (20t + \alpha)$; $R = 13$, $\tan \alpha = 2 \cdot 4$

$\therefore \alpha = 67°23' = 1 \cdot 1761$ radians

$\therefore 13 \sin (20t + 1 \cdot 1761) = 9 \cdot 1$

$\therefore \sin (20t + 1 \cdot 1761) = 0 \cdot 7$

$\therefore 20t + 1 \cdot 1761 = (44°25') = 0 \cdot 7752$ or $2 \cdot 3668$ (radians)

$\therefore \underline{20t = 1 \cdot 1907 \qquad \therefore t = 0 \cdot 0595}$

Examples 13

1. Express the following sums as products:
   (i) $\sin 80° + \sin 70°$,   (ii) $\cos 80° + \cos 30°$,   (iii) $\sin 110° + \sin 190°$.
2. Express the following differences as products:
   (i) $\sin 130° - \sin 40°$,   (ii) $\cos 40° - \cos 50°$,   (iii) $\cos 75° - \cos 25°$.
3. Express the following as products:
   (i) $\sin 7x + \sin x$,   (ii) $\sin 5x - \sin x$,   (iii) $\cos 3\theta + \cos \theta$,
   (iv) $\cos 2\theta - \cos 6\theta$,   (v) $\sin 2t + \sin t$,   (vi) $\cos 4\pi t - \cos 2\pi t$.
4. Express the following products as sums (or differences):
   (i) $2 \sin 35° \cos 15°$,   (ii) $2 \cos 65° \sin 25°$,   (iii) $2 \cos 80° \cos 35°$,
   (iv) $2 \sin 58° \sin 24°$,   (v) $2 \sin 3\theta \cos \theta$,   (vi) $2 \cos 4x \sin 3x$,
   (vii) $\cos t \sin 3t$,   (viii) $\cos 4t \cos 5t$,   (ix) $\sin 3\alpha \sin \alpha$.
5. Prove the following identities:
   (i) $\dfrac{(\sin 70° + \sin 30°)}{(\sin 70° - \sin 30°)} = \tan 50° \cot 20°$,

   (ii) $\dfrac{(\cos 75° + \cos 25°)}{(\cos 25° - \cos 75°)} = \cot 50° \cot 25°$,

   (iii) $\dfrac{(\sin 3\theta + \sin \theta)}{(\cos 3\theta + \cos \theta)} = \tan 2\theta$.

6. Prove the following identities:

  (i) $\dfrac{(\sin 5\theta - \sin \theta)}{(\sin 5\theta + \sin \theta)} = \cot 3\theta \tan 2\theta,$

  (ii) $\dfrac{(\sin 4A - \sin 2A)}{(\cos 4A + \cos 2A)} = \tan A,$

  (iii) $\dfrac{(\cos 2\theta - \cos 5\theta)}{(\sin 2\theta + \sin 5\theta)} = \tan \dfrac{3}{2} \theta.$

Solve the following equations, in each case giving solutions between 0° and 360°.

7. $6 \cos x + \sec x = 5.$

8. $3 \sec^2 \theta = 7 - 4 \tan \theta.$

9. $2 \sin^2 \theta + 3 \cos \theta = 0.$

10. $2 \sec^2 \theta = 5 \tan \theta + 3.$

11. $\cos 2\theta = 3 \sin \theta - 2.$

12. $\cos 2\theta - 5 \cos \theta = 2.$

13. $\cos 2\theta + 3 \cos \theta - 2 = 0.$

14. $3 \cos 2\theta - 20 \cos \theta + 9 = 0.$

15. $\sin x + \cos 2x = 0.$

16. $6 \cos 2\theta = \sin \theta + 5.$

17. $\cot 2\theta - 3 \tan \theta = 4.$

18. $2 \tan x - 4 \cot x = 5.$

19. $5 \cos \theta - 3 \sin \theta = 4{\cdot}3.$

20. $7 \cos \theta - 5 \sin \theta = 3{\cdot}6.$

21. $8 \sin x + 12 \cos x = 8{\cdot}9.$

22. $7 \cos x + 5 \sin x = 4{\cdot}6.$

23. $3{\cdot}5 \cos \theta + 8{\cdot}1 \sin \theta = 4{\cdot}7.$

24. $4 \cos x - 3 \sin x = 2{\cdot}4.$

25. $20 \cos \theta - 40 \sin \theta = 17.$

26. $\cos x - 2 \sin x = 2.$

27. $3 \sin 2\theta + 4 \cos 2\theta = 3{\cdot}2.$

28. $5 \cos 2\theta - 8 \sin 2\theta = 6{\cdot}3.$

29. $\sin 3\theta + \sin \theta = 0.$

30. $\cos 3x - \cos 2x = 0.$

31. $\sin 3t - \sin t = 0.$

32. $\cos 4\theta + \cos \theta = 0.$

33. Find the smallest positive value of t if $30 \sin 10t + 40 \cos 10t = 28.$

34. Find the smallest positive t to satisfy $7 \cos 20t - 5 \sin 20t = 4{\cdot}2.$

35. Solve $20 \sin 100t + 40 \cos 100t = 30$ for the smallest positive value of t.

14

Mensuration—Uniform Cross-section

14.1 Circle, Sectors and Segments

14.1.1 Circle

Circumference $= 2\pi r = \pi d$ (radius $= r$, diameter $= d$).

$$\text{Area} = \pi r^2 = \tfrac{1}{4}\pi d^2$$

Radian measure. 1 radian = Angle subtended at the centre of a circle by an arc equal to the radius.

$$\pi \text{ radians} = 180°$$

Angular speed is usually stated in radians per second or revolutions per minute.

For motion in a circle with constant speed v ft/s, if the radius of the circle is r feet, and the angular velocity is ω radians per second, then v and ω are connected by the formula $v = r\omega$. The time required to travel round a circle if the angular speed ω is constant is given by

$$T = \frac{2\pi}{\omega} = \frac{2\pi r}{v}$$

14.1.2 Sector

$$\text{Arc length } s = \frac{\theta°}{360°} \times 2\pi r$$

$$\text{Area} = \frac{\theta°}{360°} \times \pi r^2 \qquad \text{(Figure 14.1)}$$

When the angle θ is in *radians*

$$s = \frac{\theta}{2\pi} \times 2\pi r = \underline{r\theta}$$

and the area is given by

$$\text{Area} = \frac{\theta}{2\pi} \times \pi r^2 = \underline{\tfrac{1}{2}r^2\theta}$$

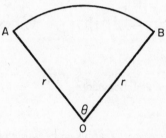

FIGURE 14.1

14.1.3 Segment

A chord AB divides the area of the circle into two segments (Figure 14.2):

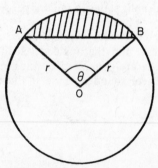

FIGURE 14.2

Minor segment (as shaded)—less than a semicircle.
Major segment—this is the rest of the circle.

Area of minor segment = Area of sector − Triangle AOB

$$= \frac{\theta}{360}\pi r^2 - \tfrac{1}{2}r \times r \times \sin\theta = \frac{r^2}{2}\left(\frac{\theta\pi}{180} - \sin\theta\right) \quad (\theta \text{ in degrees})$$

Using θ in radians, area of minor segment $= \tfrac{1}{2}r^2\theta - \tfrac{1}{2}r^2\sin\theta$

$$= \tfrac{1}{2}r^2(\theta - \sin\theta)$$

Area of major segment = Area of circle − Area of minor segment

$$= \pi r^2 - \tfrac{1}{2}r^2(\theta - \sin\theta)$$

$$= \underline{\tfrac{1}{2}r^2(2\pi - \theta) + \tfrac{1}{2}r^2\sin\theta}$$

$$= \underline{\text{Major sector} + \text{Triangle AOB}}$$

Example: The cross-section of a metal bar is a major segment of a circle. The radius of the bar is 3·2 cm and the flat is 4·8 cm wide. If the bar is 8 cm long and the density is 7·83 g/cm³, calculate the mass of the bar (Figure 14.3).

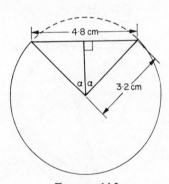

FIGURE 14.3

Let $\qquad \theta = 2\alpha; \qquad \sin\alpha = \dfrac{0\cdot9}{1\cdot2} = 0\cdot7500$

$$\therefore \ \alpha = 48°35',$$

$$\therefore \ \underline{\theta = 97°10'} = \underline{1\cdot6961 \text{ rad}}$$

Area of segment (major) $= \frac{1}{2}r^2(2\pi - \theta) + \frac{1}{2}r^2 \sin \theta$

$$= \frac{1}{2} \times (3\cdot2)^2[6\cdot284 - 1\cdot6961] + \frac{1}{2} \times (3\cdot2)^2 \times 0\cdot9922$$

$$= 5\cdot12[4\cdot5879 + 0\cdot9922]$$

$$= 5\cdot12 \times 5\cdot5801 \text{ cm}^2$$

$$= \underline{28\cdot57 \text{ cm}^2}$$

$\therefore$ Mass of bar $= 28\cdot57 \times 8 \times 7\cdot83 = \underline{1789 \text{ g.}}$

14.2 Intersecting Chords

Let two chords AB, CD of a circle intersect at O (Figure 14.4). Since $\angle CAO = \angle BDO$, $\angle ACO = \angle DBO$, $\angle AOC = \angle DOB$, the triangles AOC, DOB are *similar*.

$\therefore$ Corresponding sides are in the same ratio, i.e.

$$\frac{\text{AO}}{\text{DO}} = \frac{\text{CO}}{\text{OB}}$$

$$\therefore \underline{\text{AO} \cdot \text{OB} = \text{CO} \cdot \text{OD}}$$

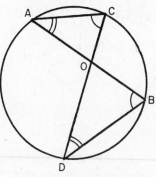

FIGURE 14.4

14.2.1 Intersecting secants (chords produced)

Let two chords produced meet at O (Figure 14.5). Since $\angle CAO = \angle BDO$, $\angle ACO = \angle OBD$ and angle O is common, the triangles

OAC, ODB are *similar*,

$$\therefore \frac{AO}{OD} = \frac{CO}{OB}$$

$$\therefore \underline{AO \cdot OB = CO \cdot OD}$$

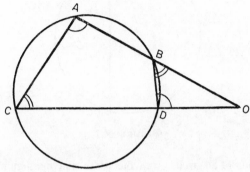

FIGURE 14.5

14.2.2 Special cases

(i) If OT is a tangent to the circle (Figure 14.6) and OBA is a secant, then

$$\underline{OT^2 = OB \cdot OA}$$

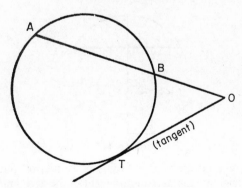

FIGURE 14.6

(ii) When the chords are at right angles (Figure 14.7), the result is still AO . OB = CO . OD.

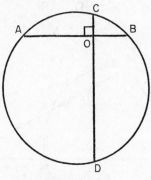

FIGURE 14.7

14.2.3 Radius of an arch, given the width and maximum height

Let maximum height be h, width $2a$, radius R (Figure 14.8). Then, using the chord theorem; $h \times (2R - h) = a \times a$

i.e.
$$2R - h = \frac{a^2}{h}$$

$$\therefore R = \frac{1}{2}\left(h + \frac{a^2}{h}\right)$$

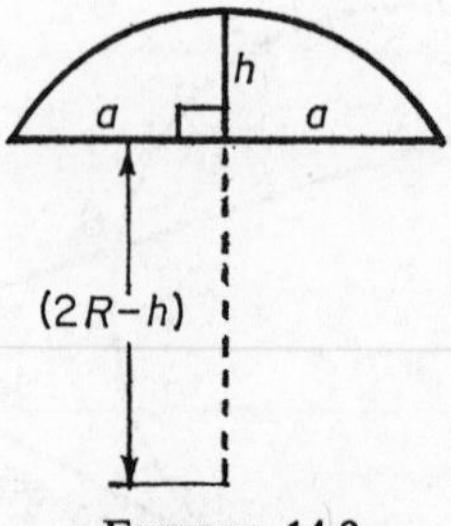

FIGURE 14.8

Example: A circular arch has a radius of 15 metres and a span of 24 metres. Calculate the maximum height of the arch and the height of the arch at a distance of 7 metres from the centre of the span.

Let h be the maximum height (Figure 14.9). Then $h(2R - h) = a^2$

$h(30 - h) = 12^2 = 144$

$h^2 - 30h + 144 = 0$ $(h - 6)(h - 24) = 0$

$\therefore$ $h = 6$ metres or 24 metres

(*Note:* 24 metres is the height of the major arc.)

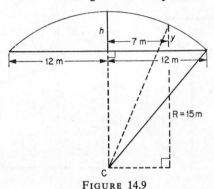

FIGURE 14.9

Let y metres be the height of the arch, 7 metres from the centre. Then $y(18 + y) = 5 \times 19 = 95$

$\therefore$ $y^2 + 18y - 95 = 0$; $y = \frac{1}{2}[-18 \pm \sqrt{(324 + 380)}]$

$y = \frac{1}{2}[-18 \pm \sqrt{(704)}] = \frac{1}{2}(-18 \pm 26{\cdot}53)$

$= 4{\cdot}265$ or $-22{\cdot}265$ metres

$\therefore$ Required height is 4·265 metres

(*Note:* 22·265 metres is the height of the major arc.)

The above example could have been done by using right-angled triangles and the theorem of Pythagoras.

14.3 Prisms

14.3.1 Volume

A *right* prism is defined as a solid with a constant cross-sectional area and generators of the surface are at right angles to the section. Such prisms may have any plane figure as the constant section, e.g. squares, rectangles, triangles, hexagons, circles, etc. The volume of a right prism is calculated as follows:

Volume of right prism = Cross-sectional area × Altitude

14.3.2 Surface areas

Surface areas of prisms may be found by adding together the face areas (and curved surface areas).

(i) Volume $= Ah$.　(ii) Volume $= \frac{1}{2}A(h_1 + h_2)$; area $B = \dfrac{A}{\cos \theta}$.

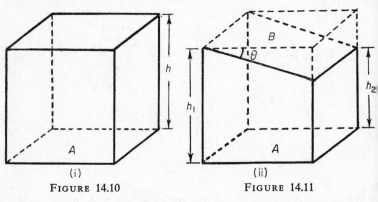

(i)

FIGURE 14.10

(ii)

FIGURE 14.11

(iii) Volume $= Ah$.　(iv) Volume $= \pi r^2 h$; Surface area $=$
$$2\pi r^2 + 2\pi rh.$$

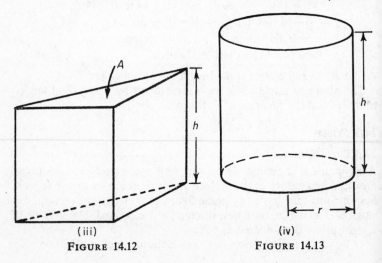

(iii)

FIGURE 14.12

(iv)

FIGURE 14.13

(v) Volume $= \frac{1}{2}\pi r^2 (h_1 + h_2)$; Area B (ellipse) $= \dfrac{\pi r^2}{\cos \theta}$.

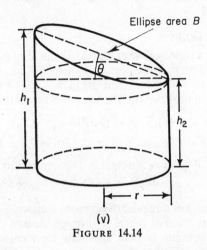

Ellipse area B

(v)

FIGURE 14.14

(vi) Volume $= Ah$, h is the perpendicular distance between the parallel faces.

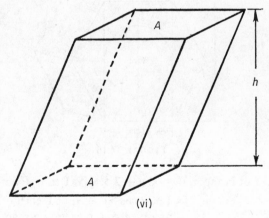

(vi)

FIGURE 14.15

Other types of prisms may be encountered, e.g. prisms with regular hexagonal form. However, if it is necessary to deal with other shapes, the same principles can be used for the calculation of volumes and surface areas.

WORKED EXAMPLES

(a) A hollow cylindrical steel shaft is 18 cm long and has internal diameter 3·5 cm and external diameter 4·5 cm. If the steel has a density of 7·83 g/cm³, find the mass.

The cross section of the shaft is an *annulus* of area

$$= \tfrac{1}{4}\pi(D^2 - d^2) = \tfrac{1}{4}\pi[(4\cdot5)^2 - (3\cdot5)^2] = \tfrac{1}{4}\pi \times 8 \times 1 = 2\pi \text{ cm}^2.$$

Volume of shaft = Cross section × Length = $2\pi \times 18 = 36\pi$ cm³

$$\therefore \text{ Mass of shaft} = \text{Volume} \times \text{Density} = 36\pi \times 7\cdot83 \text{ g}$$
$$= 36 \times 3\cdot142 \times 7\cdot83 \text{ g} = \underline{888\cdot6 \text{ g}}$$

(b) A steel bar has a regular hexagonal section. A circular hole of radius 0·5 cm is bored centrally through the bar. If the width of the flat of the hexagon is 1 cm, calculate the volume of the bar if its length is 6·5 cm (Figure 14.16).

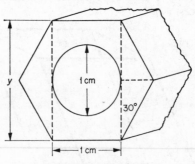

FIGURE 14.16

$$\text{Area of hexagon} = 1 \times y + 2 \times \tfrac{1}{2} \times 1 \times 1 \times \sin 120°$$
$$= 1 \times 2 \cos 30° + \sin 60° \text{ cm}^2$$
$$= 2 \times 0\cdot8660 + 0\cdot8660 = \underline{2\cdot5980 \text{ cm}^2}$$

Area of circle = $\frac{1}{4}\pi \times 1^2$ = $\underline{0\cdot7855\ cm^2}$

∴ Cross-sectional area = $2\cdot5980 - 0\cdot7855\ cm^2$

$= 1\cdot8125\ cm^2$

∴ Volume of bar = $6\cdot5 \times 1\cdot8125\ cm^3$ = $\underline{11\cdot78\ cm^3}$

(c) A tube has internal and external diameters of 3·8 cm and 4·6 cm. 45° cuts are made and two pieces joined to form a right-angle joint. Find the common section area of the joint and the volume of metal if the lengths of pipe joined have mean lengths of 15 cm and 21 cm (Figure 14.17).

Area of principal section = $\frac{1}{4}\pi(D^2 - d^2)$

$= \frac{1}{4}\pi(4\cdot6^2 - 3\cdot8^2) = \frac{1}{4}\pi(8\cdot4)(0\cdot8)\ cm^2$

$= 1\cdot68\pi = 5\cdot278\ cm^2.$

Common section area at joint = $5\cdot278/\cos 45°$

$= \underline{7\cdot464\ cm^2}$

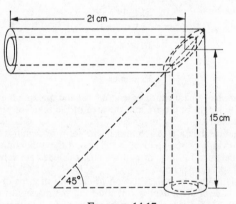

FIGURE 14.17

Volume of metal = Principal section × Mean length

$= 5\cdot278 \times 36\ cm^3 = \underline{190\ cm^3}$

(d) The cross-section of a tunnel is a major segment of a circle of radius 3·5 m, the flat base being 4·2 m wide. Find the volume of air in 120 metres of the tunnel (Figure 14.18).

Maximum height of tunnel $= 2 \cdot 8 + 3 \cdot 5 = 6 \cdot 3$ metres

$$\sin \theta = 0 \cdot 6$$

$$\therefore \quad \theta = 36°52' = 0 \cdot 6435 \text{ radians}$$

$$\text{Area of section} = \tfrac{1}{2} r^2 (2\pi - 2\theta) + 2 \cdot 8 \times 2 \cdot 1 \text{ m}^2$$

$$= 12 \cdot 25(3 \cdot 142 - 0 \cdot 6435) + 5 \cdot 88$$

$$= 36 \cdot 49 \text{ m}^2$$

$$\therefore \quad \text{Volume of air} = 120 \times 36 \cdot 49 \text{ m}^3$$

$$= \underline{4379 \text{ m}^3}$$

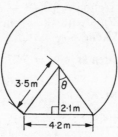

FIGURE 14.18

Examples 14

1. A circular arc has a base chord of length 8 cm and maximum height of 2 cm. Calculate the length of the arc and the area of the segment between the arc and its base chord.

2. A water channel has a cross-section in the form of a minor segment of a circle. The width of the channel is 0·8 m and the maximum depth 0·3 m. If the channel runs full at a rate of 6·5 m/s, calculate the volume of water passing any section per hour.

3. A railway tunnel has a vertical section in the form of a major segment of a circle. The base of the tunnel is 7 m wide and the maximum height is 6 m. If the tunnel is 200 m long, find (i) the volume of air in the tunnel, (ii) the curved rubbing area of the tunnel.

4. A window is in the form of a rectangle (of height h feet), surmounted by a semicircle of radius r. Express the area A and perimeter P in terms of r and h. If $h = 2$ m and the area A is 2·5 m², calculate the width of the window.

5. A cylindrical log of wood, of radius 8 cm and length 1 m, is planed down so that the section becomes a regular hexagon (which fits in the circular section exactly). Find (i) the percentage of the wood removed by planing, (ii) the volume of the hexagonal piece produced, (iii) the width of the flats.

6. A cylinder (solid) is of radius r and height h. If V is the volume, and S is the surface area, express V in terms of r and S.

7. A measuring cylinder contains 50 cm³ of water to a depth of 8 cm. Calculate the radius of the cylinder. If the cylinder is tilted without spilling so that its axis makes an angle of 30° with the vertical, find the area of the water surface.

8. A chord AB of length 5 cm is produced to a point O outside the circle so that BO = 7 cm. Calculate the length of the tangent from O to the circle.

9. A tube with internal diameter 3 cm and external diameter 3·5 cm, is suitably cut and two pieces of mean lengths 25 cm and 32 cm welded to form a right-angle joint. Calculate (i) the common section area at the joint, (ii) the external and internal surface areas of the tube, (iii) the mass of the tube if the metal has a density of 7·83 g/cm³.

10. A cylindrical tank, open at the top, is made from sheet metal of density 1·24 g/cm². If the height is 1·55 m and radius 0·9 m, find the mass of metal used in the construction of the tank. How long would it take (approx.) to fill the tank if water is fed through a pipe of diameter 5 cm at 6·5 m/s?

15

Mensuration—Non-Uniform Cross-section

15.1 Pyramids and Cones

15.1.1 Pyramids

These are three dimensional figures formed by drawing *generators* from every point on the perimeter of a *flat base* to a common point called the *vertex* (Figure 15.1). The *volume* of any such pyramid is calculated using the formula:

Volume = $\frac{1}{3}$ × Base area × *Vertical height*

The total surface area may be found by the addition of the areas of the faces and the base.

Volume = $\frac{1}{3}Ah$

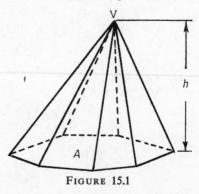

FIGURE 15.1

Right pyramid. The altitude through V passes through the *centroid* of the base.

15.1.2 Similar pyramids

Pyramids having the same shape, i.e. corresponding angles equal, corresponding sides *proportional*, have their volumes in the ratio of the cubes of corresponding dimensions. This fact is used in 15.1.3 to obtain the general formula for the volume of the *frustum* of a pyramid.

15.1.3 Frustum of a pyramid

A frustum is formed by cutting the pyramid by a *plane parallel to the base*. The portion of the pyramid removed is *similar* in shape to the original pyramid (Figure 15.2). The frustum is the part between the

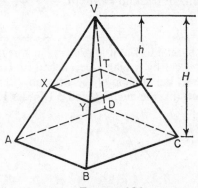

FIGURE 15.2

planes ABCD, XYZT where XYZT is parallel to the base ABCD. Let the altitude of the original pyramid be H and the altitude of the pyramid removed be h. Let the area of ABCD $= b$, and the area of XYZT $= a$. Since the two plane faces are similar in shape, their areas are proportional to the squares of any corresponding dimensions.

$$\therefore \frac{a}{b} = \left(\frac{h}{H}\right)^2$$

Volume of frustum = VABCD − VXYZT

$\therefore$ Volume of frustum $= \frac{1}{3}bH - \frac{1}{3}ah = \frac{1}{3}bH\left(1 - \frac{a}{b}\frac{h}{H}\right)$

$$= \frac{1}{3}bH\left(1 - \frac{h^2}{H^2}\frac{h}{H}\right) = \frac{1}{3}bH\left(1 - \frac{h^3}{H^3}\right)$$

$$= \frac{1}{3}bH\left(1 - \frac{h}{H}\right)\left(1 + \frac{h}{H} + \frac{h^2}{H^2}\right)$$

$$= \frac{1}{3}b(H - h)\left(1 + \frac{h}{H} + \frac{h^2}{H^2}\right)$$

Let $H - h = x$ (height of the frustum) and

$$\frac{h}{H} = \sqrt{\frac{a}{b}}$$

Volume of frustum $= \frac{1}{3}bx\left(1 + \sqrt{\frac{a}{b}} + \frac{a}{b}\right)$

$$\therefore \underline{V = \frac{1}{3}x(b + \sqrt{(ab)} + a)}$$

Example: A right pyramid of altitude 20 cm has a rectangular base 8 cm by 12 cm. It is cut by a plane, parallel to its base and 8 cm from it. Calculate (i) the volume of the frustum, (ii) the total face area of the frustum, (iii) the angles θ and ϕ (Figure 15.3).

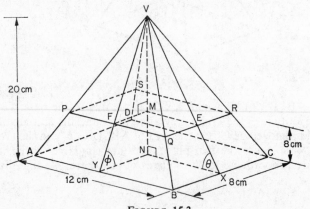

FIGURE 15.3

Let N be the centroid of the base, and M be the centroid of the top face of the frustum.

$$VN = \text{Altitude of pyramid} = 20 \text{ cm}$$

$$VM = \text{Altitude of small pyramid} = 12 \text{ cm}$$

$$\text{Area of base} = 8 \times 12 = 96 \text{ cm}^2$$

$$\frac{\text{Area of top face}}{\text{Area of base}} = \frac{VM^2}{VN^2} = \left(\frac{12}{20}\right)^2 = \frac{9}{25}$$

$$\therefore \text{Area of top face} = \frac{9}{25} \times 96 \text{ cm}^2$$

Height of frustum = 8 cm.

(i) $\therefore$ Volume of frustum $= \dfrac{1}{3} x(a + \sqrt{(ab)} + b)$

$$= \frac{1}{3} \times 8 \left[96 + \sqrt{\left(96 \times \frac{9}{25} \times 96 \right)} + \frac{9}{25} \times 96 \right]$$

$$= \frac{1}{3} \times 8 \times \left(96 + \frac{3}{5} \times 96 + \frac{9}{25} \times 96 \right)$$

$$= \frac{1}{3} \times 8 \times 96 \times \left(1 + \frac{3}{5} + \frac{9}{25} \right)$$

$$= \frac{8 \times 96 \times 49}{75} = \underline{501 \cdot 8 \text{ cm}^3}$$

(ii) By proportion

$$\frac{QR}{BC} = \frac{12}{20}$$

$$\therefore QR = \frac{3}{5} \times 8 = \underline{4 \cdot 8 \text{ cm}}$$

$$\frac{PQ}{AB} = \frac{12}{20}$$

$$\therefore PQ = \frac{3}{5} \times 12 = \underline{7 \cdot 2 \text{ cm}}$$

Area of PQRS = $7.2 \times 4.8 = 34.56$ cm² (or $\frac{9}{25} \times 96$ cm²)
Total face area of frustum = ABCD + PQRS + 2(QBCR)
$$+ 2(\text{PABQ})$$

$$VX = \sqrt{(20^2 + 6^2)} = \sqrt{436} = 20.88 \text{ cm}$$
$$VY = \sqrt{(20^2 + 4^2)} = \sqrt{(416)} = 20.40 \text{ cm}$$

By proportion

$$VE = \frac{3}{5} \times VX = \frac{3}{5} \times 20.88 = \underline{12.53 \text{ cm}}$$

$$VF = \frac{3}{5} \times VY = \frac{3}{5} \times 20.40 = \underline{12.24 \text{ cm}}$$

$$\therefore EX = VX - VE = 8.35 \text{ cm}$$
$$FY = VY - VF = 8.16 \text{ cm}$$

Area of QBCR = $\frac{1}{2}(8 + 4.8) \times 8.35 = 6.4 \times 8.35 = 53.44$ cm²
Area of PABQ = $\frac{1}{2}(12 + 7.2) \times 8.16 = 9.6 \times 8.16 = 78.34$ cm²

$$\therefore \text{ Total face area} = 96 + 34.56 + 2 \times 53.44 + 2 \times 78.34$$
$$= 130.56 + 106.88 + 156.68 = \underline{394.12 \text{ cm}^2}$$

(iii) If face VBC makes θ with the base,

$$\tan \theta = \frac{20}{6} = 3.3333$$

$$\therefore \underline{\theta = 73°18'}$$

If face VAB makes ϕ with the base

$$\tan \phi = \frac{20}{4} = 5$$

$$\therefore \underline{\phi = 78°42'}$$

15.1.4 Right circular cone

N is the centre of the base, θ the semi-vertical angle, l the slant height h the altitude, and r the base radius (Figure 15.4).

$$\text{Volume of cone} = \tfrac{1}{3}\pi r^2 h$$
$$\text{Slant height } l = \sqrt{(r^2 + h^2)}$$

$$\tan \theta = \frac{r}{h}$$

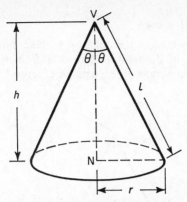

FIGURE 15.4

If the curved surface is cut down a generator and opened out, a sector of a circle radius l and arc $2\pi r$ results (Figure 15.5).

$$\text{Curved area} = \frac{2\pi r}{2\pi l} \times \pi l^2 = \pi r l$$

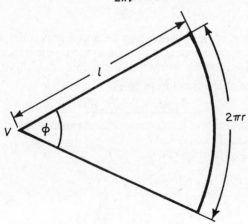

FIGURE 15.5

For a solid cone, the total surface area

$$S = \pi r^2 + \pi r l = \underline{\pi r(r + l)}$$

6

15.1.5 Frustum of a cone

This is formed by cutting the cone by a plane parallel to its base. Let the end radii of the frustum be r and R, h the altitude of the frustum, l the slant height of the frustum (Figure 15.6).

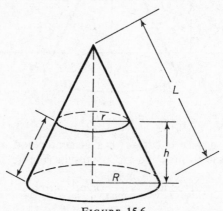

FIGURE 15.6

The volume of the frustum may be found as the difference of the volumes of the two cones. This is often the best method. Using the result obtained for the frustum of a pyramid:

$$\text{Volume of the frustum} = \tfrac{1}{3}h[\pi r^2 + \sqrt{(\pi r^2 \times \pi R^2)} + \pi R^2]$$

$$\underline{\text{Volume} = \tfrac{1}{3}\pi h(r^2 + rR + R^2)}$$

The development of the curved surface is an annulus, the difference of two sectors of radii L and l.

Curved area of frustum (Figure 15.7)

$$= \pi RL - \pi r(L - l) \qquad\qquad \left(\frac{L - l}{L} = \frac{r}{R}\right)$$

$$= \pi RL - \pi r\frac{rL}{R} = \frac{\pi L}{R}(R^2 - r^2)$$

$$= \frac{\pi L}{R}(R - r)(R + r) \qquad \left(l = L - \frac{r}{R}L = \frac{L(R - r)}{R}\right)$$

$$= \underline{\pi l(R + r)}$$

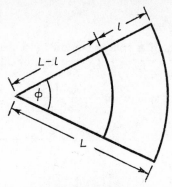

FIGURE 15.7

15.2 Sphere

Let radius of sphere be R. The volume V of the sphere $= \frac{4}{3}\pi R^3$. It can be shown that the area of a *zone* of the sphere is the same as the corresponding area of the zone of height h on the enveloping cylinder, i.e. Area of zone of sphere $= 2\pi Rh$ (Figure 15.8).

Total area (curved) of sphere $= 2\pi R \times 2R = 4\pi R^2$

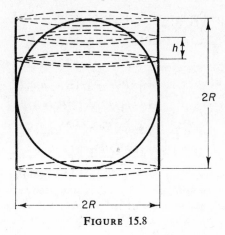

FIGURE 15.8

15.2.1 Cap of a sphere

This is the portion of a sphere cut off by a plane (Figure 15.9). Let the height of the cap $= h$. Curved area of cap $= \underline{2\pi Rh}$.

$$\text{Volume of } sector \text{ of sphere} = \frac{\text{Area of cap}}{\text{Area of sphere}} \times \frac{4}{3}\pi R^3$$

$$= \frac{2\pi Rh}{4\pi R^2} \times \frac{4}{3}\pi R^3 = \frac{2}{3}\pi R^2 h$$

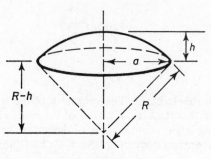

FIGURE 15.9

Volume of cap of sphere = Volume of sector − Volume of cone

$$= \tfrac{2}{3}\pi R^2 h - \tfrac{1}{3}\pi a^2(R - h)$$

$$= \tfrac{2}{3}\pi R^2 h - \tfrac{1}{3}\pi(R - h)[R^2 - (R - h)^2]$$

$$= \tfrac{2}{3}\pi R^2 h - \tfrac{1}{3}\pi(R - h)h(2R - h)$$

$$= \tfrac{1}{3}\pi h[2R^2 - (2R^2 - 3Rh + h^2)]$$

$$= \tfrac{1}{3}\pi h(3Rh - h^2)$$

$$= \tfrac{1}{3}\pi h^2(3R - h)$$

By transposition it can be shown that this volume may also be expressed as $V = \tfrac{1}{6}\pi h(3a^2 + h^2)$. It is not necessary to remember both formulae and, *in a numerical problem it may be preferable to find the volume by taking the difference of the sector and cone.*

WORKED EXAMPLES

(a) A casting is in the shape of a frustum of a cone of end radii 6 cm and 10 cm, with a central cylindrical hole of diameter 2·5 cm. Calculate the volume of the casting if its height is 9 cm.

Volume of casting = Volume of frustum

$$- \text{Volume of cylinder}$$
$$= \tfrac{1}{3}\pi h(r^2 + Rr + R^2) - \tfrac{1}{4}\pi d^2 h$$
$$= \pi h[\tfrac{1}{3}(6^2 + 60 + 100) - \tfrac{1}{4}(2 \cdot 5)^2]$$
$$= 9\pi(\tfrac{1}{3} \times 196 - \tfrac{25}{16})$$
$$= 9 \times 3 \cdot 142 \times (65 \cdot 3333 - 1 \cdot 5625)$$
$$= \underline{1803 \text{ cm}^3}$$

(b) A hemispherical bowl has a radius of 9 cm. Find the volume of water in the bowl when the depth of water is 5 cm. What is the area of the liquid surface? (Figure 15.10).

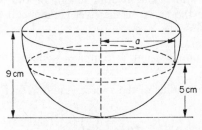

FIGURE 15.10

The water occupies a volume equal to the cap of a sphere of radius 9 cm and height 5 cm.

Volume of water $= \tfrac{1}{3}\pi h^2(3R - h) = \tfrac{1}{3}\pi \times 25 \times (27 - 5)$
$$= \tfrac{1}{3} \times \pi \times 25 \times 22 = \tfrac{1}{3}(550)\pi \text{ cm}^3$$
$$= \underline{576 \cdot 1 \text{ cm}^3}$$

Area of surface $= \pi a^2$
$$a^2 = 9^2 - 4^2 = 65$$
∴ Area of surface $= 65\pi = \underline{204 \cdot 2 \text{ cm}^2}$

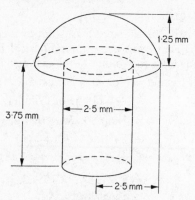

FIGURE 15.11

(c) The body of a rivet is a cylinder of length 3·75 mm and diameter 2·5 mm. The head of the rivet is a cap of a sphere of base diameter 5·0 mm. The overall length of the rivet is 5·0 mm. Calculate the mass of the rivet if the metal has a density of 2·55 g/cm³.

$$1\cdot25 \text{ mm} = \frac{1}{8} \text{ cm}, \ 3\cdot75 \text{ mm} = \frac{3}{8} \text{ cm}, \ 2\cdot5 \text{ mm} = \frac{1}{4} \text{ cm}.$$

If R is the radius of the sphere (Figure 15.11):

$$\frac{1}{8}\left(2R - \frac{1}{8}\right) = \left(\frac{1}{4}\right)^2 \quad \text{(chords)}$$

$$2R = \frac{1}{2} + \frac{1}{8} = \frac{5}{8}$$

$$\therefore R = \frac{5}{16} \text{ cm}$$

Volume of body $= \frac{1}{4}\pi d^2 h$

$$= \frac{1}{4}\pi\left(\frac{1}{4}\right)^2 \frac{3}{8}$$

$$= \frac{3\pi}{512} \text{ cm}^3$$

$$\text{Volume of head} = \frac{1}{3}\pi h^2(3R - h) = \frac{1}{3}\pi\left(\frac{1}{8}\right)^2\left(\frac{15}{16} - \frac{1}{8}\right)$$

$$= \frac{1}{3}\pi \times \frac{1}{64} \times \frac{13}{16} = \frac{13\pi}{6 \times 512}\text{ cm}^3$$

$$\therefore \text{ Volume of rivet} = \frac{\pi}{512}\left(3 + \frac{13}{6}\right) = \frac{31\pi}{6 \times 512}\text{ cm}^3$$

$$\therefore \text{ Mass of rivet} = \frac{31\pi}{6 \times 512} \times 2\cdot55 = \underline{0\cdot0809\text{ g}}$$

(d) A solid is in the form of a cylinder with conical ends. The common radius is r and the cylinder is of length h. The cones have altitudes equal to the length of the cylinder. Express the volume and total surface area of the solid in terms of r and h.

$$\text{Volume} = \pi r^2 h + 2 \times \tfrac{1}{3}\pi r^2 h = \tfrac{5}{3}\pi r^2 h$$
$$\text{Surface area} = 2\pi rh + 2\pi rl = 2\pi rh + 2\pi r\sqrt{(r^2 + h^2)}$$
$$= \underline{2\pi r[h + \sqrt{(r^2 + h^2)}]}$$

Examples 15

1. A pyramid with a square base has an altitude of 12 cm. If the side of the square base is 6 cm, find (i) the volume, (ii) the total surface area, (iii) the angle between a sloping face and the base, (iv) the angle between a sloping edge and the base.
2. A tetrahedron (a pyramid with 4 triangular faces) has a base which is an equilateral triangle of side 40 mm. The vertex is vertically above the centroid (centre of gravity) of the base and the altitude is 90 mm. Calculate (i) the volume, (ii) the total surface area, (iii) the angle between a sloping face and the base, (iv) the angle between a sloping edge and the base.
3. A solid metal cylinder, 170 mm high, diameter 55 mm, is melted down and recast in the form of a cube surmounted by a right pyramid whose height equals the edge of the cube. Find the length of the edge of the cube.
4. The parallel faces of a frustum of a pyramid are squares of sides 3 cm and 4 cm respectively, and its volume is 30 cm³. Determine (i) the height of the frustum, (ii) the height of the pyramid of which it is a part, (iii) the total surface area.
5. The mass of a frustum of a regular pyramid on a square base is 5·35 Kg. If the height of the frustum is 50 mm, the ratio of the base area to the area of the top is 4 to 1 and the density of the material is 7500 Kg/m³, find the length of a side of the base and the total surface area of the frustum.

6. A cone 20 cm high and base radius 10 cm is cut by a plane parallel to its base and 10 cm from the base. Find the ratio of the volumes of the two parts and the volume of the frustum.

7. A casting is in the form of a frustum of a cone of end radii 5 cm and 8 cm, and the height is 12 cm. A cylindrical hole of radius 3 cm runs centrally through the frustum. If the metal has a density of 7830 Kg/m³, calculate the mass of the casting.

8. A sheet metal bucket is in the form of a frustum of a cone. The inside diameters of the top and bottom are 36 cm and 27 cm respectively, and the inside depth is 36 cm. Find (i) the area of sheet metal forming the curved surface of the bucket, (ii) the volume of water contained by the bucket when the depth of water is 30 cm.

9. A casting is to be made with the dimensions shown in Figure 15.12. All sections perpendicular to XY are circles and there is to be a hole of radius 75 mm with its axis along XY. If the metal to be used weighs 76·8 KN/m³, estimate the weight of the casting in Newtons.

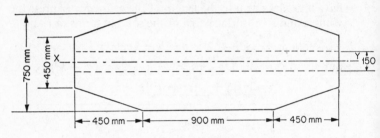

FIGURE 15.12

10. Figure 15.13 shows the section (shaded) of a collar for a shaft, the cross-sections being circular. Using the dimensions shown, calculate the volume of the metal and the weight of the collar in Newtons. (The metal weighs 76·8 KN/m³.)

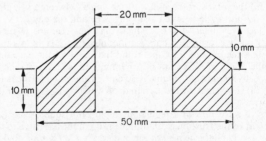

FIGURE 15.13

11. A casting is in the form of a cone of vertical height 3 cm with a segment of a sphere attached to the base. The base of the segment and the base of the cone have equal radii. The greatest height of the segment of the sphere is 1 cm, and the diameter of the sphere is 4 cm. Calculate the total surface area and weight of the casting if the metal weighs 73·58 KN/m³.

12. The head of a rivet is a segment (cap) of a sphere. The maximum height of the head is 10 mm and the base diameter is 30 mm. Calculate the weight of the head of the rivet if the metal weighs 24·5 KN/m³.

13. Figure 15.14 shows the cross section of a rivet. The head is the segment of a sphere (of radius 0·9 cm) and the maximum height of the head is 0·6 cm. Calculate (i) the total surface area, (ii) the weight of the rivet if the metal weighs 76·8 KN/m³.

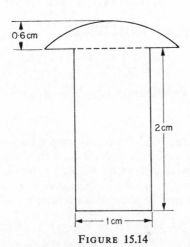

0·6 cm

2 cm

1 cm

FIGURE 15.14

14. Calculate the weight of 100 taper pins if the diameter of the small end of a pin is 5 mm and the taper is 20 mm/m. Each pin is 25 mm long and the metal weighs 76·8 KN/m³.

15. A hole of radius 20 mm is drilled centrally through a wooden sphere of radius 40 mm. Calculate the volume of the wood left.

16

Solutions of Equations by Tabulation and Graphical Methods

16.1 Functions and Equations

16.1.1 Functions

The term *function* is used widely in mathematics and subjects where mathematics is *applied*. It is important for a clear distinction to be made between *functions* and *equations*. Any expression containing a variable (represented by a letter), which may be *evaluated* for *any value* of the variable may be classed as a function.

Examples: $2x + 3$, $5x^2 + x - 1$, $x^3 + 2x^2 + x - 1$, x^n, e^x, $\log_e x$, $\sin x$, $\cos x$, $\tan x$, are all *functions* of the variable x.

16.1.2 Equations

This term relates to a statement of equality which can always, if desired, be reduced to a statement that a function (of x) is to be zero. The solutions (roots) of an equation are values of x for which the function is zero.

Examples: $2x + 5 = 0$, $3x^2 + x - 5 = 0$, $\sin x = 0$, are *equations*. The solutions are found by equating a function to zero. In simple cases such solutions (roots) may be found by *calculation* or by the use of a formula. However, in many cases which arise in practice,

158

this is not possible, but solutions can be found to *all* equations in *one variable*, by using suitable graphs.

16.1.3 Solution of equations by graphical methods

Let it be required to obtain solutions of an equation which may be represented as: $f(x) = 0$ where $f(x)$ denotes a function. Values of the function which may be written as $y = f(x)$ are calculated for different values of x, and the graph of y (vertical) against x is plotted in the *range* of values of x used. The solutions of the equation $f(x) = 0$ are those values of x at the points where the graph crosses the axis of x, since these are the values of x where $y = 0$ and $y = f(x)$. Since this is so, when tabulating values of x and y, it may often be necessary to insert additional values so that a *good estimate* may be made of the value of x *where the graph crosses the axis of x.*

16.1.4 Tabulation of function values

Since $f(x)$ *depends on x, if $y = f(x)$, then x is referred to as the independent variable and y is referred to as the dependent variable.*

Example: Tabulate the values of the function $x^3 - 2x^2 - 5x + 6$ for values of x from -5 to $+5$ in steps of one unit.

Note: For ease of tabulation it is convenient to break the function down as shown in the table below:

x	-5	-4	-3	-2	-1	0	1	2	3	4	5
x^3	-125	-64	-27	-8	-1	0	1	8	27	64	125
$-2x^2$	-50	-32	-18	-8	-2	0	-2	-8	-18	-32	-50
$-5x$	25	20	15	10	5	0	-5	-10	-15	-20	-25
$y = x^3 - 2x^2 - 5x + 6$	-144	-70	-24	0	8	6	0	-4	0	18	56

It is clear from this table that there are 3 values of x for which the function is zero. Therefore it follows (without plotting) that three solutions of the equation $x^3 - 2x^2 - 5x + 6 = 0$ are $x = -2, 1$ or 3. In fact these are the *only* solutions, as a *cubic equation* cannot have more than 3 roots.

16.1.5 Change of sign of a function

From observation of the table of values in 16.1.4. it can be seen that as the value of x increases through a root, the *sign of the function changes* from positive to negative or negative to positive. This result is important and may be used to find a range of values of x in which a root lies.

Theorem: If $f(x)$ is *continuous* between $x = a$ and $x = b$ and $f(a)$ and $f(b)$ are of opposite signs, then there is at least *one* real root of the equation $f(x) = 0$ between $x = a$ and $x = b$.

Example: Locate the three real roots of the equation

$$x^3 - 3x + 1 = 0.$$
$$\text{Let } f(x) = x^3 - 3x + 1$$
$$f(-2) = -8 + 6 + 1 = -1$$
$$f(-1) = -1 + 3 + 1 = +3$$
$$f(0) = +1$$
$$f(1) = 1 - 3 + 1 = -1$$
$$f(2) = 8 - 6 + 1 = +3$$

Since $f(-2)$ and $f(-1)$ are of opposite sign $f(x) = 0$ has a root between -2 and -1

$f(0)$ and $f(1)$ are of opposite sign, $\therefore f(x) = 0$ has a root between 0 and 1

$f(1)$ and $f(2)$ are of opposite sign, $\therefore f(x) = 0$ has a root between 1 and 2

Hence $f(x) = 0$ has roots in the ranges -2 to -1; 0 to 1; and 1 to 2.

16.2 Quadratic and Cubic Equations

16.2.1 Solution of quadratic equations

Graphical methods may be used to solve $ax^2 + bx + c = 0$, when a, b and c are given numerical values.

Example: Solve the equation $2x^2 + 3x - 3 = 0$.

Method (i). Let $y = f(x) = 2x^2 + 3x - 3$

$$f(-3) = 18 - 9 - 3 = +6$$
$$f(0) = -3$$
$$f(1) = 2 + 3 - 3 = +2$$

$\therefore$ The equation has roots between -3 and 0, 0 and 1. It would be sufficient to plot the graph of y against x from $x = -3$ to $+1$. However, a table of values will be constructed for x from -3 to $+2$ as follows:

x	-3	-2	-1	0	1	2	$\frac{1}{2}$	$1\frac{1}{2}$	$-2\frac{1}{2}$
$2x^2$	18	8	2	0	2	8	$\frac{1}{2}$	$4\frac{1}{2}$	$12\frac{1}{2}$
$3x$	-9	-6	-3	0	3	6	$1\frac{1}{2}$	$4\frac{1}{2}$	$-7\frac{1}{2}$
$y = 2x^2 + 3x - 3$	6	-1	-4	-3	2	11	-1	6	2

(*Note:* The additional values of x used to evaluate $f(x)$. This is particularly important near points where the graph will cross the x-axis. From the graph (Figure 16.1) the solutions of the equation are the values of x at points A and B.)

Solutions: $x = -2 \cdot 19,\ 0 \cdot 69$

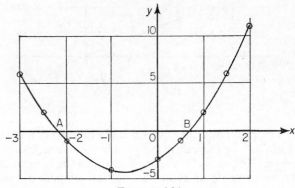

FIGURE 16.1

Method (ii).

$$2x^2 + 3x - 3 = 0 \qquad \text{may be written as;}$$

$$2x^2 = -3x + 3 \qquad \text{or} \qquad x^2 = -\frac{3}{2}x + \frac{3}{2}$$

∴ The solutions of the equation may be found by plotting *two* graphs, i.e.

$$(a) \qquad y = x^2 \qquad \text{and} \qquad (b) \qquad y = -\frac{3}{2}x + \frac{3}{2}$$

This method produces quicker results but *may* not be so accurate. The values of x and y for (a) may be plotted immediately and (b) is a straight line which may be plotted using two points only. The solutions are the values of x at the points P and Q (Figure 16.2).

Solutions: $x = -2.19$ or 0.69

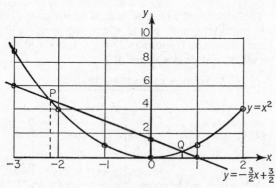

FIGURE 16.2

The *two* graph method may be used in the solution of any equation in one variable. In general, it will not give the same accuracy as a single graph. This is due to the angle at which the graphs intersect. An intersection angle of about 40°–60° is preferable for accurate *reading* at intersections.

16.2.2 Solution of a cubic equation

Example: Solve the equation $x^3 - 3x + 1 = 0$.
    Let $y = f(x) = x^3 - 3x + 1$.

Method (i).

$$f(-2) = -1$$
$$f(-1) = +3$$
$$f(0) = +1$$
$$f(1) = -1$$
$$f(2) = +3$$

∴ Using the theorem on location of roots, there are roots of the equation $f(x) = 0$ in the ranges: -2 to -1; 0 to 1; 1 to 2. Hence it is sufficient to plot a graph in the range -2 to $+2$ for x. Values of x are tabulated for steps of 0.5 in x.

x	-2	-1.5	-1.0	-0.5	0	0.5	1.0	1.5	2.0
x^3	-8	-3.375	-1.0	-0.125	0	0.125	1.0	3.375	8.0
$-3x$	6	4.5	3.0	1.5	0	-1.5	-3.0	-4.5	-6.0
$y = x^3 - 3x + 1$	-1	2.125	3.0	2.375	1	-0.375	-1.0	-0.125	3.0

The solutions of $x^3 - 3x + 1 = 0$ are the values of x at the points A, B and C (see Figure 16.3), i.e.

$$x = -1.95, +0.33, +1.52$$

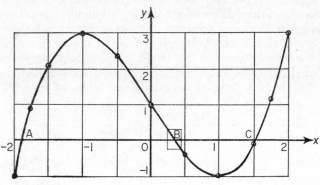

FIGURE 16.3

Method (*ii*). Write the equation in the form $x^3 = 3x - 1$. If the two graphs of $y = x^3$ and $y = 3x - 1$ are plotted, then the required solutions are the values of x at the points of intersection of the two graphs (see Figure 16.4).

Solutions of $x^3 - 3x + 1 = 0$ are approximately $x = -1\cdot9$, $+0\cdot3$, $1\cdot5$.

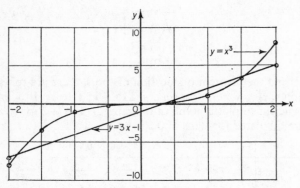

FIGURE 16.4

16.3 Enlargements

In order to obtain better estimates of roots of equations by a graphical method, it is necessary to attempt to *read* the value of x at the *intersection* of the graph with the x-axis. To do this a small portion of the graph containing the estimated root is plotted on large scales. If only a small range of x values is considered, the graph obtained is *almost a straight line*. For greater accuracy, three points should be plotted. For the small portion indicated by the rectangle surrounding B in Figure 16.3, tabulate accurately the values of y as follows:

x	0·25	0·3	0·35
x^3	0·0156	0·0270	0·0429
$-3x$	−0·7500	−0·9000	−1·0500
$y = x^3 - 3x + 1$	0·2656	0·1270	−0·0071

From the enlargement a better estimate of the middle root of the equation is $x = 0 \cdot 347$.

(*Note:* The plot of the small portion of the graph is almost a straight line (Figure 16.5).)

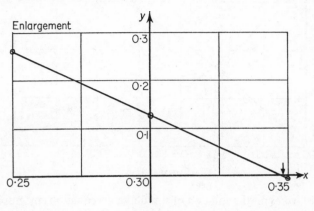

FIGURE 16.5

WORKED EXAMPLE

Using a graphical method, find a solution of the equation $e^{+2x} \sin x = 1$ between $x = 0$ and $1 \cdot 4$.

This is a case where a two graph method is preferable. Write the equation as $\sin x = e^{-2x}$. Plot the graphs of $y = \sin x$ and $y = e^{-2x}$ in the range $x = 0$ to $1 \cdot 5$ (Figure 16.6). It should be noted that the angle is in *radian measure*. Function values: (x in radians)

x	0	0·2	0·4	0·6	0·8	1·0	1·2	1·4
$\sin x$	0	0·199	0·389	0·565	0·717	0·841	0·932	0·982
e^{-2x}	1	0·670	0·449	0·301	0·202	0·135	0·091	0·061

The solution of the equation is the value of x corresponding to the point of intersection of the two graphs.

Solution: $x = 0 \cdot 445$

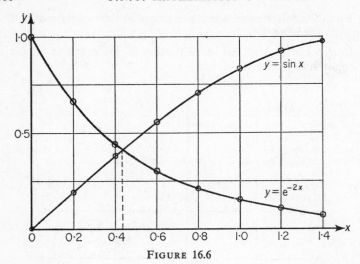

FIGURE 16.6

Special Notes on the solution of simultaneous equations by graphical methods.

1. The solutions of two linear equations of the forms $ax + by = c$ and $Ax + By = C$ may be obtained by plotting the two straight line graphs which represent the equations. The solutions are the values of x and y at the point of intersection.

2. More general simultaneous equations may be solved by plotting two graphs. For example, the equations $xy = c$ and $x^2 + y^2 = r^2$. By plotting the two graphs which these equations represent, their solutions are found as the corresponding values of x and y at the points of intersection.

Examples 16

1. Tabulate the values of the function $x^2 - x - 5$ for values of x from -3 to $+3$. Using the graph of the function, solve the equations (i) $x^2 - x - 5 = 0$, (ii) $x^2 - x - 3 = 0$.

2. Plot the function $x^2 - 2x$ between $x = -2$ and $+3$. Hence solve the equation $x^2 - 2x = 2$. Plot $y + 2x = 2$ on the same scales and hence solve the simultaneous equations $x^2 - 2x = y$ and $y + 2x = 2$.

3. Obtain graphically solutions of the equation $x^2 = 8x + 5$, if all the three real roots lie between $x = -4$ and $+4$. Determine the largest root correct to two decimal places using an enlargement.

4. Solve the equation $x^3 - 4x - 2 = 0$ graphically.

5. Find, using one or two graphs, the solutions of $2x^3 - 7x - 3 = 0$.

6. Using one or two suitable graphs and values of x from -4 to $+4$, find the three roots of the equation $x^3 = 9x - 4$. From the graphs find the range of values of x for which x^3 is greater than $9x - 4$.

7. Plot, on the same scales, the functions $2x^3$ and $x^2 + 7x - 6$, for values of x from $-2 \cdot 5$ to $+2 \cdot 5$. Hence find the roots of $2x^3 - x^2 - 7x + 6 = 0$.

8. Plot the graph of the function $y = x^3 - 2x^2 - 2x + 1$ for values of x from -2 to $+3$. Hence solve $x^3 - 2x^2 - 2x + 1 = 0$. By plotting an enlargement, determine the middle root to 3 decimal places.

9. Using two graphs, find a solution of the equation $e^x = x^2$. (Use values of x from -3 to $+3$.) Use an enlargement to find the root more accurately.

10. Using values of x between -2 and $+2$, find solutions of the equation $5e^x = 4x + 6$. (Plot $y = e^x$ and $y = \frac{1}{5}(4x + 6)$.)

11. By plotting a suitable graph (or graphs), find a solution of the equation $9 \log_{10} x = 2(x - 1)$ between $x = 1$ and $x = 5$.

12. Plot the graph of $y = \sin x$ from $x = 0$ to 3 (radians). Hence find two solutions of the equation $4 \sin x = x + 1$ in the given range. Give the results in radians and degrees.

13. Obtain a root of the equation $e^{-x} = \sin x$ between $x = 0$ and $\pi/2$, using a graphical plot. Using an enlargement, determine the root more accurately.

14. Determine a solution of $e^x = 2 \cos x$ between $x = 0$ and $x = \pi/2$.

15. On the same scales, plot the graphs of $xy = 2$ (rectangular hyperbola) and $x^2 + y^2 = 9$ (circle), using values of x from -4 to $+4$. Hence find the four pairs of solutions of the equations $xy = 2$, $x^2 + y^2 = 9$.

17

Reduction of Laws to Linear Forms and their Determination

17.1 Linear Law

If two variables x and y are connected by a law of the form $y = mx + c$, then the graph of y (vertical) against x (horizontal) will be a *straight line*. Hence a law like the form $y = mx + c$ is called a *linear law*. The constant $m = slope$ (*or gradient*) of the graph and may be determined by $m = \dfrac{BN}{AN}$ (see Figure 17.1). The constant $c = intercept$ made by the graph on the vertical axis. In some cases

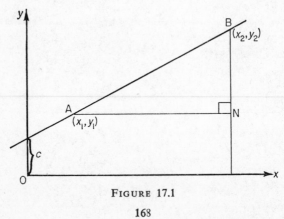

FIGURE 17.1

168

c cannot be read off directly, but m can always be *calculated*, hence c can be calculated, using the value obtained for m.

An alternative method of finding the constants m and c is as follows:

Let the values of the coordinates at A and B be (x_1, y_1) and (x_2, y_2). If the law is

$$y = mx + c$$

Then at A $\qquad\qquad y_1 = mx_1 + c \qquad\qquad\qquad\qquad$ (i)

and at B $\qquad\qquad y_2 = mx_2 + c \qquad\qquad\qquad\qquad$ (ii)

These two equations may be solved to find m and c.

Subtract (i) from (ii), then $y_2 - y_1 = m(x_2 - x_1)$

$$\therefore \; m = \frac{y_2 - y_1}{x_2 - x_1}$$

Substitute this value for m into (i), then:

$$c = y_1 - mx_1 = y_1 - \left(\frac{y_2 - y_1}{x_2 - x_1}\right)x_1$$

$$= \frac{y_1(x_2 - x_1) - x_1(y_2 - y_1)}{x_2 - x_1}$$

$$c = \frac{y_1 x_2 - x_1 y_2}{x_2 - x_1}$$

It is not necessary to memorize these values for m and c. In particular cases use one of the two *methods* to determine m and c.

The equation of the line may be written down as follows. If a general point P on the line has coordinates (x, y) (see Figure 17.2), then the triangles BNA and PLB are *similar*. Ratios of corresponding sides of similar triangles are equal, hence

$$\frac{PL}{BN} = \frac{BL}{AN}$$

$$\therefore \; \frac{y - y_2}{y_2 - y_1} = \frac{x - x_2}{x_2 - x_1}$$

This form, when rearranged, gives the necessary equation.

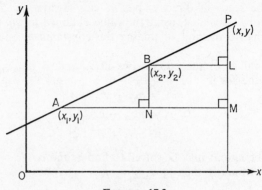

FIGURE 17.2

Examples:

(i) Write down the linear law connecting x and y, if it is of the form
$y = mx + c$, given that the points A(1,3) and B(3,7) lie on the line.

The slope of the line

$$m = \frac{BN}{AN} = \frac{7 - 3}{3 - 1} = \frac{4}{2} = 2$$

$$\therefore \text{ Law is } y = 2x + c$$

But $y = 3$ when $x = 1$

$$\therefore 3 = 2 \times 1 + c = 2 + c$$

$$\therefore c = 1$$

$$\therefore \underline{\text{The law is } y = 2x + 1}$$

(ii) The law connecting load (W N) and effort (P N) is thought
to be of the form $P = aW + b$. If $P = 8$ N when $W = 27$ N,
and $P = 13$ N when $W = 39$ N determine the law. Since
$P = aW + b$, using $P = 8$, $W = 27$

$$8 = 27a + b \qquad \qquad (i)$$

using $P = 13$, $W = 39$

$$13 = 39a + b \qquad \qquad (ii)$$

Hence $12a = 5$

$$\therefore a = \frac{5}{12}$$

$$b = 8 - 27 \times \frac{5}{12} = 8 - \frac{45}{4} = -\frac{13}{4}$$

$$\therefore \text{Law is } P = \frac{5}{12} W - \frac{13}{4}$$

(iii) Write down the linear equation connecting the two variables s and t, given $s = 9$ when $t = 2$, $s = 21$ when $t = 5$. The equation may be written down at once as

$$\frac{s - 21}{21 - 9} = \frac{t - 5}{5 - 2}$$

$$\therefore s - 21 = \frac{12}{3}(t - 5) \quad \text{or} \quad \underline{s = 4t + 1}$$

17.2 Reduction of Laws to Linear Form

The principal use for the linear law, in practical subjects, is in the estimation of approximate laws connecting two variable quantities, e.g. distance and time, pressure and volume, temperature and time, concentration and temperature, friction and normal pressure, etc. In most cases, when a graph is plotted, it will not be a straight line graph. Now a *straight line graph is the only one about which precise statements may be made*. Hence, in order to establish an assumed law, it is necessary to *change the variables* so that an approximate linear law may be established.

Illustrations of the change of variable technique to produce a *linear law*.

(i) Reduce the law $y = ax^2 + b$ to *linear* form.
Let $X = x^2$, i.e. $X =$ Square of the x values, then

$$y = aX + b$$

Hence the graph of y against X will be a straight line.

(ii) Reduce the law $y = m\sqrt{x} + c$ to linear form.

Let $X = \sqrt{x}$, i.e. $X =$ Square root of the x values, then

$$y = mX + c$$

Hence the graph of y against X will be a straight line.

(iii) Reduce $y = \dfrac{a}{x} + bx$ to linear form.

$$xy = a + b(x^2)$$

Let $Y = xy =$ values of products of the variables and $X = x^2$, then $Y = a + bX$. Hence a linear law is produced and a and b can be determined.

The original graphs of laws (i), (ii), (iii) would be curved and it would not be possible to decide that the assumed laws were of correct form. However, by plotting the new variables, straight lines would be produced and definite statements may be made about the lines.

Numerical illustrations of the change of variable techniques will be given in the following example. Further illustrations of a more complex nature will be dealt with in Chapter 18.

Example: The following values of x and y are thought to obey a law of the approximate form $y = ax^2 + b$. Show that this is so, and determine possible values for a and b, and hence the approximate law.

x	1	2	3	4	5	6
y	$-3 \cdot 10$	$-1 \cdot 48$	$1 \cdot 14$	$4 \cdot 85$	$9 \cdot 65$	$15 \cdot 43$

In order to *establish* the law, it is necessary to change the variable. Let $X = x^2$, then the law reduces to $y = aX + b$. Therefore plotting y against X should produce approximately a line.

Values of x^2 are 1, 4, 9, 16, 25, 36.

After plotting the points, using the new variables, it is seen that the points lie almost on a straight line (Figure 17.3). *The best line to fit among the points is drawn* (so that positive and negative vertical difference approximately cancel each other out in total). Since the graph is linear, the original law assumed is approximately correct.

(*Note:* This is the object of obtaining the straight line.)

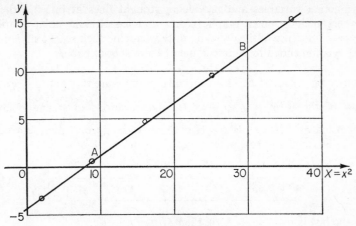

FIGURE 17.3

The law of the *graph* is now determined. At the two points A and B *on the graph*, when $X = 10$, $y = 1.7$, $X = 30$, $y = 12.5$.

∴ If the linear law is $y = aX + b$

then $\qquad\qquad\qquad 1.7 = 10a + b \qquad\qquad\qquad$ (i)

and $\qquad\qquad\qquad 12.5 = 30a + b \qquad\qquad\qquad$ (ii)

Hence $20a = 10.8$ ∴ $\underline{a = 0.54}$

$$b = 1.7 - 10a = 1.7 - 5.4 = \underline{-3.7}$$

∴ The approximate linear law is $y = 0.54X - 3.7$.

∴ The approximate law connecting y and x is

$$\underline{y = 0.54x^2 - 3.7}$$

17.3 Special Graph Papers

In addition to the standard uniform scale graph papers ($\frac{1}{2}$ inch 1 inch, centimetre), many special papers are now produced, on which the scales may not be uniform. These include many papers on which are marked logarithmic scales (as on a slide rule). The different papers may be used to establish certain laws directly, i.e. by plotting the actual variables and producing straight lines at once. Other papers include polar graph papers and logarithmic polar graph papers. Because of the difficulty of reproducing such scales, students are recommended to handle some of these special papers.

WORKED EXAMPLE. Two variables p and v are thought to obey a law of the form $p = \dfrac{c}{\sqrt{v}} + K\sqrt{v}$. Observations of p and v are recorded as follows. Show that the law is approximately correct and determine approximate values for c and K.

v	1	5	10	15	20
p	6·50	11·85	16·28	19·75	22·70

If the law is $p = \dfrac{c}{\sqrt{v}} + K\sqrt{v}$, then $p\sqrt{v} = c + Kv$.

Let $y = p\sqrt{v}$, then $y = c + Kv$.

Plot values of y against v. An approximate straight line should result.

$\sqrt{v}$	1	2·236	3·162	3·873	4·472
$y = p\sqrt{v}$	6·50	26·53	51·46	76·55	101·42

Since the graph obtained is linear (Figure 17.4), the assumed law is approximately of correct form.

$$y = c + Kv$$

$$K = \frac{BN}{AN} = \frac{101\cdot3 - 26\cdot2}{15} = 5\cdot007$$

$$\therefore K \text{ is approximately } \underline{5}$$

when $v = 10$, $y = 51\cdot5$

$$\therefore c = 51\cdot5 - 10 \times 5 = \underline{1\cdot5}$$

$\therefore$ Linear law is approximately $y = 1\cdot5 + 5v$

Hence $\qquad p\sqrt{v} = 1\cdot5 + 5v$

$$\therefore \text{ The law is approximately } p = \frac{1\cdot5}{\sqrt{v}} + 5\sqrt{v}$$

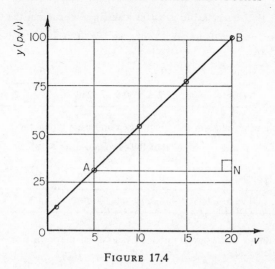

FIGURE 17.4

Examples 17

1. The following values of x and y are thought to obey a law of the form $y = ax^2 + b$. By drawing a suitable graph, show that this is so and estimate likely values of a and b.

x	1	2	3	4
y	4·1	8·3	15·3	25·3

2. Show that the law $y = a + \dfrac{b}{x}$ is satisfied by the values given, and estimate values of a and b.

x	4	5	6	7	8
y	1·13	1·23	1·29	1·34	1·37

3. Verify that x and y are connected approximately by the law $y = a + bx^2$ and estimate the values of a and b.

x	19	25	31	38	44
y	1900	3230	4900	7330	9780

4. A load W N is applied to a bar at a distance x cm from the fulcrum in an experiment on moments. Verify the law $W = \dfrac{a}{x} + b$ and estimate a and b.

x(cm)	8	10	12	14	16	18
W(N)	48	38·2	30·8	26·1	22	20·4

5. The following values of two quantities x and y are thought to be connected by a law $y = a + \dfrac{b}{x}$. Show that this is so and determine a and b.

x	0·2	0·3	0·4	0·8	1·0	2·0	4·0
y	40·5	24·5	16·3	4·0	1·6	−3·3	−5·8

6. Show that x and y are connected by a law of the form $y = \dfrac{1}{a + bx}$ and estimate a and b.

x	80	120	140	180	220	280
y	5·37	3·67	3·18	2·51	2·09	1·65

7. Verify that the given values obey a law of the form $y = a + \dfrac{b}{x^2}$ and obtain likely values for a and b.

x	2	3	4	5
y	1·940	1·862	1·835	1·822

8. The values shown in the table obey a law of the form $y = a\sqrt{x} + b$. Verify that this is so and estimate a and b.

x	400	600	800	1,000	1,400	1,800
y	0·210	0·223	0·235	0·245	0·262	0·277

9. The current i milliamperes flowing through a diode valve is thought to obey a law of the form $i = av + bv^2$ where v is the anode voltage in volts. Find possible values for a and b and verify that the law is approximately true.

v (V)	0	20	40	60	80	100
i(mA)	0	2·2	8·4	18·6	32·8	51·0

10. The distance s metres travelled by a car in time t seconds is recorded as follows:

t(sec)	5	10	15	20	25
s(metres)	137·5	350	637·5	1000	1437·5

Show that the law connecting s and t is of the form $s = at + bt^2$ and find possible values of a and b.

11. The following values of V and r are connected by a law of the form $V = Ar + \dfrac{B}{r}$. Show that this is so and estimate the values of A and B

r	2	4	6	8	10
V	55	72·5	98·3	126·2	155

12. The following values of s and t are suspected to follow a law $s = at^n$. Plot log s against log t and from the approximate line determine n(slope) and a (log a = Intercept on log s-axis)

t	5	10	15	20	25
s	64·9	183·3	336·9	518·7	724·7

18

Reduction of Laws like $y = ax^n$, $y = ae^{bx}$

18.1 Reduction of $y = ax^n$

As explained in Chapter 17, in order to *show* that two variables obey a stated law, it is necessary to establish a *linear law*. If x and y obey a law like $y = ax^n$, then they will also obey a law like $\log_{10} y = \log_{10} a + n \log_{10} x$. Let $Y = \log_{10} y$, $X = \log_{10} x$, $A = \log_{10} a$, then the law simplifies to $Y = A + nX$, i.e. a linear law. Therefore given a set of corresponding values of x and y, tabulate the logarithms and plot a graph of $Y(\log y)$ against $X(\log x)$. If the graph obtained is approximately a straight line, then the assumed law is approximately of correct form and the constants a and n can be determined using the straight line graph.

Example: The relation between pressure $P(\text{KN/m}^2)$ and volume $V(\text{m}^3)$ is thought to be of the form $PV^n = C$, where n and C are constants. Use the following experimental values to show that this is so and estimate likely values of n and C.

P	7·2	12·6	22·1	56·8	200
V	9	6	4	2	0·8
$\log P$	0·8573	1·1004	1·3444	1·7543	2·3010
$\log V$	0·9542	0·7782	0·6021	0·0310	$\bar{1}$·9031

Plot $\log P$ (vertical) against $\log V$ (horizontal) (see Figure 18.1).

$$\log P + n \log V = \log C$$
$$\log P = -n \log V + \log C$$

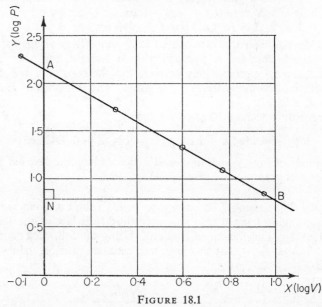

FIGURE 18.1

Since the graph of $\log P$ against $\log V$ is linear the assumed law is approximately of the correct form.

From the graph when $\log V = 0$

$$\log P = \log C = 2 \cdot 1600$$
$$\therefore\ C = \text{antilog } 2 \cdot 16 = \underline{144 \cdot 5}$$

$$\text{Slope of graph} = -n = -\frac{\text{AN}}{\text{NB}}$$

$$\therefore\ n = \frac{2 \cdot 16 - 0 \cdot 79}{1 \cdot 0} = 1 \cdot 37$$

$$\therefore\ \log P = -1 \cdot 37 \log V + 2 \cdot 16$$

$$\therefore\ \underline{PV^{1 \cdot 37} = 144 \cdot 5}\ \text{is the approximate law}$$

18.2 Reduction of $y = ae^{bx}$

If two variables x and y obey a law like $y = ae^{bx}$, then, taking logarithms *to base* e, $\log_e y = \log_e a + bx$.
Let $Y = \log_e y$, $A = \log_e a$, then $\underline{Y = A + bx}$.
Hence, to establish the exponential law, plot $Y(\log_e y)$ against x. If the graph obtained is approximately a straight line, then the assumed law is approximately correct, and the constants a, b can be determined from the straight line graph. The slope of this graph would give b.

If logarithms to base 10 are used, then

$$\log_{10} y = \log_{10} a + bx \log_{10} e = \log_{10} a + 0.4343bx.$$

Plot values of $\log_{10} y$ against x and hence deduce the law *but* the slope of this graph would give $0.4343\,b$.

Example: The tension $T\,(\text{N})$ in a rope coiled round a drum varies with the angle of lap θ (radians) according to a law of the form $T = T_0 e^{\mu\theta}$ (μ is coefficient of friction). Using the following experimental values, show that this is so and estimate possible values of T_0 and μ.

θ (radian)	1	3	5	7	9	12
$T\,(\text{N})$	30.9	47.0	71.5	108.7	165.5	310.8
$\log_e T$	3.4308	3.8502	4.2697	4.6889	5.1090	5.7391

If the assumed law is of correct form, then $\log_e T = \log_e T_0 + \mu\theta$. Plot values of $\log_e T$ against θ (Figure 18.2). Since the graph obtained is approximately linear the assumed law is approximately correct. From the graph, $\log_e T_0 = \text{Intercept} = 3.2200$

$$\therefore \underline{T_0 = 25.03}$$

$$\mu = \text{Slope of graph} = \frac{\text{BN}}{\text{NA}} = \frac{5.75 - 3.43}{11} = 0.211$$

$\therefore$ Law connecting T and θ is approximately $\underline{T = 25e^{0.211\theta}}$.

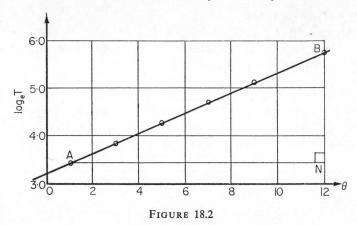

FIGURE 18.2

18.3 Note with Reference to the Laws $y = ax^n$, $y = ae^{bx}$

When estimating a possible law connecting two variables represented by pairs of experimental values, it must be remembered that observations are usually subject to *experimental and observational errors*, in addition to other *random errors*. These errors usually combine and hence, whilst an exact law may connect the variables, when the graphs are plotted exact graphs are not always obtained. Estimations are usually made of the *best graphs* to fit among the plotted points. Because of this, the *constants estimated* are subject to further errors, i.e. different estimates of the constants are obtained. With care in plotting, estimation and reading the estimates should not differ significantly.

The above types of law may be established by plotting actual observations on logarithmic papers. The law $y = ax^n$ may be established by plotting x and y on logarithmic paper which has *both* scales logarithmic. The law $y = ae^{bx}$ may be established by plotting x and y on paper which has a uniform scale on the horizontal axis but a logarithmic scale on the vertical axis. An example on the exponential law will be dealt with using logarithms to base 10 (see worked example (*b*).)

WORKED EXAMPLES

(a) Show that the observed values (see table) of the variables x and y obey a law of the form $y = Ax^m$ and estimate values for A and m.

x	5	10	15	20	25
y	17·40	29·25	39·65	49·20	58·10
$\log x$	0·6990	1·0000	1·1761	1·3010	1·3979
$\log y$	1·2405	1·4661	1·5982	1·6920	1·7642

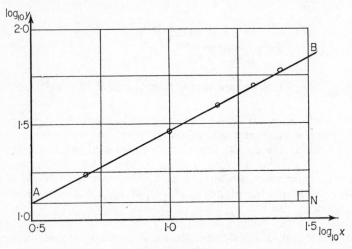

FIGURE 18.3

If the law is $y = Ax^m$, then $\log y = \log A + m \log x$.

Plot values of $\log y$ (vertical) against $\log x$ (horizontal) (Figure 18.3). Since the graph obtained is approximately linear, therefore the assumed law is approximately of correct form. From the linear graph

$$m = \text{Slope of graph} = \frac{\text{BN}}{\text{AN}} = \frac{1·85 - 1·10}{1·0} = 0·75$$

Since the intercept cannot be read off, log A is calculated.

$\log A = \log y - m \log x$ (when $\log x = 1$, $\log y = 1{\cdot}4700$)

$\qquad = 1{\cdot}4700 - 0{\cdot}75 \times 1 = 0{\cdot}7200$

$\therefore$ $A = $ antilog $0{\cdot}7200 = 5{\cdot}248$

$\therefore$ <u>Law is approximately $y = 5{\cdot}25x^{0{\cdot}75}$</u>

(b) In an undamped motion, the distance s metres travelled in t seconds is given by $s = ae^{kt}$. Using the tabulated data, show that this is so and estimate a and k.

t (sec)	1	5	10	15	20
s (metres)	8·12	8·62	9·30	10·02	10·80
$\log_{10} s$	0·9096	0·9355	0·9685	1·0009	1·0334

(In this example logarithms to base 10 are used)

If the law is $s = ae^{kt}$ then

$$\log_{10} s = \log_{10} a + kt \log_{10} e = \log_{10} a + 0{\cdot}4343kt$$

$\therefore$ If the assumed law is of correct form, the graph of $\log_{10} s$ against t should be linear (see Figure 18.4).

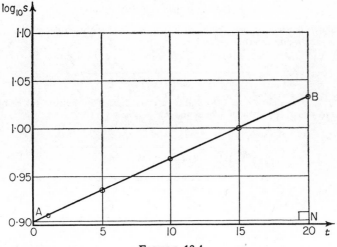

FIGURE 18.4

Since graph is linear $\therefore$ assumed law is of correct form.

$$\text{Slope of graph} = \frac{1 \cdot 034 - 0 \cdot 904}{20} = \frac{BN}{AN} = 0 \cdot 0065$$

$$\therefore \ 0 \cdot 4343k = 0 \cdot 0065$$

$$\therefore \ k = \frac{0 \cdot 0065}{0 \cdot 4343} = 0 \cdot 014\ 96$$

$$\log_{10} a = \text{Intercept} = 0 \cdot 904 \ \therefore \ a = 8 \cdot 017$$

$$\therefore \ \text{The law is approximately } s = 8e^{0 \cdot 015t}$$

Examples 18

1. The following pairs of values of x and y are thought to obey a law of the form $y = ax^n$. Show that this is so and estimate a and n.

x	2	3·5	4·2	7	9·1
y	20·8	195	407	3,120	8,960

2. Determine likely values of a and k if the following values of x and y obey a law of the form $y = ax^k$.

x	5	7·3	8·2	9·6
y	2·4	0·769	0·543	0·337

3. Show that the following pairs of values of x and y obey a law of the form $y = ae^{bx}$, and determine a and b.

x	0·5	0·8	1·3	2·8	3·2
y	99	54	20	1	0·49

4. Obtain possible values of a and k in order that the following values of x and y may approximately obey the law $y = ae^{kx}$.

x	2·4	3·6	4·8	5·3	6·9
y	1·16	2·06	3·75	4·9	10·7

5. The following are the values of span (in cm) and deflection (in cm) on steel rods all of the same cross-sectional dimensions used as beams:

Span L (cm)	30·5	46	61	76	92
Deflection d (cm)	0·15	0·55	1·19	2·32	4·07

If d and L are connected by a law of the form $d = kL^n$, determine k and n.

6. During a gas engine test of a given mass of gas contained in a cylinder, the following values of pressure (p KN/m²) and volume (v m³) were recorded:

p	100	75	60	40	30
v	2·300	2·824	3·312	4·425	5·435

Show that the gas law is $pv^n = c$, and estimate n and c.

7. The quantity Q (m³/s) of water discharged through an orifice under various pressure heads H (metres) are obtained as follows:

H	2·2	1·8	1·4	1·1	0·8	0·6
Q	8·90	8·03	7·23	6·4	5·5	4·85

Show that the discharge law is $Q = aH^n$, and estimate the likely values of a and n.

8. The torque T (Nm) and angle of twist θ (degrees) obtained experimentally in a torsion test are given as:

T (Nm)	850	900	950	1000	1050	1100	1150	1200
θ (°)	11·6	14·0	16·6	19·8	22·9	26·5	30·6	38·2

Show that the law connecting T and θ is $T = a\theta^n$, and estimate likely values of a and n.

9. A liquid is heated in a calorimeter to a certain temperature, and allowed to cool. The temperature is recorded every 4 minutes as follows (no record was made at the start):

t (min)	4	8	12	16	20
θ (°C)	98·3	77·4	60·8	47·9	37·7

The law of cooling is in the form $\theta = Ae^{-kt}$. Obtain likely values for A and k and estimate the initial temperature.

10. The speed v m/s of a particle after t seconds is recorded and the following results obtained:

t (sec)	1·0	1·5	2·0	2·5	3·0	3·5	4·0
v (m/s)	2·7	6·1	10·8	16·9	24·3	33·1	43·2

If v is given by $v = at^n$, estimate the values of a and n.

11. Show that the given values of M and t are related by a law of the form $M = ae^{bt}$, and estimate possible values of a and b.

t	2·3	3·1	4·0	4·9	5·9	7·2
M	10·5	13·0	16·8	21·9	28·6	41·7

12. The population N (in millions) in a certain country at different times (t) in years ($t = 0$ corresponds to 1935) is given in the following table:

t (years)	0	5	10	15	20	25
N (millions)	4·8	5·3	5·8	6·4	7·1	7·9

It is thought that $N = ae^{kt}$. Estimate possible values of a and k. Using your result, calculate the estimate of the population in 1970, assuming that the indicated trend continues.

19

Approximate Numerical Methods

19.1 Approximate Methods

In many practical problems it is not possible to obtain *a precise result*, hence in many cases it is necessary to use approximate numerical methods. In the solution of problems using digital computers, the methods of approximation are invaluable. It is essential to understand the nature of *approximate methods*. In any given problem it is possible to obtain a result correct to any number of significant figures by using a number of stages of approximation. Examples of methods of approximation have already been illustrated, e.g.

 (i) *Logarithmic calculations*, where results are initially obtained correct to four significant figures.
 (ii) *Binomial approximations*, where results can be obtained to any number of significant figures by taking suitable *orders of* approximation.
 (iii) Determination of the *roots of equations* (not solvable by formulae).
 (iv) Determination of *approximate laws* connecting variables.

The approximate determination of areas and volumes will be illustrated in the present chapter.

19.1.1 Approximate determination of areas and volumes

Since, in many cases, a plane area, or a solid, cannot be divided into *regular shapes* whose areas (or volumes) can be calculated with

187

precise formulae, approximations are made, i.e. areas or volumes of shapes which are *approximately equal to* the required area (or volume) are found.

19.1.2 Theorems of Guldin (or Pappus)

These were discovered separately by Guldin (or Pappus) about the same time. They relate to the volume (and surface) of a solid formed when a given plane area is rotated about an axis in the *plane of the area*. The theorems may be used to estimate volumes (or surfaces) when given areas (or arcs), the position of whose centres of gravity are known are rotated about an axis. Alternatively, they may be used to estimate the positions of centres of gravity of plane areas (or arcs).

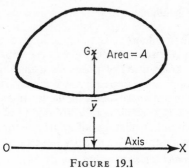

FIGURE 19.1

Theorem (i): see Figure 19.1

If a plane area A be rotated through 360° about an axis in the plane of the area (not intersecting the area), then the volume V swept out (formed) by A = Area A × Path of the centre of gravity of A

i.e. $$V = A \times 2\pi\bar{y}$$

where $\bar{y}$ is the distance of the centre of gravity of A from the axis OX.

Theorem (ii): see Figure 19.2

If a plane arc l be rotated through 360° about an axis in the plane of the arc (not intersecting the arc), then the area S swept out

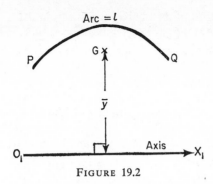

FIGURE 19.2

(formed) by l = Arc length l × Path of centre of gravity of l

i.e. $$S = l \times 2\pi\bar{y}$$

where $\bar{y}$ is the distance of the centre of gravity of l from the axis O_1X_1.

Examples:

(i) A right-angled triangle ABC (angle B = 90°) is rotated through 360° about BC. If AB = 4 cm, BC = 3 cm, calculate the position of the centre of gravity of ABC relative to BC (Figure 19.3), and the area of the curved surface of the cone formed (Figure 19.4).

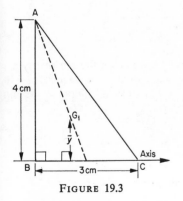

FIGURE 19.3

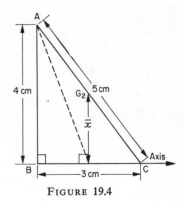

FIGURE 19.4

Area of triangle = 6 cm²
Length of AC = 5 cm.

Let C. of G. of area be G_1 at $\bar{y}$ cm from BC.

C. of G. of arc (AC) is $\frac{1}{2} \times 4 = 2$ cm $= \bar{x}$ from BC(G_2).

The solid formed is a cone of height 3 cm and radius 4 cm. Volume of cone $= \frac{1}{3}\pi r^2 h = \frac{1}{3} \times \pi \times 4^2 \times 3 = 16\pi$ cm³. Using Theorem (i) $16\pi = $ Area $\times 2\pi\bar{y} = 6 \times 2\pi \times \bar{y}$

$$\therefore \bar{y} = \frac{4}{3} \text{ cm} = \frac{1}{3} \times \text{altitude}$$

$\therefore$ G of area lies $\frac{1}{3}$ way along the median AD.

Curved area of the cone $=$ length of arc $\times 2\pi\bar{x} = 5 \times 2\pi \times 2 = 20\pi$ cm². (From Chapter 15, curved area $= \pi r l = \pi \times 4 \times 5 = 20\pi$ cm².)

(ii) By considering the rotation of a semicircle of radius r about its diameter, determine the positions of the centres of gravity of the area and arc (Figures 19.5 and 19.6).

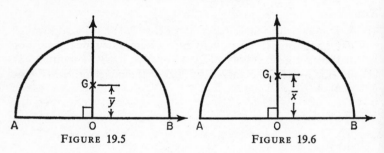

FIGURE 19.5   FIGURE 19.6

By symmetry the centres of gravity both lie on the *central radius*. Let G of the area be $\bar{y}$ from AB, G_1 of the arc be $\bar{x}$ from AB. The solid formed by rotation is a sphere of radius r. Using Theorem (i)

$$\text{Volume} = \tfrac{4}{3}\pi r^3 = \tfrac{1}{2}\pi r^2 \times 2\pi \times \bar{y}$$

$$\therefore \bar{y} = \frac{4r}{3\pi}$$

Using Theorem (ii) Surface $= 4\pi r^2 = \pi r \times 2\pi\bar{x}$

$$\therefore \bar{x} = \frac{2r}{\pi}$$

19.2 Standard Rules

19.2.1 Mid-ordinate rule

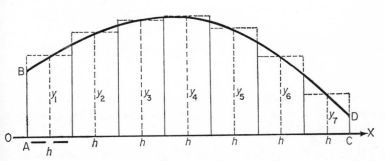

FIGURE 19.7

Let the area between the curve, the ordinates AB, CD and the axis OX be required. Let $y_1, y_2, \ldots, y_7$ be the ordinates at the mid-points of the equal intervals of size h. The area required is approximately equal to the sum of the areas of the rectangles of equal width h and heights $y_1, y_2, \ldots, y_7$, i.e.

$$\text{Area} \simeq hy_1 + hy_2 + \ldots + hy_7$$

$$\text{Area} \simeq h(y_1 + y_2 + \ldots + y_7)$$

$$\text{Area} \simeq \text{Width of interval} \times \text{Sum of mid-ordinates}$$

These ordinates must be measured or read off from a graphical plot (Figure 19.7).

19.2.2 Trapezoidal rule

To estimate the area between the curve, the end ordinates and the axis OX, read off the ordinates indicated (at each end of the equal intervals). The area is approximately equal to the sum of the

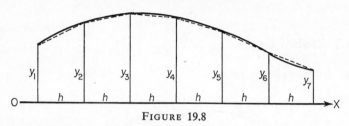

FIGURE 19.8

trapezia indicated (Figure 19.8), i.e.

Area $\simeq \frac{1}{2}h(y_1 + y_2) + \frac{1}{2}h(y_2 + y_3) + \ldots + \frac{1}{2}h(y_6 + y_7)$

Area $\simeq \frac{1}{2}h[y_1 + y_7 + 2(y_2 + y_3 + y_4 + y_5 + y_6)]$

Area $\simeq \frac{1}{2}$(Spacing) $\times$ (Sum of first and last ordinates

$+$ Twice the remaining ordinates)

19.2.3 Simpson's rule

This is the most useful of the rules for estimating an area approximately, since the rule is established on the assumption that a *curve* passes through the tops of the ordinates (Figure 19.9). In order to use the rule an *even number of intervals* must be used (i.e. *an odd number of ordinates*).

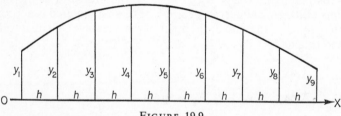

FIGURE 19.9

Let $h = $ spacing of ordinates.

For *three* ordinates, Area $\simeq \frac{1}{3}h(y_1 + 4y_2 + y_3)$

For any number of ordinates (odd)

Area $\simeq \frac{1}{3}h(y_1 + 4y_2 + y_3) + \frac{1}{3}h(y_3 + 4y_4 + y_5) + \ldots$

$+ \frac{1}{3}h(y_7 + 4y_8 + y_9)$

Area $\simeq \frac{1}{3}h[y_1 + y_9 + 2(y_3 + y_5 + y_7) + 4(y_2 + y_4 + y_6 + y_8)]$

Area $\simeq \frac{1}{3}$(Spacing) $\times$ [Sum of first and last ordinates

$+ 2$(Remaining odd ordinates) $+ 4$(Sum of even ordinates)]

19.2.4 Determination of volumes

The same formulae may be used, but cross-sectional areas are used instead of ordinates.

19.2.5

Any number of intervals may be used to apply any of the three rules but, *when using Simpson's rule*, an *odd* number of ordinates *must* be used.

19.3 Mean and Root Mean Square Values

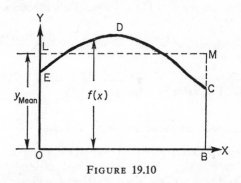

FIGURE 19.10

Let the area under the graph of $y = f(x)$, between ordinates at O and B, be A. If LM (Figure 19.10) be drawn parallel to OX, so that the area of the rectangle OBML is equal to Area of OBCDE, then OL = Height of rectangle is the *mean value* of $f(x)$ between O and B. To calculate y_{Mean}:

$$y_{\text{Mean}} = \frac{\text{Area under graph}}{\text{Length of axis (OB)}}$$

Similarly, if values of $[f(x)]^2$ are calculated and plotted, the '*squared function*' graph is obtained (Figure 19.11). If ST be drawn parallel to OX so that the area of the rectangle OBTS is equal to area of OBPQR, then OS = Height of rectangle is the *mean value* of

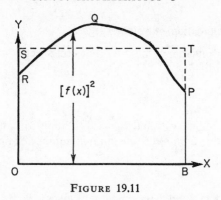

FIGURE 19.11

$[f(x)]^2$ i.e. mean square of $f(x)$. To calculate the *mean square* value of $f(x)$:

$$\text{Mean square} = \frac{\text{Area under 'squared function' graph}}{\text{Length of axis (OB)}}$$

The *root mean square* (R.M.S.) value of $f(x)$ is the square root of this value, i.e. R.M.S. value $= \sqrt{(\text{mean square})}$.

19.3.1 Applications of mean and R.M.S. values

(i) *Electrical Engineering*—mean currents in components. R.M.S. values of currents and voltages used in *Alternating current* theory and calculations. They arise because Power $\propto$ (Current)^2.

(ii) *Mechanical Engineering*—centre of gravity calculations (mean values), mean pressures, average forces, etc. *Radius of gyration* of a body about an axis is the R.M.S. value of distances from the axis.

(iii) *Statistical Calculations*—the mean value is a measure of central location. R.M.S. value is a measure of *dispersion* or scattering of data.

WORKED EXAMPLES (Graphical work omitted in these examples)

(a) From a graph of y (cm) against x (cm) 11 ordinates are read off at intervals of 0·5 cm, as follows:

　　0·82, 1·36, 2·06, 2·56, 2·74, 2·68, 2·36, 1·72, 0·94, 0·52, 0·32.

Estimate $\bar{y}$, the distance of the centre of gravity of the area from the x-axis, and estimate the volume swept out when the area is rotated about the x-axis through 360°. (*Note:* $\bar{y}$ is found by using the first moment of area about the axis. This is approximately 9·20 cm³.)

Let the ordinates be $y_1, y_2, y_3, \ldots, y_{11}$,
then $$y_1 + y_{11} = 1·14$$
$$y_2 + y_4 + y_6 + y_8 + y_{10} = 8·84$$
$$y_3 + y_5 + y_7 + y_9 = 8·10$$
Applying Simpson's rule
$$\text{Area} = \tfrac{1}{3}h(F + L + 2O + 4E)$$
$$\begin{aligned}
\text{Area} &= \tfrac{1}{3} \times 0·5(1·14 + 2 \times 8·10 + 4 \times 8·84) \\
&= \tfrac{1}{3} \times 0·5 \ (1·14 + 16·20 + 35·36) \ \text{cm}^2 \\
&= \tfrac{1}{3} \times 0·5 \times 52·70 = \tfrac{1}{3} \times 26·35 = \underline{8·783 \ \text{cm}^2}
\end{aligned}$$

$\bar{y} \simeq$ First Mom. of area/Area $= 9·20/8·783 = 1·047$ cm.

Volume of revolution $= A \times 2\pi\bar{y} = 8·783 \times 2\pi \times 1·047$
$$= \underline{57·81 \ \text{cm}^3}$$

(b) From a graph of force against distance, the following values of force (N) at intervals of 5 metres are obtained:

x(m)	0	5	10	15	20	25	30
F(N)	16·7	19·4	18·3	12·1	9·7	10·9	14·0

Estimate the work done by the variable force over the 30 metres interval and the average force.

(*Note:* Work done by the force = Area below graph in Joules.) Using Simpson's rule:

Work done by force = Area under graph
$$\begin{aligned}
&= \tfrac{1}{3} \times h[F_1 + F_7 + 2(F_3 + F_5) + 4(F_2 + F_4 + F_6)] \\
&= \tfrac{1}{3} \times 5[16·7 + 14·0 + 2(18·3 + 9·7) + 4(19·4 + 12·1 + 10.9)] \\
&= \tfrac{1}{3} \times 5(30·7 + 2 \times 28·0 + 4 \times 42·4) \\
&= \tfrac{1}{3} \times 5(30·7 + 56·0 + 169·6) \\
&= \tfrac{1}{3} \times 5 \times 256·3 \\
&= 85·43 \times 5 = 427·15 \\
&= \underline{427 \ \text{Joule}} \ \text{(nearest Joule)}
\end{aligned}$$

$$\text{Average force} = \frac{\text{Work done}}{\text{Distance}} = \frac{427 \cdot 15}{30}$$

$$= 14 \cdot 24 \qquad = 14 \cdot 2 \text{ N} \quad \text{(nearest } 0 \cdot 1 \text{ N)}$$

(c) The following empirical values of a function $f(x)$ are obtained in an experimental investigation for given values of x. Estimate the mean value and R.M.S. value of $f(x)$ over the given range.

x	0	2	4	6	8	10	12	14	16	18	20
$f(x)$	20·1	17·2	18·0	21·0	23·9	25·7	26·0	24·0	20·0	17·8	17·0
$[f(x)]^2$	404·0	296·0	324·0	441·0	571·0	660·5	676·0	576·0	400·0	317·0	289

Using Simpson's rule, area under the graph $y = f(x)$ is given by

$$\text{Area} = \frac{1}{3} \times h(F + L + 2O + 4E)$$

$$= \frac{2}{3}(20 \cdot 1 + 17 \cdot 0 + 2 \times 87 \cdot 9 + 4 \times 105 \cdot 7)$$

$$= \frac{2}{3}(37 \cdot 1 + 175 \cdot 8 + 422 \cdot 8) = \frac{2}{3} \times 635 \cdot 7$$

$$= \frac{1271 \cdot 4}{3} = \underline{423 \cdot 8} \text{ sq. units}$$

$$\text{Mean value of } f(x) = \frac{\text{Area under graph}}{\text{Total length of axis}} = \frac{423 \cdot 8}{20} = \underline{21 \cdot 19}$$

Area under graph of $y = [f(x)]^2$

$$= \frac{2}{3}(404 \cdot 0 + 289 \cdot 0 + 2 \times 1971 \cdot 0 + 4 \times 2290 \cdot 5)$$

$$= \frac{2}{3}(693 \cdot 0 + 3942 \cdot 0 + 9162 \cdot 0) = \frac{2}{3} \times 13\,797 \cdot 0$$

$$= \frac{1}{3} \times 27\,594 = \underline{9198} \text{ units}$$

$$\text{Mean square value of } f(x) = \frac{9198}{20} = \underline{459 \cdot 9}$$

$$\therefore \text{ R.M.S. value of } f(x) = \sqrt{(\text{Mean square})} = \sqrt{459 \cdot 9} = \underline{21 \cdot 44}$$

(d) The frustum of a cone has an altitude h and end radii of r and R. Using 3 sections and Simpson's rule, obtain the *formula* for the volume of the frustum.

(*Note:* When ordinates or cross sectional areas are quadratic functions of distance along the axis, Simpson's rule will give the exact result.)

By proportion the radius of the middle section of the frustum $= \frac{1}{2}(r + R)$.

Let $A = \pi r^2$, $B = \pi R^2$, $M = \pi \left(\dfrac{r + R}{2}\right)^2$

To use Simpson's rule, the 'h' of the formula $= \frac{1}{2}h(h')$

$\therefore$ Volume of frustum $= \frac{1}{3}h'(A + B + 4M)$

$$= \frac{1}{2}\frac{h}{3}\left[\pi r^2 + \pi R^2 + 4\pi\left(\frac{r + R}{2}\right)^2\right]$$

$$= \frac{\pi h}{6}\left[r^2 + R^2 + (r^2 + 2rR + R^2)\right]$$

$$= \frac{\pi h}{6}\left[2r^2 + 2R^2 + 2Rr\right] = \frac{2\pi h}{6}\left[r^2 + R^2 + Rr\right]$$

$$\therefore \underline{V = \frac{1}{3}\pi h(r^2 + R^2 + Rr)}$$

Examples 19

1. The following empirical values of $y = f(x)$ for equal intervals of 1 unit in x are obtained:

x	0	1	2	3	4	5	6	7	8	9	10
y	9·5	12·3	16·3	18·5	17·6	14·1	10·5	7·8	5·8	4·5	4·0

Plot the graph of $y = f(x)$. From your graph read off the mid-ordinate values at the mid-points of the ten intervals. Estimate the area under the graph between $x = 0$ and $x = 10$, using the mid-ordinate rule. Estimate the mean value of y and the approximate volume formed if the area is rotated through 360° about the x-axis. (First moment of area $= 764\cdot5$ unit³.)

2. Using the ordinates given in Question 1, estimate the area under the graph using (a) the trapezoidal rule, (b) Simpson's rule.

3. During an experimental investigation on a gas in a cylinder, the following values of pressure and volume are recorded:

v (m³)	2	3	4	5	6	7
p (KN/m²)	350	233·3	175	140	116·7	100

Plot the graph of pressure against volume. Read off the pressures at 2·5, 3·5, 4·5, 5·5, 6·5 m³. Using the 11 ordinates estimate, the work done in Joules, during the expansion from 2 to 7 m³ (using Simpson's rule) and estimate the mean pressure during the expansion.

4. The cross-sectional areas of a solid at constant intervals of 0·5 cm are 0, 1, 2·8, 4·9, 7·2, 10, 13·9, 18, 22·8, 29·0, 38·2 cm². Estimate the volume of the solid, using Simpson's rule. What would be the radius of a solid of uniform circular cross section of the same length having the same volume?

5. In an experiment with a model ship, the resistance to motion, R N is found to vary with the speed v m/min as follows:

v	100	120	140	160	180	200	220
R	0·78	0·84	0·95	1·12	1·37	1·80	2·63

Determine (using Simpson's rule) the average resistance for speeds between 100 and 220 m/min.

6. The current I amp in an electrical circuit varies with time t seconds as shown in the table:

t (s)	0	10	20	30	40	50	60	70	80	90	100
I (A)	3·5	4·6	5·7	5·9	5·4	4·6	3·9	3·1	2·5	1·6	0·8

Using Simpson's rule, estimate the quantity (Q coulombs) of electricity passed during the 100 seconds, and the average current. Estimate also the R.M.S. value of the current.

7. The following table gives the speed of a car at one second intervals from rest. Plot a graph of speed v against t and estimate the distance travelled, using (i) the mid-ordinate rule (8 ordinates), (ii) Simpson's rule (9 ordinates). Find the average speed in m/s and Km/h, using (ii).

t (s)	0	1	2	3	4	5	6	7	8
v (m/s)	0	8·75	12·55	16·30	21·35	22·50	21·60	17·30	12·60

8. Plot the graph of $y = 5 \sin \theta$ for values of θ from 0° to 180° in steps of 18°. Using Simpson's rule estimate the area under the graph and deduce the approximate value of the mean of $5 \sin \theta$ in this range. $\left(\text{Note: Interval } h = \dfrac{\pi}{10} . \right)$

9. Plot the graph of $y = \dfrac{20}{x}$ for values of x from 1 to 5 in steps of 0·5. Read off

the 9 equally spaced ordinates and estimate the area under the graph, using Simpson's rule. Use your result to find an approximate value for the mean value of y and deduce the approximate volume swept out by the area when it is rotated through 360° about the x-axis. (First Moment of area = 160 unit³.)

10. The turning moment (torque) on a shaft is a function of θ (radians) and is given for values of θ in intervals of $\pi/6$ radians as follows:

θ	0	$\pi/6$	$\pi/3$	$\pi/2$	$2\pi/3$	$5\pi/6$	π
Torque (N m)	6	7·54	9·73	12	13·73	14·46	14

Estimate the mean torque on the shaft using Simpson's rule as θ varies from 0 to π radians.

11. The acceleration of a racing car in m/s² at 2 second intervals is shown in the following table:

t	0	2	4	6	8	10	12	14	16	18	20
f	3·73	3·50	3·30	3·03	2·83	2·67	2·50	2·33	2·13	1·73	1·50

Estimate the speed of the car after 20 seconds (using Simpson's rule) in kilometre/hour. What is the average acceleration of the car?

12. An anchor ring has a circular cross-section of radius 6 cm and the mean diameter of the ring is 24 cm. Using the theorem of Pappus, calculate (i) the weight of the ring if the metal weighs 76·8 KN/m³, (ii) the total surface area of the ring (in cm²).

20

Tabulation of Polynomial Functions

20.1 Function Tabulation

All the common mathematical tables are examples of the tabulation of *numerical values* of a function, for increasing values of the argument (independent variable) x.

Examples: Logarithms—tabulated numerical values of the function

$$y = \log_{10} x$$

Squares—tabulated numerical values of x^2.

Similarly, square roots ($y = \sqrt{x}$), reciprocals ($y = 1/x$), sines ($y = \sin x$) and so on.

20.1.1 General tabulation of functions

Numerical values of any function may be tabulated. Normally functions are tabulated for uniform *increments* (or *finite differences*) in x. In addition 'differences columns' are provided to estimate intermediate values of the function. In four-figure tables, these differences are usually employed to adjust for the fourth significant figure (or in some cases the fourth decimal place). With higher tables e.g. five, six, seven and nine-figure tables, the *differences* may be quite large numbers. In order to estimate intermediate values the principle of *proportional parts* is used. The differences are examples of *first-order finite differences*. For greater accuracy of estimation, *higher orders* of finite differences may be used.

20.1.2 Polynomial functions

A polynomial of degree n in the variable x is of the form $y = a_1x^n + a_2x^{n-1} + a_3x^{n-2} + \ldots + a_n$, i.e. is the sum of terms containing integral powers of x.

Examples: $ax^2 + bx + c$ is a quadratic polynomial.

$ax^3 + bx^2 + cx + d$ is a cubic polynomial, etc.

20.1.3 Tabulation of numerical values of a polynomial

Example: Tabulate the values of $2x^3 + 3x^2 + 5x - 2$ for values of x from 0 to 1 in steps of 0·1.

x	0	0·1	0·2	0·3	0·4	0·5	0·6	0·7	0·8	0·9	1·0
$2x^3$	0	0·002	0·016	0·054	0·128	0·250	0·432	0·686	1·024	1·458	2·000
$3x^2$	0	0·030	0·120	0·270	0·480	0·750	1·080	1·470	1·920	2·430	3·000
$5x$	0	0·500	1·000	1·500	2·000	2·500	3·000	3·500	4·000	4·500	5·000
$f(x)$	−2	−1·468	−0·864	−0·176	0·608	1·500	2·512	3·656	4·944	6·388	8·000

20.2 Finite Differences

20.2.1 Notation

If x increases by Δx, then the corresponding first-order finite difference in y is Δy, the second-order finite difference in y is $\Delta^2 y$, the third-order difference $\Delta^3 y$ and so on.

Example: Tabulate the function $y = x^3$ and write down the finite differences up to the fourth order, using values of x from 0 to 10 in steps of one unit.

x	0	1	2	3	4	5	6	7	8	9	10
y	0	1	8	27	64	125	216	343	512	729	1000
Δy		1	7	19	37	61	91	127	169	217	271
$\Delta^2 y$			6	12	18	24	30	36	42	48	54
$\Delta^3 y$				6	6	6	6	6	6	6	6
$\Delta^4 y$					0	0	0	0	0	0	0

It should be noted that the fourth-order differences are all *zero*, the third-order differences constant.

20.2.2 Polynomials

If the values of a polynomial of degree n for equal increments in x are tabulated and the finite differences written down, the differences of order $n + 1$ vanish. When a tabulated function is given for equal steps in x, and the $(n + 1)$th order differences all vanish, then it may be deduced that the values given are numerical values of a polynomial of degree n. In practical problems, if the differences of order $n + 1$ are very small, then the function is approximately a polynomial of degree n.

20.2.3 Interpolation

This describes the process of estimating intermediate values of a function by using finite differences.

Example: If $f(0 \cdot 120) = 1 \cdot 7652$, $f(0 \cdot 125) = 1 \cdot 7666$, use proportional parts (first-order differences) to estimate $f(0 \cdot 123)$.

For an increase $0 \cdot 005$ in x:

$$\Delta f = 1 \cdot 7666 - 1 \cdot 7652 = 0 \cdot 0014$$

By simple proportion, the difference to add to $f(0 \cdot 120)$ will be

$$\frac{3}{5} \times 0 \cdot 0014 = \frac{0 \cdot 0042}{5} = 0 \cdot 000\,84$$

$$\therefore f(0 \cdot 123) = 1 \cdot 7652 + 0 \cdot 000\,84 = \underline{1 \cdot 766\,04}$$

20.2.4 Interpolation in mathematical tables

Example: Using 4-figure tables, estimate the value of tan 60°39′45″.

tan 60°36′ = $1 \cdot 7747$, difference for 3′ = 36, difference for 4′ = 48
45″ = $\frac{3}{4}$′, therefore additional difference to add to difference for 3′
is $\frac{3}{4} \times (48 - 36) = 9$.

$$\therefore \tan 60°39′45″ = 1 \cdot 7747 + 36 + 9 = \underline{1 \cdot 7792}$$

20.3 Deduction of Simple Polynomial Functions

Examples: (i) Show that the following tabulated values of y obey a polynomial function and find the function.

x	0	1	2	3	4	5	6	7	8
y	-1	4	13	26	43	64	89	118	151
Δy		5	9	13	17	21	25	29	33
$\Delta^2 y$		4	4	4	4	4	4	4	
$\Delta^3 y$			0	0	0	0	0	0	

Since the third-order differences vanish, it can be deduced that y is a quadratic function of x. Let $y = ax^2 + bx + c$.
When $x = 0$, $y = -1$

$$\therefore\ \underline{-1 = c}$$

When $x = 1$, $y = 4$

$$\therefore\ 4 = a + b + c$$

$$\underline{a + b = 5}$$

When $x = 2$, $y = 13$

$$\therefore\ 13 = 4a + 2b + c$$

$$\underline{4a + 2b = 14}$$

Hence $a = 2$, $b = 3$, $c = -1$.

$$\therefore\ \underline{y = 2x^2 + 3x - 1}$$

(ii) Show that the following tabulated values of y obey a cubic polynomial:

x	0	0·1	0·2	0·3	0·4	0·5	0·6	0·7	0·8	0·9	1·0
y	$-2 \cdot 000$	$-1 \cdot 468$	$-0 \cdot 864$	$-0 \cdot 176$	0·608	1·500	2·512	3·656	4·944	6·388	8·000
Δy		0·532	0·604	0·688	0·784	0·892	1·012	1·144	1·288	1·444	1·612
$\Delta^2 y$			0·072	0·084	0·096	0·108	0·120	0·132	0·144	0·156	0·168
$\Delta^3 y$				0·012	0·012	0·012	0·012	0·012	0·012	0·012	0·012
$\Delta^4 y$					0	0	0	0	0	0	0

Since the fourth-order differences all vanish, therefore the values of y, as tabulated, obey a polynomial of degree three, i.e. a cubic polynomial. It will be seen that the actual polynomial is $y = 2x^3 + 3x^2 + 5x - 2$ [see 20.1.3].

WORKED EXAMPLES

(a) Tabulate the values of x^4 for values of x from 0 to 8 in steps of 1 unit. Write down the finite differences for x^4 up to the fifth order.

x	0	1	2	3	4	5	6	7	8
$y = x^4$	0	1	16	81	256	625	1296	2401	4096
Δy		1	15	65	175	369	671	1105	1695
$\Delta^2 y$			14	50	110	194	302	434	590
$\Delta^3 y$				36	60	84	108	132	156
$\Delta^4 y$					24	24	24	24	24
$\Delta^5 y$						0	0	0	0

(b) Show that the following tabulated values of y obey a quadratic polynomial and hence find y as a function of x.

x	0	1	2	3	4	5	6
y	5	6	13	26	45	70	101
Δy		1	7	13	19	25	31
$\Delta^2 y$			6	6	6	6	6
$\Delta^3 y$				0	0	0	0

Since the third-order differences vanish, y is a quadratic function of x. Let $y = ax^2 + bx + c$.

$x = 0$; $5 = c$

$x = 1$; $6 = a + b + c$

$$\underline{a + b = 1}$$

$x = 2$; $13 = 4a + 2b + c$

$$\underline{4a + 2b = 8}$$

$2a + b = 4$

hence $a = 3$, $b = -2$

$$\therefore \underline{y = 3x^2 - 2x + 5}$$

(c) Given $(2 \cdot 10)^3 = 9 \cdot 2610$, $(2 \cdot 12)^3 = 9 \cdot 5281$, use interpolation to estimate the value of $(2 \cdot 115)^3$.

$\Delta y = 0 \cdot 2671$ for increase of $0 \cdot 02$ in x.

For increase $0 \cdot 015$ in x

$$\Delta y = \frac{15}{20} \times 0 \cdot 2671 = 0 \cdot 2003$$

Hence

$$(2 \cdot 115)^3 \simeq 9 \cdot 2610 + 0 \cdot 2003 = \underline{9 \cdot 4613}$$

(If 4 figure logarithms are used, $(2 \cdot 115)^3 = 9 \cdot 4610$)

(d) Use 4 figure tables to estimate $\log_e 1 \cdot 1864$.

$\log_e 1 \cdot 186 = 0 \cdot 1707$, finite difference = 9 (6 to 7 change)

$$\therefore \text{ Difference to add for } 0 \cdot 0004 \simeq \frac{2}{5} \times 9 = 3 \cdot 6$$

$$\therefore \log_e 1 \cdot 1864 = 0 \cdot 170 \ 70 + 0 \cdot 000 \ 36 = \underline{0 \cdot 171 \ 06}$$

Examples 20

1. Tabulate the numerical values of $x^3 - 2x + 3$ for values of x from 0 to 8 in steps of 1 unit. Write down the finite differences for the function as far as the fourth-order differences.

2. By tabulating the finite differences, show that the following values of y obey a polynomial in x. Find this polynomial function.

x	0	1	2	3	4	5	6	7	8
y	-7	0	13	32	57	88	125	168	217

3. Use proportional parts to estimate the value of $f(0 \cdot 267)$ given $f(0 \cdot 26) = 3 \cdot 7864$ and $f(0 \cdot 27) = 3 \cdot 7896$.

4. From four figure tables, $\tan 20°30' = 0 \cdot 3739$ and $\tan 20°35' = 0 \cdot 3756$. Use proportional parts to estimate $\tan 20°33'$.

5. Using the principle of proportional parts, estimate $\sqrt{2 \cdot 55}$ given $\sqrt{2 \cdot 530} = 1 \cdot 591$, $\sqrt{2 \cdot 570} = 1 \cdot 603$.

6. The following values of s (metres) are tabulated experimentally for values of t (seconds) from 1 to 8 seconds.

t	1	2	3	4	5	6	7	8
s	2·10	2·65	3·40	4·35	5·50	6·85	8·40	10·15

By tabulating the finite differences for s, show that s is a quadratic function of t, and find the function.

7. The following numerical values of $f(x)$ are obtained experimentally. By tabulating the finite differences for $f(x)$, estimate the approximate type of polynomial for $f(x)$.

x	1	2	3	4	5	6	7	8
$f(x)$	16·01	51·98	104·03	171·95	256·02	355·96	472·01	603·97

8. Show that the following numerical values of y obey a cubic polynomial function, and find the function.

x	0	1	2	3	4	5	6	7	8	9	10
y	2	3	12	35	78	147	248	387	570	803	1,092

9. From exponential tables $e^{0·15} = 1·1618$, $e^{0·16} = 1·1735$. Using interpolation (proportional parts), estimate the value of $e^{0·154}$.

10. Show that the following numerical values of θ obey a law of the form $\theta = at^2 + bt + c$, and find the law.

t	0	0·2	0·4	0·6	0·8	1·0
θ	4	3·08	2·32	1·72	1·28	1·0

21

Tabulation of Functions and Increments

21.1 Finite Increments

The relationships between relative increases of a dependent and independent variable will now be considered. The consideration of such relationships between increases (or increments) leads to the *differential calculus*. Investigation of tabulated values of a function or a graphical plot leads to ideas of approximate rates of change of functions over an interval of the independent variable. From such approximate rates of change it is possible, using *limiting processes*, to obtain values for *instantaneous rates of change* of functions at specific values of the independent variable.

Example: Tabulate the values of $y = x^2$ for steps of 0·1 in x from $x = 1$ to 2. Calculate the values of

$$\frac{\text{Increment of } y}{\text{Increment of } x}$$

for each of the intervals of 0·1 in x.

x	1	1·1	1·2	1·3	1·4	1·5	1·6	1·7	1·8	1·9	2·0
$y = x^2$	1	1·21	1·44	1·69	1·96	2·25	2·56	2·89	3·24	3·61	4·0
Increment in y		0·21	0·23	0·25	0·27	0·29	0·31	0·33	0·35	0·37	0·39
$\dfrac{\text{Increment of } y}{\text{Increment of } x}$		2·1	2·3	2·5	2·7	2·9	3·1	3·3	3·5	3·7	3·9

It will be seen that the ratios calculated are simply related as follows:
 (i) The ratios increase at a constant rate or the values of the ratios are a linear function of x.
(ii) In each case the ratio of the increments is exactly twice the mid-value of x.

21.2 Functional Notation for Increments

In order to represent a general increment in a variable, a special notation is used. An increase (increment) in x will be represented by δx (read as delta x). A corresponding increase in y, where y is a function of x will be represented by δy. During the interval δx the *average rate of of change of y with respect to x* is given by

$$\frac{\text{Increment of } y}{\text{Increment of } x} = \frac{\delta y}{\delta x}$$

This ratio gives the average increase of y for unit increase in x during the interval δx. If $y = f(x)$ (i.e. y is a function of x) then, if x increases by δx, $f(x)$ increases to $f(x + \delta x)$.

Hence δy = Increment of y corresponding to an increment δx in x

$$= f(x + \delta x) - f(x).$$

$$\therefore \quad \frac{\delta y}{\delta x} = \frac{f(x + \delta x) - f(x)}{\delta x}$$

= Average rate of change of y with respect to x

Example: If $y = x^2 + 3x + 5$, find an expression for the average rate of change of y with respect to x.

Let $y = f(x) = x^2 + 3x + 5$.

If x increases by δx and y increases correspondingly by δy, then the value of x increases to $x + \delta x$, and y increases correspondingly to $y + \delta y$.

Then $\delta y = f(x + \delta x) - f(x)$

$$= [(x + \delta x)^2 + 3(x + \delta x) + 5] - (x^2 + 3x + 5)$$

$$= [x^2 + 2x\delta x + (\delta x)^2 + 3x + 3\delta x + 5] - (x^2 + 3x + 5)$$

$$\therefore \quad \delta y = 2x\delta x + 3\delta x + (\delta x)^2$$

dividing by δx

$$\frac{\delta y}{\delta x} = 2x + 3 + \delta x = \text{Average rate of change of } y$$

(*Note:* The increased value of the function $f(x + \delta x)$ is obtained by replacing x in the given function by $x + \delta x$. δx must be treated as an independent quantity. The special case when δx tends to zero will be dealt with in more detail later. In this example it should be noted that when $\delta x = 0$, the rate of change is $2x + 3$, i.e. is independent of δx and is a function of x only.)

Example: For the function $y = x^3$, tabulate the values of y for $x = 2\cdot0$, $2\cdot10$, $2\cdot08$, $2\cdot06$, $2\cdot04$, $2\cdot02$, $2\cdot01$, $2\cdot001$. Obtain the values of $\delta y/\delta x$ to two decimal places for an initial value of $x = 2$ and increments of $0\cdot10$, $0\cdot08$, $0\cdot06$, $0\cdot04$, $0\cdot02$, $0\cdot01$, $0\cdot001$ in x. What is the likely value of the rate of change when $x = 2$?

x	$f(x) = x^3$	δx	δy	$\dfrac{\delta y}{\delta x}$
2·00	8·0000			
2·10	9·2610	0·10	1·2610	12·61
2·08	8·9989	0·08	0·9989	12·48
2·06	8·7416	0·06	0·7416	12·36
2·04	8·4896	0·04	0·4896	12·24
2·02	8·2424	0·02	0·2424	12·12
2·01	8·1206	0·01	0·1206	12·06
2·001	8·0120	0·001	0·0120	12·00

From the manner in which $\delta y/\delta x$ is changing, it would seem that the most likely value of $\delta y/\delta x$ when $x = 2$ would be 12·00. It will be shown later that this is the correct value.

21.3 Estimation of Approximate Rates of Change Using Standard Tables

Using the principles already laid down, approximate rates of change for any tabulated function values may be readily obtained for stated intervals or increments in the argument x.

Example: Using standard four figure tables, tabulate values of $\log_e x$ for values of x from 2 to 2·5 in steps of 0·1. Evaluate $\delta y/\delta x$ for each step of 0·1 and compare the results with the values of $1/x$ at the mid-points of the intervals.

x	$y = \log_e x$	δx	δy	$\delta y/\delta x$	Mid-x	$1/x$
2·0	0·6931					
		0·10	0·0488	0·488	2·05	0·4878
2·10	0·7419					
		0·10	0·0466	0·466	2·15	0·4651
2·20	0·7885					
		0·10	0·0444	0·444	2·25	0·4444
2·30	0·8329					
		0·10	0·0426	0·426	2·35	0·4255
2·40	0·8755					
		0·10	0·0408	0·408	2·45	0·4082
2·50	0·9163					

It will be seen that columns 5 and 7 almost agree to three decimal places. It can be shown that the exact rate of change of $y = \log_e x$ with respect to x is $1/x$ at the value x.

WORKED EXAMPLES

(a) If $y = 3x^2 + 2x - 7$, find the values of y when $x = 3$ and 3·05, and evaluate $\delta y/\delta x$ for this increment in x.

$$y = f(x) = 3x^2 + 2x - 7; \; f(3) = 26$$
$$\delta x = 0·05; \; f(x + \delta x) = f(3 + 0·05) = 3(3·05)^2 + 2(3·05) - 7$$
$$= 3 \times 9·3025 + 2(3·05) - 7 = 27·0075$$
$$\delta y = f(x + \delta x) - f(x) = 1·0075$$

$$\therefore \frac{\delta y}{\delta x} = \frac{1·0075}{0·05} = \underline{20·15}$$

(*b*) From standard four figure tables, estimate the average rate of change of sin *x* between *x* = 0·5 and 0·6 (radians). How does this value compare with cos *x* when *x* = 0·55 (radians)?

0·5 rad = 28°39′; 0·6 rad = 34°23′; 0·55 rad = 31°31′
$f(x) = \sin x$; $f(0·5) = \sin 28°39′ = 0·4795$
$f(0·6) = \sin 34°23′ = 0·5647$

$$\delta y = f(x + \delta x) - f(x) = 0·5647 - 0·4795 = 0·0852$$

$$\delta x = 0·6 - 0·5 = 0·1; \quad \frac{\delta y}{\delta x} = \frac{0·0852}{0·1} = \underline{0·852}$$

From cosine tables cos 0·55 = cos 31°31′ = $\underline{0·8524}$

The average rate of change and the cosine are almost equal. It can be shown that the exact rate of change of sin *x* (*x* radians) at a value *x* is cos *x*.

(*c*) If *s* metres is the distance travelled by a body in time *t* seconds and $s = 0·5t^2 + 1·5t + 1·7$, tabulate the values of *s* for *t* = 0 to 5 in steps of one second, and estimate the average velocity ($\delta s/\delta t$) during each second.

t	*s*	δs	δt	$\delta s/\delta t$ m/s
0	1·7			
		2·0	1·0	2·0
1	3·7			
		3·0	1·0	3·0
2	6·7			
		4·0	1·0	4·0
3	10·7			
		5·0	1·0	5·0
4	15·7			
		6·0	1·0	6·0
5	21·7			

This method of analysis is very useful in the practical estimation of velocities from distance–time graphs. In this example, since the distance is an exact quadratic function of time, it is seen that the velocity obtained is a linear function of time. This could have been deduced by finite differences (as in Chapter 20). The increments used are indeed finite differences.

Examples 21

1. From tables of logarithms to base 10, log $3 \cdot 56 = 0 \cdot 5514$, log $3 \cdot 58 = 0 \cdot 5539$. Use first order interpolation (proportional parts) to estimate log $3 \cdot 573$.

2. During an experimental investigation, two values of V are obtained for values of the independent variable t. $V_1 = 82 \cdot 32$ when $t = 0 \cdot 3$, $V_2 = 67 \cdot 39$ when $t = 0 \cdot 4$. Use interpolation to estimate the value of V when $t = 0 \cdot 36$.

3. If $y = 5x^2 - 2x + 3$, find the average rate of change of y with respect to x between $x = 3$ and $x = 3 \cdot 2$.

4. If $f(x) = x^3$ and x increases by δx, find the value of $f(x + \delta x)$. Hence obtain the average rate of change of $f(x)$ between x and $x + \delta x$. Use your result to find the average rate of change of x^3 between $x = 4$ and $x = 4 \cdot 3$.

5. From standard tables, write down the values of $f(x) = \log_{10} x$ for values of x from 3 to 4 in steps of $0 \cdot 2$ in x. Hence obtain the values of the average rates of change of $f(x)$ in the 5 intervals of $0 \cdot 2$ for x.

6. The following experimental values of p and v are obtained:

v	5	10	15	20	25
p	250	125	83·3	62·5	50

Find the average rate of change of p with respect to v in the four equal intervals of v. (*Note:* These will all be negative since p decreases as v increases.)

7. The following values of e^t are given for values of t from $t = 0 \cdot 5$ to $t = 1 \cdot 5$, in steps of $0 \cdot 2$ for t. Calculate the average rates of change of e^t with respect to t in the five equal intervals of t. Compare the values obtained with the values of e^t for the middle values of t in the intervals.

t	0·5	0·7	0·9	1·1	1·3	1·5
e^t	1·649	2·014	2·460	3·004	3·669	4·482

8. Tabulate values of $f(x) = \cos x$ (x in radians) for $x = 0 \cdot 5$, $0 \cdot 6$, $0 \cdot 7$, $0 \cdot 8$. Estimate the average rate of change of $f(x)$ in the three equal intervals. Compare the results with values of $-\sin x$ for the mid-values of x in the three equal intervals. (*Note:* The rates of change will all be negative since $\cos x$ decreases as x increases.)

9. The distance s (metres) is connected with time t (seconds) by the formula $s = 3 \cdot 5 \sqrt{t} + 9 \cdot 5$. Find the values of s for $t = 0, 2, 4, 6, 8, 10$ seconds, and estimate the average speed in metres per second, for each of the 2 second intervals.

10. Given $y = 5x^2 + 6x - 3$, find the expression for the average rate of change of y ($\delta y / \delta x$) in terms of x and δx. What is the limiting value of $\delta y / \delta x$ as δx tends to zero?

22

Slopes and Gradients of Graphs

22.1 Slope (Gradient) of a Graph

Figure 22.1 shows the sketch of a portion of the graph of $y = f(x)$. Let P and Q be two points on the graph such that P is the point (x, y), Q is the point $(x + \delta x, y + \delta y)$, then the side PR of the

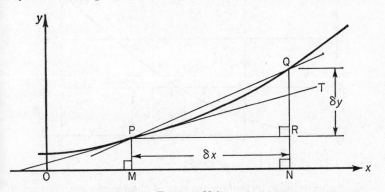

FIGURE 22.1

triangle PRQ is δx (increment in x) and side RQ is δy (the corresponding increment in y). The slope (gradient) of the chord PQ is a measure of the average slope (gradient) of the *curve* between P and Q. It is equal to the slope of a *tangent* to the graph at a point on the graph between P and Q.

$$\text{Average gradient} = \frac{\text{QR}}{\text{PR}} = \frac{\delta y}{\delta x}$$

213

8

As the point Q is made to approach P (fixed), the slope of the chord PQ *approaches the slope of the tangent PT to the graph at P.* The slope of the tangent measures the *instantaneous rate of change of y with respect to x.* A special symbol is used for this (see Chapter 23).

22.2 Instantaneous Rates of Change

These may be obtained *approximately* by using chords, i.e. using an average rate of change during an interval which contains the instant at which the rate of change is required.

Example: Estimate the instantaneous rate of change of $y = x^2$ at the point on the graph of the function where $x = 2$.

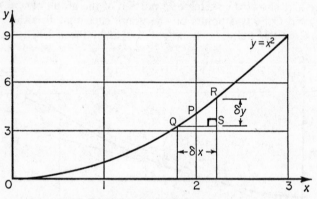

FIGÙRE 22.2

The approximate instantaneous rate of change of y with respect to x is measured by the slope of the chord QR (see Figure 22.2). In order to estimate the slope as accurately as possible, Q and R are chosen fairly near to P. In general, the points are chosen so that they are at equal horizontal distances from P and fairly near to P. From a plotted graph the values of y were read off at $x = 1.8$ and $x = 2.2$. The values of y obtained were 3.24 and 4.84. Hence

$$\delta x = 2.2 - 1.8 = 0.4; \quad \delta y = 4.84 - 3.24 = 1.60$$

$\therefore$ Rate of change of y, when $x = 2$

= Slope of tangent to the graph at the point P

$$= \frac{\delta y}{\delta x} \text{ (approximately)} = \frac{1\cdot 60}{0\cdot 40} = \underline{4\cdot 0}$$

(*Note:* This actually gives the correct rate of change.)

22.3 Distance–Time, Speed–Time, Acceleration–Time Graphs

Velocity is defined as the *rate of change of displacement*. If the motion is in a straight line, then the displacement is the *distance* from a fixed point and the velocity magnitude (speed) is the rate of change of distance with respect to time. From a graphical plot of distance s against time t, the speeds at various times may be estimated by obtaining average speeds over small time intervals. These average speeds may be estimated as in 22.2. The estimated speeds can be plotted graphically to give a speed–time graph.

Acceleration is defined as the *rate of change of velocity*. Hence, using averages, the accelerations at various times may be estimated and an acceleration–time graph plotted. The method will be illustrated in the following example.

Example: The distances, in metres travelled by a racing car, from rest, are recorded as follows:

Distance (s metres)	0	27	75	144	246	400
Time (t seconds)	0	2	4	6	8	10

Plot the distance–time, speed–time and acceleration–time graphs for the motion. What is the minimum acceleration during the period? Using the principles stated earlier, the speeds at 1, 3, 5, 7, 9 seconds are estimated approximately. 1 second intervals are used, centred on these times and the estimates of speed found are:

Speed (v m/s)	13	25	34	48	77
Time (t seconds)	1	3	5	7	9

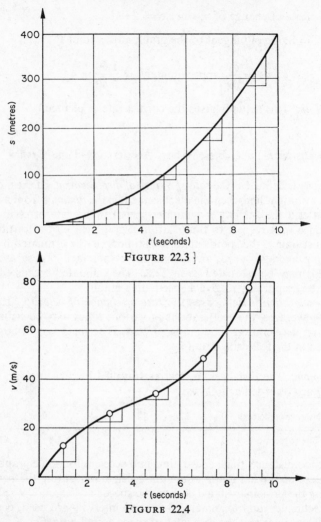

FIGURE 22.3

FIGURE 22.4

The accelerations at 1, 3, 4, 5, 7, 9 seconds are estimated as before and the following values are obtained:

Acceleration (f m/s²)	10	5	3·8	4·4	10·6	16
Time (t seconds)	1	3	4	5	7	9

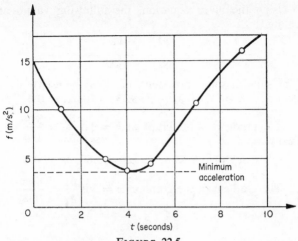

FIGURE 22.5

From the graph (Figure 22.5) the minimum acceleration occurs at 4·4 seconds and is about 3·7 m/s².

WORKED EXAMPLES

(a) During a cooling test, the following temperatures ($T°$C) are recorded at times t (minutes). Without plotting a graph, estimate the rate of cooling at 2, 6, 10, 14, 18 minutes.

t (min)	0	4	8	12	16	20
T (°C)	100	81·9	67·0	54·9	44·9	36·8

Rate of cooling is measured by $-\delta T/\delta t$ as T is falling. Values of $-\delta T$ in the given intervals of 4 minutes are:

$$18·1, \quad 14·9, \quad 12·1, \quad 10·0, \quad 8·1$$

δt may be taken as 4 minutes in each case.

∴ The approximate rates of cooling at 2, 6, 10, 14, 18 minutes are given by $\dfrac{18·1}{4}, \dfrac{14·9}{4}, \dfrac{12·1}{4}, \dfrac{10·0}{4}, \dfrac{8·1}{4}$ deg C/min

i.e. $4·52, 3·72, 3·02, 2·50, 2·02$ deg C/min

(b) The equation of a graph is $y = 3x^2 + 4x + 7$. Estimate the values of the gradient of the curve when (i) $x = 2$, (ii) $x = 5$.

Using the given equation, the following values are calculated:

x	1·8	2·2	4·8	5·2
y	23·92	30·32	95·32	108·92

(any suitable small increments of x may be used)
near $x = 2$, $\delta y = 30{\cdot}32 - 23{\cdot}92 = 6{\cdot}40$, $\delta x = 0{\cdot}4$

$\therefore$ The gradient of the graph at $x = 2$ is $\dfrac{\delta y}{\delta x} = \dfrac{6{\cdot}40}{0{\cdot}4} = \underline{16{\cdot}0}$
near $x = 5$,

$$\delta y = 108{\cdot}92 - 95{\cdot}32 = 13{\cdot}60, \quad \delta x = 0{\cdot}4$$

$\therefore$ The gradient of the graph at $x = 5$ is $\dfrac{\delta y}{\delta x} = \dfrac{13{\cdot}60}{0{\cdot}4} = \underline{34{\cdot}0}$

Examples 22

1. Plot the graph of the function $y = 2x^2 + x + 3$ between $x = 0$ and $x = 5$. Using suitable small intervals for x, estimate the gradient of the curve at the points where $x = 0{\cdot}5$, $1{\cdot}0$, $1{\cdot}5$, $2{\cdot}0$, $2{\cdot}5$, $3{\cdot}0$, $3{\cdot}5$, $4{\cdot}0$, $4{\cdot}5$. Plot the values of the gradient against x. (This is called the derived curve.)

2. Plot the graph of $y = 5e^{0{\cdot}1x}$ between $x = 0$ and $x = 10$. Using suitable chords estimate the slopes of the tangents to the curve at the points where $x = 2, 4, 6, 8$ to two decimal places.

3. Without plotting the graph, estimate the slopes of the tangents to the graph of $y = x^2 e^x$ at the points where (i) $x = 1$, (ii) $x = 2$.

4. Plot the graph of $y = 10 \log_{10} x$ for values of $x = 1, 2, 4, 6, 8, 10$ and, using suitable chords, estimate the gradient of the curve at the points where $x = 3, 5, 7, 9$ (to two decimal places).

5. The distance s (metres) travelled by a particle in time t (seconds) is given in the following table:

t	0	1	2	4	6	8	10
s	0	29·0	46·5	70·0	84·0	93	100

Plot the graph of s (vertical) against t. Using suitable chords, estimate the speed v at times $1, 2, 4, 6, 8, 9$ seconds. Plot the speed–time graph and hence, using suitable chords, deduce the acceleration–time graph.

6. The temperature $T\,°C$ of a cooling body at time t minutes is noted as follows:

t (min)	0	4	8	12	16	20
$T\,(°C)$	200	170·4	145·2	123·8	106·2	89·9

Plot the graph of T against t (the cooling curve), and, using suitable chords, estimate the rate of cooling (in deg C/min) when $t = 4, 8, 12, 16$.

7. Plot the graph of $y = \dfrac{5}{x}$ for values of x from 0·5 to 5·0 in steps of 0·5. From your graph, using suitable chords, estimate the gradient of the graph when $x = 1, 2, 3, 4$.

8. The height h metres of a body projected vertically with velocity 18 m/s, after time t seconds, is given by $h = 18t - 4\cdot905t^2$.

Plot the graph of h against t for values of t between $t = 0$ and 4 in steps of 0·5 second. Using suitable chords, estimate the vertical velocity when $t = 0\cdot5, 1\cdot0, 1\cdot5, 2\cdot0, 2\cdot5$, seconds. From your graph estimate (i) the maximum height reached, (ii) the average acceleration in the four intervals. What significance can be given to the results?

23

Plots of Functions and Derivatives from First Principles

23.1 Plots of Functions

The plotting of functions in graphical form has already been dealt with. In some cases it is possible to carry out a rough sketch of the graph of a function when certain essential facts are known; e.g.
  (i) Where the graph will cross the x and y-axes.
 (ii) Where the ordinate y has stationary values (maxima and minima).
(iii) How the gradient of the graph varies.
 (iv) Where the *asymptotes* of the graph (if any) lie.
(An *asymptote* is a line which the graph approaches but never crosses.) Some of these facts may be readily obtained when a deeper knowledge of the *differential calculus* has been obtained. Turning values (or stationary values) may be estimated by plotting a graph between suitable values of x.

23.1.1 Graphical determination of turning values

From a graphical plot the turning values of a function $f(x)$ may be estimated and the values of x at which they occur.

Example: By plotting the function $4x^3 - 3x^2 - 36x + 9$, determine its stationary values (Figure 23.1).

(*Note:* Intermediate values of x are used to estimate more precisely.)

x	-3	-2	-1	0	1	2	3	$-1\frac{1}{2}$
y	-18	37	38	9	-26	-43	-18	$42\frac{3}{4}$

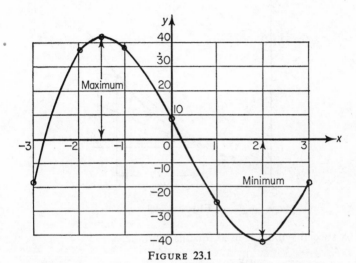

FIGURE 23.1

From the graph the stationary values of $f(x)$ are 42·75 (when $x = -1\cdot5$) (maximum), and $-43\cdot0$ (when $x = 2$) (minimum).

[*Note:* The stationary values are *values of y* (*or f(x)*).]

23.2 Differentiation from First Principles

In Chapter 22 the idea of the rate of change of y with respect to x was introduced. In order to determine the gradient of a graph (slope of a tangent) at a point, estimates were made using chords or approximate rates of change.

Now consider the meaning of the value of $\delta y/\delta x$ as δx tends to zero. $\delta y/\delta x$ was defined earlier as the average rate of change of y, with respect to x, over the interval δx. If this is taken as the gradient of a chord of the graph $y = f(x)$, then, as $\delta x \to 0$, the *slope* of the chord PQ approaches the slope of the tangent PT, at P, hence the limiting value of $\delta y/\delta x$ as δx tends to zero may be defined as the gradient of the tangent to the graph at P (or the gradient of the *curve* at P). (See Figure 23.2.)

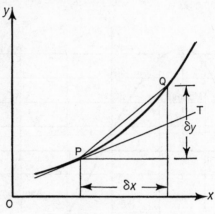

FIGURE 23.2

A special symbol is used for this limit, i.e.

$$\frac{\mathrm{d}y}{\mathrm{d}x} \text{ (read as dee } y \text{ by dee } x)$$

and may be defined as follows

$$\frac{\mathrm{d}y}{\mathrm{d}x} = \text{Limit of } \frac{\delta y}{\delta x} \text{ as } \delta x \text{ tends to zero}$$

or

$$\frac{\mathrm{d}y}{\mathrm{d}x} = \lim_{\delta x \to 0} \left(\frac{\delta y}{\delta x} \right)$$

The description used for $\mathrm{d}y/\mathrm{d}x$ may depend on the type of problem. *Basically* $\mathrm{d}y/\mathrm{d}x$ *measures the instantaneous rate of change of y with respect to x.*

Other descriptions of $\mathrm{d}y/\mathrm{d}x$ are:

(i) The differential coefficient of y with respect to x.
(ii) The derivative of y with respect to x.

(iii) The derived function.
(iv) The gradient of the function.
 (v) The gradient (slope) of a graph.
(vi) The gradient (slope) of a tangent to a graph.
Any one of these descriptions may be used in a problem.

Example: Determine, from first principles, the derivative of y with respect to x when $y = x^2$.

Let x increase by δx, and y increase correspondingly by δy, then $y + \delta y = (x + \delta x)^2$, but $y = x^2$

$$\therefore \quad \delta y = (x + \delta x)^2 - x^2 = x^2 + 2x\delta x + (\delta x)^2 - x^2$$
$$\delta y = 2x\delta x + (\delta x)^2$$

Divide by δx; then

$$\frac{\delta y}{\delta x} = 2x + \delta x$$

as δx approaches (tends to) zero this approaches the value $2x$. Hence it may be stated that:

$$\frac{dy}{dx} = \lim_{\delta x \to 0}\left(\frac{\delta y}{\delta x}\right) = 2x$$

23.2.1 Derivative of $y = f(x)$ from first principles

Let $y = f(x)$, x increase by δx and y increase correspondingly by δy. Then

$$\delta y = f(x + \delta x) - f(x)$$

$$\therefore \quad \frac{\delta y}{\delta x} = \frac{f(x + \delta x) - f(x)}{\delta x}$$

$$\therefore \quad \frac{dy}{dx} = \lim_{\delta x \to 0}\left(\frac{\delta y}{\delta x}\right) = \lim_{\delta x \to 0}\left[\frac{f(x + \delta x) - f(x)}{\delta x}\right]$$

In general, with simple algebraic functions, this limit is fairly easily found, as $f(x + \delta x) - f(x)$ has δx as a factor. With more difficult functions, special limits need to be used. However, the *method* is general for obtaining dy/dx *from first principles*.

Examples:

(i) Find dy/dx from first principles when $y = 2x^2 + 3x + 1$.

Let x increase by δx and y increase correspondingly by δy, then

$$\delta y = f(x + \delta x) - f(x)$$
$$= 2(x + \delta x)^2 + 3(x + \delta x) + 1 - (2x^2 + 3x + 1)$$
$$= 4x\delta x + 2(\delta x)^2 + 3\delta x$$

Divide by δx, then $\delta y/\delta x = 4x + 3 + 2\delta x$ \hfill (1)

$$\therefore \frac{dy}{dx} = \lim_{\delta x \to 0}\left(\frac{\delta y}{\delta x}\right) = 4x + 3$$

(*Note:* This is, in fact, obtained by putting $\delta x = 0$ in the right-hand side of (1).)

(ii) If $y = 5/x^2$, obtain dy/dx from first principles.

Let x increase by δx and y increase correspondingly by δy.

$$\delta y = f(x + \delta x) - f(x)$$
$$= \frac{5}{(x + \delta x)^2} - \frac{5}{x^2} = \frac{5x^2 - 5(x + \delta x)^2}{(x + \delta x)^2 x^2}$$
$$= \frac{5[x^2 - \{x^2 + 2x\delta x + (\delta x)^2\}]}{(x + \delta x)^2 x^2} = \frac{5[-2x\delta x - (\delta x)^2]}{(x + \delta x)^2 x^2}$$
$$\therefore \frac{\delta y}{\delta x} = \frac{-5(2x + \delta x)}{(x + \delta x)^2 x^2}.$$
$$\therefore \frac{dy}{dx} = \lim_{\delta x \to 0}\left(\frac{\delta y}{\delta x}\right) = \frac{-5 \times 2x}{x^2 \times x^2} = -\frac{10}{x^3}$$

23.2.2 Derivative of x^n

General rule for the derivative of x^n.

Let $y = x^n$, δx and δy corresponding increments then

$$\delta y = (x + \delta x)^n - x^n = x^n\left(1 + \frac{\delta x}{x}\right)^n - x^n$$
$$= x^n\left[1 + n\frac{\delta x}{x} + \frac{n(n - 1)}{1 \times 2}\left(\frac{\delta x}{x}\right)^2 + \ldots\right] - x^n$$

$$\therefore \ \delta y = nx^{n-1}\delta x + \frac{n(n-1)}{2}x^{n-2}(\delta x)^2 + \ldots + \text{terms contain-}$$

ing at least $(\delta x)^3$

Divide by δx:

$$\frac{\delta y}{\delta x} = nx^{n-1} + \text{terms containing } (\delta x) \text{ at least}$$

As $\delta x \to 0$ all the terms on the R.H.S. (except the first) $\to 0$.

$$\therefore \ \frac{\mathrm{d}y}{\mathrm{d}x} = \lim_{\delta x \to 0}\left(\frac{\delta y}{\delta x}\right) = nx^{n-1}$$

This rule may be used to write down the derivative of *any power of x.*

Examples:

(i) $y = x^3 + 3x^2 + 7x + 5;$ $\quad \dfrac{\mathrm{d}y}{\mathrm{d}x} = 3x^2 + 6x + 7$

(ii) $s = t^3 + 5t^2 + 3;$ $\quad \dfrac{\mathrm{d}s}{\mathrm{d}t} = 3t^2 + 10t$

(iii) $y = 2\sqrt{x} + \dfrac{3}{\sqrt{x^3}} = 2x^{\frac{1}{2}} + 3x^{-\frac{3}{2}}$

$$\frac{\mathrm{d}y}{\mathrm{d}x} = 2 \times \tfrac{1}{2}x^{-\frac{1}{2}} + 3\left(-\frac{3}{2}\right)x^{-\frac{5}{2}} = \frac{1}{\sqrt{x}} - \frac{9}{2\sqrt{x^5}}$$

(*Note:* (1) To use the rule, each term must be put in the form x^n.
(2) Powers of *any* variable may be differentiated using the same *rule*.)

WORKED EXAMPLES

(*a*) Determine the values of x and y when $\mathrm{d}y/\mathrm{d}x = 0$, if

$$y = 4x^3 - 3x^2 - 36x + 11.$$

$$\frac{\mathrm{d}y}{\mathrm{d}x} = 4 \times 3x^2 - 3 \times 2x^1 - 36 = 6(2x^2 - x - 6) = 0$$

When $\qquad\qquad 2x^2 - x - 6 = 0$

$$(2x + 3)(x - 2) = 0$$

$$\therefore \ \frac{\mathrm{d}y}{\mathrm{d}x} = 0 \quad \text{when } x = 2 \text{ or } -\frac{3}{2}$$

When $x = 2$

$$y = 4(2)^3 - 3(2)^2 - 36(2) + 11 = \underline{-41}$$

When $x = -\dfrac{3}{2}$

$$y = 4\left(-\frac{3}{2}\right)^3 - 3\left(-\frac{3}{2}\right)^2 - 36\left(-\frac{3}{2}\right) + 11 = \underline{44\tfrac{3}{4}}$$

[*Note:* These are the *stationary values* of y, i.e. stationary values of $y = f(x)$ are obtained when $dy/dx = 0$.]

(b) Find the equations of the tangents to the curve $y = x^3$ at the points where (i) $x = 1$, (ii) $x = -2$.

Slope of the tangent at (x, y) is measured by dy/dx.

$$\frac{dy}{dx} = 3x^2$$

∴ Slope of tangent at $x = 1$ is $+3$ and slope of tangent at $x = -2$ is $+12$.

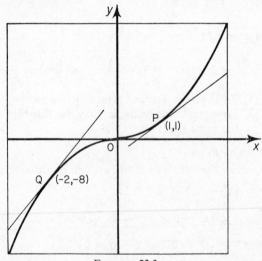

FIGURE 23.3

The equation of a straight line of slope m, passing through the point (x_1, y_1) is $y - y_1 = m(x - x_1)$

∴ at P(1,1) the equation of the tangent (line) is

$$y - 1 = 3(x - 1)$$

or
$$y = 3x - 2$$

and at Q(−2,−8), the equation of the tangent (line) is

$$y - (-8) = 12[x - (-2)]$$
$$y + 8 = 12(x + 2)$$

or
$$y = 12x + 16$$

Examples 23

1. Plot the function $y = x^2 - 4x + 5$ between $x = 0$ and 4. From the graph, estimate the minimum value of y and the value of x at which it occurs.
2. By plotting the function $y = x^3 - 3x^2 - 9x + 5$ for values of x between −2 and +4, estimate the turning values of the function and the values of x at which these occur.
3. Find, from first principles, the derivative of y with respect to x when $y = 5x^2 + 3x + 6$.
4. Use first principles to find the differential coefficient of the function $3/x$.
5. From first principles find the derivative of

$$y = 3x^2 + \frac{1}{x^2}.$$

6. Using the general rule for differentiating x^n, write down the derivatives of the following functions:

   (i) x^4, (ii) $\sqrt{x}$, (iii) $\frac{1}{x^4}$, (iv) $3x^4 - 3x^3 + 7x^2 + 4x + 5$.

7. Write down the derivatives of:

   (i) $4t^3$, (ii) $\sqrt[3]{x^4}$, (iii) $\theta^3 + 4\theta^2 - 3\theta$, (iv) $u^4 + \frac{1}{u^4}$.

8. If $y = 2x^3 - 3x^2 - 72x + 5$, find the values of x when $dy/dx = 0$. Hence calculate the turning values of y.
9. Find the equation of the tangent of $y = 3x^2 - 2x + 5$ at $x = 1$.
10. The distance s metres travelled in time t seconds is given by

$$s = t^3 + 3t^2 - 4t + 3.$$

Find the expressions for the velocity and acceleration in terms of t.
11. The height s metres risen by a body projected upwards with velocity 25 m/s is given by $s = 25t - 4\cdot905t^2$. Find the time when $ds/dt = 0$ and hence the maximum height.
12. For the function $y = 4x^3 + 15x^2 - 72x + 7$, find the equation of the tangent to the curve at the point where $x = 2$, and determine the stationary values of y.

24

Derivatives of x^n

24.1 Derivatives of x^n

24.1.1 First derivative of x^n

In order to write down the derivatives of simple functions of x, the rule for differentiating x^n (already obtained in Chapter 23) is quoted. The rule is as follows:
If $y = x^n$

$$\frac{\mathrm{d}y}{\mathrm{d}x} = nx^{n-1}$$

Alternatively the rule may be written as

$$\frac{\mathrm{d}}{\mathrm{d}x}(x^n) = nx^{n-1}$$

where n may be any *real* number.

24.1.2 Derivative of ax^n, where a is a constant

Since a derivative is a *rate of change*, it is clear that
Rate of change of (constant $\times x^n$) = Constant $\times$ Rate of change of x^n

$$\frac{\mathrm{d}}{\mathrm{d}x}(ax^n) = anx^{n-1} = nax^{n-1}$$

24.1.3 The second derivative

Symbolically, since this is the second rate of change of $y = f(x)$, the second derivative may be written as $\dfrac{d}{dx}\left(\dfrac{dy}{dx}\right)$. This is usually abbreviated to $\dfrac{d^2y}{dx^2}$ (read as dee 2y by dee x squared).

Examples:

(i) Write down the first and second derivatives of $3x^2 - 6x + 7$.
Let $y = 3x^2 - 6x + 7$

$$\frac{dy}{dx} = 6x - 6$$

$$\frac{d^2y}{dx^2} = 6$$

(ii) Find the second derivative, with respect to t, of $1/t^2$.

Let $s = \dfrac{1}{t^2} = t^{-2}$

$$\frac{ds}{dt} = -2t^{-3}$$

$$\frac{d^2s}{dt^2} = \frac{d}{dt}\left(-2t^{-3}\right) = -2 \times (-3) \times t^{-4} = \frac{6}{t^4}$$

(iii) If $y = 2x^3 + 3x^2 - 12x + 5$, find the values of d^2y/dx^2 when $dy/dx = 0$.

$$\frac{dy}{dx} = 6x^2 + 6x - 12$$

$$= 6(x^2 + x - 2) = 6(x + 2)(x - 1)$$
$$= 0 \text{ when } (x + 2)(x - 1) = 0; \text{ i.e. when } \underline{x = -2 \text{ or } +1}$$

$$\frac{d^2y}{dx^2} = \frac{d}{dx}(6x^2 + 6x - 12) = 12x + 6$$

When $x = 1$ $\dfrac{d^2y}{dx^2} = 12 \times 1 + 6 = \underline{+18}$

When $x = -2$ $\dfrac{d^2y}{dx^2} = 12 \times (-2) + 6 = \underline{-18}$

24.2 Velocity and Acceleration

If s (distance) is expressed as a function of t (time), then

Velocity $= v =$ Rate of change of distance $= ds/dt$
Acceleration $= f =$ Rate of change of velocity $= dv/dt$

Acceleration is therefore the 2nd rate of change of distance with respect to time, and hence

$$f = \frac{dv}{dt} = \frac{d}{dt}\left(\frac{ds}{dt}\right) = \frac{d^2s}{dt^2}$$

Examples:

(i) If the distance, s metres, travelled by a body in t seconds, is given by $s = 30t - 4\cdot905t^2$, what is the velocity after $\frac{3}{4}$ second, and what can be deduced about the acceleration?

$$s = 30t - 4\cdot905t^2$$

$$\text{Velocity } v = \frac{ds}{dt} = 30 - 9\cdot81t \text{ m/s}$$

when $t = \frac{3}{4}$

$$v = 30 - 9\cdot81 \times \frac{3}{4} = 30 - 7\cdot3575 = 22\cdot6425 \text{ m/s}$$

$$f = \frac{dv}{dt} = -9\cdot81 \text{ m/s}^2$$

i.e. the acceleration is constant (actually *retardation*).

(ii) The distance, s cm, travelled by a body in time t seconds is given by $s = 2t^3 - 15t^2 + 24t + 8$.

Find (*a*) at what times the velocity is zero (i.e. body is at rest),
(*b*) the acceleration at these times,
(*c*) the time when the acceleration is zero.

$s = 2t^3 - 15t^2 + 24t + 8$

$$\text{Velocity } v = \frac{ds}{dt} = 6t^2 - 30t + 24 = 6(t^2 - 5t + 4) \text{ cm/s}$$

$$\text{Acceleration } f = \frac{dv}{dt} = 12t - 30 \text{ cm/s}^2$$

(a) Body is at rest when $v = 0$, i.e. $6(t^2 - 5t + 4) = 0$

$6(t - 4)(t - 1) = 0$, i.e. <u>when $t = 1$ or 4 seconds</u>

(b) When $t = 1$

Acceleration $= 12 \times 1 - 30 = -18 \text{ cm/s}^2$

When $t = 4$

Acceleration $= 12 \times 4 - 30 = 18 \text{ cm/s}^2$

(*Note:* A negative acceleration is equivalent to *retardation*.)

(c) The acceleration is zero when $dv/dt = 0$, i.e.

$12t - 30 = 0$, when <u>$t = 2\frac{1}{2}$ seconds</u>

24.3 Maxima and Minima (Stationary Values)

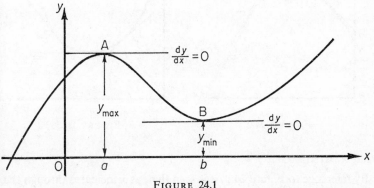

FIGURE 24.1

Let the graph of $y = f(x)$ be as shown in Figure 24.1. At points like A and B the function y is said to have stationary (or turning) values. At such points the rate of change of y is instantaneously zero, i.e.

$$\frac{dy}{dx} = 0 \text{ at stationary values of } y$$

To distinguish between maxima and minima, the rate of change of dy/dx is considered.

AT A MAXIMUM:

By reference to Figure 24.2, it is seen that, as x increases through the value of x at a *maximum*, dy/dx changes from *positive to zero to negative*, i.e.

The rate of change of dy/dx is *negative*

or

$$\frac{d}{dx}\left(\frac{dy}{dx}\right) = \frac{d^2y}{dx^2}$$

is *negative at a maximum value of y*.

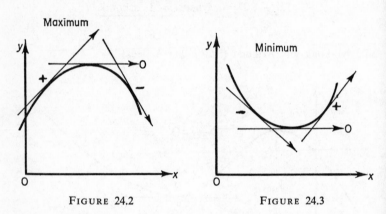

FIGURE 24.2   FIGURE 24.3

AT A MINIMUM:

By reference to Figure 24.3, it is seen that, as x increases through the value of x at a *minimum*, dy/dx changes from *negative to zero to positive*, i.e. the rate of change of dy/dx is *positive*

or

$$\frac{d}{dx}\left(\frac{dy}{dx}\right) = \frac{d^2y}{dx^2}$$

is *positive at a minimum value of y*.

Example: Determine the maximum and minimum values of the function $2x^3 + 3x^2 - 36x + 7$.

Let $y = 2x^3 + 3x^2 - 36x + 7$

$$\frac{dy}{dx} = 6x^2 + 6x - 36 = 6(x^2 + x - 6)$$

$$\frac{d^2y}{dx^2} = 12x + 6$$

y has stationary values when $dy/dx = 0$
i.e. when $6(x^2 + x - 6) = 0$

$$(x + 3)(x - 2) = 0$$

$\therefore$ Stationary values occur when $x = 2$ or -3

when $x = +2$

$$\frac{d^2y}{dx^2} = 12 \times 2 + 6 = +30, \text{ i.e. } positive$$

$\therefore$ y is a minimum when $x = 2$
Minimum value of $y = 2(2)^3 + 3(2)^2 - 36(2) + 7 = -37$
when $x = -3$,

$$\frac{d^2y}{dx^2} = -12 \times 3 + 6 = -30, \text{ i.e. } negative$$

$\therefore$ y is a maximum when $x = -3$
Maximum value of $y = 2(-3)^3 + 3(-3)^2 - 36(-3) + 7 = +88$

WORKED EXAMPLES

(a) Obtain the derivative of $(2\sqrt{x} + 1)^2$.
Let $y = (2\sqrt{x} + 1)^2 = 4x + 4\sqrt{x} + 1 = 4x + 4x^{\frac{1}{2}} + 1$

$$\frac{dy}{dx} = 4 + 4 \times \tfrac{1}{2}x^{-\frac{1}{2}} = 4 + \frac{2}{\sqrt{x}}$$

(b) Write down the derivative of $(t + 1)^3 - t^2 + t - 2$.

Let $s = (t + 1)^3 - t^2 + t - 2 = t^3 + 3t^2 + 3t + 1 - t^2 + t - 2$

$s = t^3 + 2t^2 + 4t - 1$

$$\therefore \frac{ds}{dt} = 3t^2 + 4t + 4$$

(c) The distance s metres travelled by a body in time t seconds is given by $s = 30\sqrt{t} + 40/\sqrt{t}$. Find the velocity and acceleration at time $t = 4$ seconds.

$$s = 30t^{\frac{1}{2}} + 40t^{-\frac{1}{2}}$$

$$\text{Velocity} = \frac{ds}{dt} = \frac{1}{2} \times 30t^{-\frac{1}{2}} + 40\left(-\frac{1}{2}\right)t^{-\frac{3}{2}}$$

$$v = 15t^{-\frac{1}{2}} - 20t^{-\frac{3}{2}}$$

$$\text{Acceleration} = \frac{dv}{dt} = -15 \times \tfrac{1}{2}t^{-\frac{3}{2}} - 20\left(-\frac{3}{2}\right)t^{-\frac{5}{2}}$$

$$f = -\frac{15}{2\sqrt{t^3}} + \frac{30}{\sqrt{t^5}}$$

when $t = 4$,

$$\text{Velocity} = \frac{15}{\sqrt{4}} - \frac{20}{\sqrt{64}} = \frac{15}{2} - \frac{20}{8} = \underline{5\,\text{m/s}}$$

$$\text{Acceleration} = -\frac{15}{2\sqrt{64}} + \frac{30}{\sqrt{4^5}} = -\frac{15}{16} + \frac{30}{32} = \underline{0\,\text{m/s}^2}$$

(d) Determine the maximum and minimum values of $5x + \dfrac{20}{x} + 7$.

$$\text{Let } y = 5x + \frac{20}{x} + 7$$

$$\frac{dy}{dx} = 5 - \frac{20}{x^2}$$

$$\frac{d^2y}{dx^2} = \frac{40}{x^3}$$

The stationary values of y occur when $dy/dx = 0$, i.e. when

$$5 - \frac{20}{x^2} = 0, \; x^2 = 4, \; \underline{x = \pm 2}$$

When $x = +2$

$$\frac{d^2y}{dx^2} = +\frac{40}{2^3} = +5, \text{ i.e. } positive$$

$\therefore$ y is a minimum when $x = +2$

$$\underline{\text{Minimum } y = +27}$$

When $x = -2$

$$\frac{d^2y}{dx^2} = -\frac{40}{2^3} = -5, \text{ i.e. } negative$$

$\therefore$ y is a maximum when $x = -2$

$$\underline{\text{Maximum } y = -13}$$

Examples 24

1. Write down the derivatives of:
    (i) $5x^4$, (ii) $\frac{8}{x^3}$, (iii) $3\sqrt{t}$, (iv) $\sqrt[3]{x}$, (v) $\theta^2 + 3\theta + 2$.

2. Write down the differential coefficients of:
    (i) $(2x + 1)^2$, (ii) $(x^2 - 1)^2$, (iii) $(t - 1)(t + 2)$, (iv) $\theta^2(3\theta + 2)$.

3. Obtain the first and second derivatives in each case of:
    (i) $7x^3$, (ii) $(t^2 - 1)^2$, (iii) $5\theta(2\theta - 1)$.

4. Write down $\frac{dy}{dx}$ when $y = \sqrt{x^3} + \frac{2}{x^2} + 5x$.

5. Write down $\frac{ds}{dt}$ and $\frac{d^2s}{dt^2}$ when $s = 3t^4 + 6t^2 + 7$.

6. Find the value of x when $dy/dx = 0$, if $y = 5x^2 - 2x + 3$. What is the value of d^2y/dx^2?

7. The distance s metres travelled in time t seconds by a moving body is given by $s = 0.5t^2 + 5.8t + 3.2$. Find the velocity and acceleration at time $t = 5$ seconds.

8. A shaft turns through an angle θ radians in time t seconds, where $\theta = 6t^2 - 3t + 5$. Find the angular velocity and acceleration at time $t = 5$ seconds.

9. The distance s cm travelled in t seconds by a moving body is given by $s = 4t^3 - 21t^2 + 18t + 21$.
    Find (i) the velocity and acceleration when $t = 2$ seconds,
        (ii) the times at which the velocity is zero,
        (iii) the acceleration at these times,
        (iv) the time when the acceleration is zero.

10. Obtain the stationary value of $4x^2 - 8x + 3$. Is this a maximum or a minimum?

11. Obtain the stationary value of $5 + 6x - 3x^2$. Is this a maximum or a minimum?

12. What is the sign of the derivative of the function $2x^2 - 3x + 5$ when (i) $x = \frac{1}{2}$, (ii) $x = 2$. For what value of x is the derivative zero?

13. Find the maximum and minimum values of $2x^3 - 9x^2 - 60x + 11$.

14. Determine the maximum and minimum values of $x + \dfrac{4}{x}$.

15. A rectangular plate has to have a perimeter of 40 cm. Find the dimensions of the plate so that its area shall be a maximum.

16. An open rectangular tray is to be formed from a rectangular plate measuring 20 cm by 30 cm by cutting squares of side x cm from each corner and turning up the edges. Find x so that the volume of the tray is a maximum.

NOTE: **Maxima and Minima**

In some problems involving stationary values it may happen that the second derivative is zero. With such problems it is necessary to investigate **higher** derivatives to decide whether a particular function value is a maximum or a minimum. Such problems are outside the scope of this volume but may be met with in Higher National Certificate work.

25

Derivatives of Functions by Substitution

25.1 Function of a Function

In order to obtain the derivatives of many functions, it is possible to use a substitution, and hence find the required derivative by multiplying simple derivatives together. The rule used is called the *'function of a function'* rule.

RULE:

Let $y = f(z)$ where z is a function of x, i.e. $z = z(x)$. Let δx, δy, δz be corresponding finite increments of x, y and z. then

$$\frac{\delta y}{\delta x} = \frac{\delta y}{\delta z} \times \frac{\delta z}{\delta x}$$

(since δz may be cancelled when it is finite). This statement is exact and it is reasonable to assume that the result is true in the limit as δx, δy and δz all tend to zero, i.e.

$$\lim_{\delta x \to 0} \frac{\delta y}{\delta x} = \lim_{\delta z \to 0} \frac{\delta y}{\delta z} \times \lim_{\delta x \to 0} \frac{\delta z}{\delta x}$$

or

$$\underline{\frac{\mathrm{d}y}{\mathrm{d}x} = \frac{\mathrm{d}y}{\mathrm{d}z} \times \frac{\mathrm{d}z}{\mathrm{d}x}}$$

Examples:

(i) Find dy/dx when $y = (5x + 4)^3$.

    Let $z = 5x + 4$, then $y = z^3$

$$\frac{dy}{dz} = 3z^2, \frac{dz}{dx} = 5$$

$$\therefore \frac{dy}{dx} = \frac{dy}{dz} \times \frac{dz}{dx} = 3z^2 \times 5 = 15z^2 = \underline{15(5x + 4)^2}$$

(ii) Find the derivative of $\dfrac{4}{\sqrt{(x^2 + 1)}}$.

Let

$$y = \frac{4}{\sqrt{(x^2 + 1)}} \quad \text{and} \quad z = x^2 + 1$$

Then

$$y = \frac{4}{\sqrt{z}} = 4z^{-\frac{1}{2}}$$

$$\frac{dy}{dz} = 4\left(-\frac{1}{2}\right)z^{-\frac{1}{2}-1} = -2z^{-\frac{3}{2}}$$

$$\frac{dz}{dx} = 2x$$

$$\frac{dy}{dx} = \frac{dy}{dz} \times \frac{dz}{dx} = -2z^{-\frac{3}{2}}2x$$

$$= -4xz^{-\frac{3}{2}} = -4x(x^2 + 1)^{-\frac{3}{2}}$$

$$= -\frac{4x}{(x^2 + 1)^{\frac{3}{2}}} = -\underline{\frac{4x}{\sqrt{[(x^2 + 1)^3]}}}$$

(*Note:* When using the method of substitution, any letter may be used as the new variable. The letter used does not affect the *method.*)

(iii) Find the derivative of $\sqrt{(x^3 + 1)}$.

    Let $y = \sqrt{(x^3 + 1)}$, and $u = x^3 + 1$

Then $y = \sqrt{u} = u^{\frac{1}{2}}$

$$\frac{dy}{du} = \frac{1}{2} u^{-\frac{1}{2}}$$

$$\frac{du}{dx} = 3x^2$$

$$\frac{dy}{dx} = \frac{dy}{du} \times \frac{du}{dx} = \frac{1}{2} u^{-\frac{1}{2}} 3x^2 = \frac{3}{2} x^2 u^{-\frac{1}{2}}$$

$$= \frac{3}{2} x^2 (x^3 + 1)^{-\frac{1}{2}} = \frac{3x^2}{2\sqrt{(x^3 + 1)}}$$

25.2 Exponential Functions

25.2.1 Derivative of e^x

e^x may be defined as an infinite series as follows:

$$e^x = 1 + \frac{x}{1!} + \frac{x^2}{2!} + \frac{x^3}{3!} + \frac{x^4}{4!} + \dots \text{ to infinity}$$

$$(4! = 1 \times 2 \times 3 \times 4 \dots \text{etc.})$$

If $y = e^x$, then

$$\frac{dy}{dx} = 0 + \frac{1}{1!} + \frac{2x}{2!} + \frac{3x^2}{3!} + \frac{4x^3}{4!} + \dots$$

$$= 1 + \frac{x}{1!} + \frac{x^2}{2!} + \frac{x^3}{3!} + \dots \text{ to infinity}$$

i.e. the same infinite series as used to define e^x,

$$\therefore \frac{dy}{dx} = e^x$$

or

$$\frac{d}{dx} (e^x) = e^x$$

(*Note:* This is a special property of exponential functions, i.e. the rate of change of the function is proportional to the function.)

25.2.2 Derivative of $\log_e x$

So long as δx and δy are finite, it is clear that

$$\frac{\delta y}{\delta x} = \frac{1}{\delta x/\delta y}$$

and hence it may be assumed that the result is true as δx and δy both tend to zero, i.e.

$$\frac{dy}{dx} = \frac{1}{dx/dy}$$

Let $y = \log_e x$, then $x = e^y$

$$\frac{dx}{dy} = e^y = x$$

$$\therefore \frac{dy}{dx} = \frac{1}{x} \quad \text{or} \quad \frac{d}{dx}(\log_e x) = \frac{1}{x}$$

Examples:

(i) Find dy/dx if $y = e^{4x}$. Let $z = 4x$, then $y = e^z$

$$\frac{dy}{dz} = e^z; \quad \frac{dz}{dx} = 4$$

$$\frac{dy}{dx} = \frac{dy}{dz} \times \frac{dz}{dx} = e^z \times 4 = 4e^{4x}$$

(ii) Find dy/dx if $y = \exp(3x^2) = e^{3x^2}$.
Let $u = 3x^2$, then $y = e^u$

$$\frac{dy}{du} = e^u; \quad \frac{du}{dx} = 6x$$

$$\frac{dy}{dx} = \frac{dy}{du} \times \frac{du}{dx} = e^u(6x) = 6xe^{3x^2}$$

(iii) Obtain the derivative of $\log_e(x^2 + 1)$.
Let $y = \log_e(x^2 + 1)$ and $z = x^2 + 1$, then $y = \log_e z$.

$$\frac{dy}{dz} = \frac{1}{z}; \quad \frac{dz}{dx} = 2x$$

$$\frac{dy}{dx} = \frac{dy}{dz} \times \frac{dz}{dx} = \frac{1}{z}(2x) = \frac{2x}{x^2 + 1}$$

(iv) Obtain the derivative of $y = 6 \log_{10} (x^3 - 1)$.

Let $z = x^3 - 1$

$$y = 6 \log_{10} z = 6 \times 0 \cdot 4343 \times \log_e z$$

$$\therefore \frac{dy}{dz} = 6 \times 0 \cdot 4343 \frac{1}{z}$$

$$\frac{dz}{dx} = 3x^2$$

$$\frac{dy}{dx} = \frac{dy}{dz} \times \frac{dz}{dx} = 6 \times 0 \cdot 4343 \times \frac{1}{z} 3x^2 = \frac{7 \cdot 8174 x^2}{(x^3 - 1)}$$

(*Note:* It is necessary to convert to logarithms to base e to differentiate logarithms to any other base.)

25.3 Trigonometrical Functions

25.3.1 Derivatives of sin x, cos x (x in radians)

At this stage, these will be stated without rigorous proof. If *x is in radians*, it can be shown that:

(i) $\frac{d}{dx} (\sin x) = \cos x$, (ii) $\frac{d}{dx} (\cos x) = -\sin x$

By extracting numerical values from the tables, these can be verified approximately. The *signs* are verified by the manner in which the tabular values vary or by considering the slopes of the tangents to the graphs of $y = \sin x$ and $y = \cos x$.

25.3.2 Approximate verification

Verify approximately that $\frac{d}{dx} (\sin x) = \cos x$ when $x = 0 \cdot 3$ radians.

From the tables sin 0·28 rad = 0·2764; sin 0·32 rad = 0·3146

If $y = \sin x$, $\delta y = 0 \cdot 3146 - 0 \cdot 2764 = 0 \cdot 0382$

$$\delta x = 0 \cdot 32 - 0 \cdot 28 = 0 \cdot 04$$

$$\frac{\delta y}{\delta x} = \frac{0 \cdot 0382}{0 \cdot 04} \qquad = 0 \cdot 9550 \quad [\cos 0 \cdot 3 \text{ rad} = 0 \cdot 9554]$$

$$\therefore \text{ Result is verified approximately}$$

Examples: Obtain the derivatives of (i) sin nx, (ii) cos nx.

(i) $$y = \sin nx$$

Let $z = nx$, $y = \sin z$.

$$\frac{dy}{dz} = \cos z, \qquad \frac{dz}{dx} = n$$

$$\therefore \frac{dy}{dx} = \frac{dy}{dz} \times \frac{dz}{dx} = n \cos z$$

$$= n \cos nx$$

(ii) $$y = \cos nx$$

Let $z = nx$, $y = \cos z$.

$$\frac{dy}{dz} = -\sin z, \qquad \frac{dz}{dx} = n$$

$$\frac{dy}{dx} = \frac{dy}{dz} \times \frac{dz}{dx} = -n \sin z$$

$$= -n \sin nx$$

$$\therefore \frac{d}{dx}(\sin nx) = n \cos nx; \qquad \frac{d}{dx}(\cos nx) = -n \sin nx$$

WORKED EXAMPLES

(*a*) Differentiate $y = \sqrt[3]{(9x + 4)}$.

Let
$$z = 9x + 4; \qquad y = \sqrt[3]{z} = z^{\frac{1}{3}}$$

$$\frac{dy}{dz} = \tfrac{1}{3}z^{-\frac{2}{3}} \qquad \frac{dz}{dx} = 9$$

$$\frac{dy}{dx} = \frac{dy}{dz} \times \frac{dz}{dx} = \tfrac{1}{3}z^{-\frac{2}{3}} \times 9 = 3(9x + 4)^{-\frac{2}{3}} = \frac{3}{\sqrt[3]{[(9x + 4)^2]}}$$

(*b*) Find ds/dt when $s = e^{\sqrt{t}}$.

Let $u = \sqrt{t} = t^{\frac{1}{2}}$; $s = e^u$

$$\frac{ds}{du} = e^u; \qquad \frac{du}{dt} = \tfrac{1}{2}t^{-\frac{1}{2}} = \frac{1}{2\sqrt{t}}$$

$$\frac{ds}{dt} = \frac{ds}{du} \times \frac{du}{dt} = e^u \times \frac{1}{2\sqrt{t}} = \frac{1}{2\sqrt{t}}e^{\sqrt{t}}$$

(c) Write down dV/dx when $V = 5 \log_e \sqrt{(x^3 + 1)}$.

$$V = 5 \log_e \sqrt{(x^3 + 1)} = 5 \times \frac{1}{2} \log_e (x^3 + 1) = \frac{5}{2} \log_e (x^3 + 1)$$

Let $\qquad\qquad z = x^3 + 1; \qquad V = \frac{5}{2} \log_e z$

$$\frac{dV}{dz} = \frac{5}{2} \times \frac{1}{z}; \qquad \frac{dz}{dx} = 3x^2$$

$$\frac{dV}{dx} = \frac{dV}{dz} \times \frac{dz}{dx} = \frac{5}{2} \times \frac{1}{z} \times 3x^2 = \underline{\frac{15x^2}{2(x^3 + 1)}}$$

(d) Write down the derivative of $\sin x°$.

Let $\qquad y = \sin x° = \sin \left(\frac{\pi}{180} x \right) \qquad \left(x° = \frac{\pi x}{180} \text{ radians} \right)$

Substitute $\qquad z = \frac{\pi}{180} x; \qquad y = \sin z$

$$\frac{dy}{dz} = \cos z; \qquad \frac{dz}{dx} = \frac{\pi}{180}$$

$$\frac{dy}{dx} = \frac{dy}{dz} \times \frac{dz}{dx} = \cos z \times \frac{\pi}{180} = \frac{\pi}{180} \cos \frac{\pi x}{180} \text{ rad} = \underline{\frac{\pi}{180} \cos x°}$$

(e) Find a turning value of $y = 4 \sin x + 3 \cos x$.

$$\frac{dy}{dx} = 4 \cos x - 3 \sin x = 0 \text{ for a stationary value of } y,$$

when $4 \cos x = 3 \sin x$, $\tan x = \frac{4}{3}$

∴ A turning value of y occurs when $x = 53°8'$

$$\frac{d^2y}{dx^2} = -4 \sin x - 3 \cos x, \text{ this is negative when } x = 53°8'$$

∴ y is a maximum when $\sin x = \frac{4}{5}$, $\cos x = \frac{3}{5}$

∴ Maximum value of $y = 4 \times \frac{4}{5} + 3 \times \frac{3}{5} = \underline{5}$

Examples 25

1. Find dy/dx when $y = (x^3 + 1)^4$.
2. Write down dy/dx when $y = 5/(x^2 - 1)^3$.
3. Using the substitution rule, find ds/dt when $s = \sqrt{(t^2 + 1)}$.
4. Obtain the derivative of e^{5x}.

5. Write down the differential coefficient of $e^{-0.5t}$.
6. If $y = 4 \log_e (x^2 + 4)$ write down dy/dx.
7. Find the rate of increase of $(x^2 - 1)^{\frac{1}{2}}$ when $x = 1.2$.
8. Obtain the derivative of $1/\sqrt{(t^3 - 1)}$ and find its numerical value when $t = 2$.
9. Write down the derivative of e^{4x} and find its value when $x = 0.1$.
10. Using suitable substitutions, find the rates of change of:
    (i) sin $5x$, (x in radians),
    (ii) sin $5x$, (x in degrees).
11. Using suitable substitutions, find the derivatives of:
    (i) $(x^2 + 3x)^{\frac{1}{2}}$, (ii) e^{3t}, (iii) $10 \log_e (x^2 + 4)$.
12. If $s = 5/(t + 1)$, write down ds/dt and d^2s/dt^2.
13. If $y = 9 \log_e x - \frac{1}{2}x^2$, find the value of x when dy/dx is zero.
14. Write down the derivatives of the following functions with respect to the appropriate variable:
    (i) $e^{-2x} + \log_e (3x - 1)$,   (ii) $\sin 2\theta + 3 \cos 2\theta$,
    (iii) $(2t + 1)^3 + \log_e 3t$,   (iv) $\sqrt[3]{(3x^2 + 1)}$.
15. During the oscillation of a particle, the displacement s of the particle in time t is given by $s = a \sin \omega t$, where a and ω are constants. Show that $d^2s/dt^2 + \omega^2 s = 0$.
16. The angle θ radians turned through in time t seconds by a shaft under damping is given by $\theta = Ae^{-Kt}$, where A and K are constants. Write down the expression for the angular velocity and show that $\dfrac{d^2\theta}{dt^2} - K^2\theta = 0$.
17. The voltage v volts induced across an inductance of L henrys is given by $v = L\dfrac{di}{dt}$ where i is the current in amp. If $i = 50 \sin (100\pi t)$, find the value of v when $L = 0.01$ henry (the angle is in radians).
18. Find a value of t when $ds/dt = 0$ if $s = 5 \sin 20t + 15 \cos 20t$. Hence obtain a stationary value of s and state whether the value is a maximum or a minimum.
19. Find the value of x for which y has a stationary value when $y = e^{2x} - 5x$. Show that this value of y is a minimum and find its numerical value.
20. Obtain the slopes of the graph of $y = 5 \log_{10} x$ when $x = 2, 5, 10$ (to 3 significant figures).

26

Integration

This may be treated as either (i) the reverse of the process of differentiation or (ii) the process of finding areas under graphs. *Applications* of integration to problems use mainly the second treatment.

Consider the statement: $dy/dx = 3x^2$. The process of finding the function, $y = f(x)$, whose derivative is $3x^2$, is called *integration*. From previous work, it follows that y could be equal to x^3. However, since the derivative of a constant is zero, it is possible to add *any* constant C to x^3 and the derivative of the function would still be $3x^2$; i.e. the result is $y = x^3 + C$, where C is an *arbitrary* constant.

To denote the process of *integration*, a special symbol (like an elongated S) is used, i.e.

$$y = \int 3x^2 \, dx = x^3 + C$$

This statement is *read* as: y equals the integral of $3x^2$ *with respect to* x, or y is the integral of $3x^2$ *dee x*.

The result $y = x^3 + C$ is called the *indefinite integral*, since C is an *arbitrary* constant. If a definite value of y is given for a particular value of x, then a particular value of C may be found, e.g. suppose that $y = 5$, when $x = 2$, then $5 = 2^3 + C$, or $C = -3$; therefore the *definite* result is $y = x^3 - 3$, and this result is called the *definite integral*.

245

9

26.1 General Rules

By considering the results which have been obtained for derivatives of functions, it is possible to deduce the results:

(i) $\quad \int x^n \, dx = \dfrac{x^{n+1}}{n+1} + C \qquad$ (n not equal to -1)

(ii) $\quad \int \dfrac{1}{x} \, dx = \log_e x + C \qquad$ (special case of (i) when $n = -1$)

(iii) $\quad \int e^x \, dx = e^x + C$

(iv) $\quad \int \cos x \, dx = \sin x + C \qquad$ (x in radians)

(v) $\quad \int \sin x \, dx = -\cos x + C \qquad$ (x in radians)

26.2 Integral Curves

The indefinite integral, containing the arbitrary constant C, represents an infinite set of graphs (curves) called the *integral curves*. All the integral curves cross any line parallel to the y-axis at the same angle, i.e. $\dfrac{dy}{dx}$ is the same for each of the integral curves. C is the intercept of the general curve on the y-axis (Figure 26.1).

Examples—using the general rules:

(i) Find y in terms of x if $dy/dx = 2x^2 + 4x + 1$, and $y = 7$ when $x = 1$.

$$y = \int (2x^2 + 4x + 1) \, dx = 2\,\frac{x^3}{3} + 4\,\frac{x^2}{2} + x + C$$

$$= \tfrac{2}{3}x^3 + 2x^2 + x + C$$

Using the given values:

$$7 = \frac{2}{3} \times 1^3 + 2 \times 1^2 + 1 + C = 3\frac{2}{3} + C$$

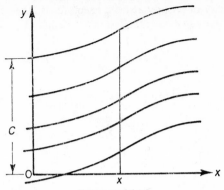

FIGURE 26.1

$$\therefore\ C = 7 - 3\tfrac{2}{3} = 3\tfrac{1}{3}$$

$\therefore$ The definite integral is $y = \tfrac{2}{3}x^3 + 2x^2 + x + 3\tfrac{1}{3}$

(ii) The slope of the curve $y = f(x)$ is $2x - 1$, and the curve passes through the point (2,5). Find the equation of the curve.

Slope of the curve $= \mathrm{d}y/\mathrm{d}x = 2x - 1$

$$\therefore\ y = \int (2x - 1)\,\mathrm{d}x = x^2 - x + C$$

Since the curve passes through (2,5)

$$\therefore\ 5 = 2^2 - 2 + C = 2 + C$$
$$\therefore\ C = 3$$

Hence the equation of the curve is $y = x^2 - x + 3$

(iii) Find y in terms of x when $\dfrac{\mathrm{d}y}{\mathrm{d}x} = \dfrac{3}{x} + 2x + 1$ and $y = 3$ when $x = 1$.

$$y = \int \left(\frac{3}{x} + 2x + 1\right) \mathrm{d}x = 3 \log_e x + x^2 + x + C$$

Using the given values:

$$3 = 3 \log_e 1 + 1^2 + 1 + C \quad (\log_e 1 = 0)$$
$$\therefore\ 3 = 0 + 2 + C \quad \text{or} \quad C = 1$$
$$\therefore\ y = 3 \log_e x + x^2 + x + 1$$

(iv) The velocity of a body at time t seconds is $30 - 10t$ m/s. Find the distance s metres travelled in t seconds.

$$\text{Velocity} = v = \frac{ds}{dt} = 30 - 10t$$

$$\therefore \ s = \int (30 - 10t)\, dt = 30t - 5t^2 + C$$

If $s = 0$ when $t = 0$; $0 = C$.

Hence $$s = 30t - 5t^2$$

26.3 Definite Integral Between Limits

In many *applications* of integration it is necessary to find the *total* effect between two definite values of the *independent* variable. This can be represented by $\int_a^b f(x)\, dx$, read as the integral of $f(x)$ dee x between the limits a and b. a is called the *lower limit* of integration, and b is called the *upper limit* of integration.

If $F(x)$ is the indefinite integral of the function $f(x)$, then

$$\int_a^b f(x)\, dx = [F(x)]_a^b = F(b) - F(a)$$

Note the meaning of the last term—the change of $F(x)$ as x changes from a to b. In this expression it is unnecessary to include the arbitrary constant.

Examples:

(i) Evaluate

$$\int_1^3 (2x + 1)\, dx = [x^2 + x]_1^3 = (3^2 + 3) - (1^2 + 1)$$
$$= 12 - 2 = \underline{10}$$

(ii) $\int_2^5 \frac{1}{x}\, dx = [\log_e x]_2^5 = \log_e 5 - \log_e 2 = \log_e \frac{5}{2} = \underline{\log_e (2\cdot 5)}$

(iii) $\displaystyle\int_2^4 (x-1)^2 \, dx = \int_2^4 (x^2 - 2x + 1) \, dx = \left[\frac{x^3}{3} - x^2 + x\right]_2^4$

$$= \left(\frac{4^3}{3} - 4^2 + 4\right) - \left(\frac{2^3}{3} - 2^2 + 2\right) = \frac{56}{3} - 10 = 8\frac{2}{3}$$

26.3.1 Areas under graphs by integration

Let $y = f(x)$ be plotted graphically (see Figure 26.2). To determine the area under the graph, *Simpson's rule* could be used, by dividing the area into an even number of strips of equal widths. This is a good *approximate method* of finding the area.

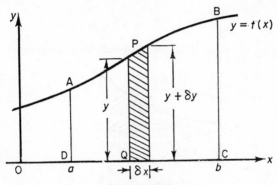

FIGURE 26.2

Let PQ be a strip of width δx. The area of the strip (if $f(x)$ is increasing) will be between the areas of two rectangles of heights y and $y + \delta y$. If δA represents the area of the strip, then

$$y \, \delta x < \delta A < (y + \delta y) \, \delta x$$

Divide by δx:

$$y < \frac{\delta A}{\delta x} < y + \delta y$$

As $\delta x \to 0$,

$$\frac{\delta A}{\delta x} \to \frac{dA}{dx}, \qquad y + \delta y \to y$$

$$\therefore \text{ as } \quad \delta x \to 0, \qquad \frac{\mathrm{d}A}{\mathrm{d}x} = y$$

$$\therefore \ A = \int_a^b y \, \mathrm{d}x = \int_a^b f(x) \, \mathrm{d}x$$

i.e. the area between the curve, the x-axis and the ordinates at $x = a$ and $x = b$ is given by the integral of the function between the limits for x.

Example: Find the area between the curve $y = 3x^2 + 1$, the x-axis and the ordinates at $x = 1$ and $x = 4$.

The area required is shown shaded in Figure 26.3.

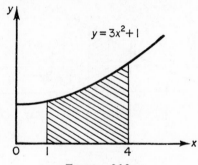

FIGURE 26.3

Using integration:

$$\text{Area} = \int_1^4 y \, \mathrm{d}x = \int_1^4 (3x^2 + 1) \, \mathrm{d}x$$

$$= [x^3 + x]_1^4 = (4^3 + 4) - (1^3 + 1)$$

$$= 68 - 2 = \underline{66 \text{ sq. units}}$$

(*Note:* The actual units will depend on the quantities plotted graphically. Basically the integral represents units of area, but discretion must be used in any given problem.)

WORKED EXAMPLES

(a) Find y as a function of x if $dy/dx = x^2 - 1$ and $y = 4$ when $x = -1$.

$$y = \int (x^2 - 1)\,dx = \frac{x^3}{3} - x + C$$

$$\therefore\ 4 = \frac{(-1)^3}{3} - (-1) + C = -\frac{1}{3} + 1 + C$$

$$\therefore\ \underline{C = 3\tfrac{1}{3}}$$

$$\therefore\ y = \tfrac{1}{3}x^3 - x + 3\tfrac{1}{3} \quad \text{or} \quad \underline{y = \tfrac{1}{3}(x^3 - 3x + 10)}$$

(b) Evaluate $\displaystyle\int_1^3 (x^3 - 3x + 2)\,dx$.

$$\int_1^3 (x^3 - 3x + 2)\,dx = \left[\frac{x^4}{4} - \frac{3x^2}{2} + 2x\right]_1^3$$

$$= \left(\frac{3^4}{4} - \frac{3 \times 3^2}{2} + 2 \times 3\right) - \left(\frac{1^4}{4} - \frac{3 \times 1^2}{2} + 2 \times 1\right)$$

$$= \frac{80}{4} - \frac{24}{2} + 4 = \underline{12}$$

(c) Evaluate $\displaystyle\int_1^4 \frac{1}{\sqrt{x}}\,dx$.

$$\int_1^4 x^{-\frac{1}{2}}\,dx = \left[\frac{x^{\frac{1}{2}}}{\frac{1}{2}}\right]_1^4$$

$$= 2[x^{\frac{1}{2}}]_1^4 = 2(4^{\frac{1}{2}} - 1^{\frac{1}{2}}) = 2(2 - 1) = \underline{2}$$

(d) Find the area under the graph of $y = 5/x$, above the x-axis between the ordinates $x = 1$ and $x = 6$.

The area required is shown shaded in Figure 26.4.

$$\text{Area} = \int_1^6 y\,dx = \int_1^6 \frac{5}{x}\,dx$$

$$= [5 \log_e x]_1^6 = 5 \log_e 6 - 5 \log_e 1$$

$$= 5 \log_e 6 = 5 \times 1\cdot7918 = \underline{8\cdot959 \text{ sq. units}}$$

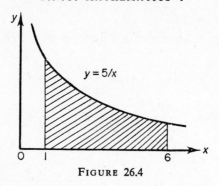

FIGURE 26.4

(e) Evaluate

$$\int_0^{\pi/4} \cos x \, dx = [\sin x]_0^{\pi/4} = \sin \pi/4 - \sin 0$$

$$= 0{\cdot}7071 - 0 = \underline{0{\cdot}7071}$$

Examples 26

1. If $dy/dx = 2x + 3$ and $y = 6$, when $x = 2$, find y in terms of x.
2. The acceleration dv/dt of a body at any time t seconds is $32 - 6t$ m/s². Express the velocity v as a function of t if $v = 20$ when $t = 0$.
3. The slope of the tangent to the graph of $y = f(x)$ is $3x^2 + 2x - 1$ at the point (x, y). Find y as a function of x if $y = 3$ when $x = -1$.
4. Given $dy/dx = x + 1/x$ and $y = 4$ when $x = 1$, express y as a function of x.
5. Obtain the indefinite integral of $x^3 + 2x^2 - x + 1$.
6. Write down the indefinite integrals of (i) $3/\sqrt{x}$, (ii) $x^{3/2}$.
7. Evaluate the definite integral $\int_1^3 (x^2 + x) \, dx$.
8. Evaluate the definite integral $\int_2^4 (4x^3 + 2x - 1) \, dx$.
9. The velocity of a particle at time t seconds is given by $v = ds/dt = 45 - 12t$ m/s. If $s = 0$ when $t = 0$, find s in terms of t and hence find the distance travelled in 3 seconds from $t = 0$.
10. Find the numerical value of $\int_0^4 (x + 1)^2 \, dx$.
11. Evaluate $\int_1^9 3\sqrt{x} \, dx$.

12. Evaluate $\int_0^{\pi/4} \sin x \, dx$ (x in radians).

13. Sketch the graph of the function $y = x^2 + 2x$ between $x = 0$ and $x = 5$. Use integration to determine the area between the graph, the x-axis and the ordinate $x = 5$.

14. Find, by integration, the area under the graph of $y = x^3$, above the x-axis, between $x = 1$ and $x = 3$.

15. Plot the graph of $y = x^2 + 3$ between $x = 0$ and $x = 5$. Using Simpson's rule, and 11 ordinates, find the area between the graph, the x-axis and the ordinates at $x = 0$ and $x = 5$. Obtain the exact area by integration.

27

Revision Examples

27.1 Examples on Chapters 1–5

1. Use logarithms to evaluate $(1 \cdot 93)^{1 \cdot 42} \times (0 \cdot 356)^{-0 \cdot 53}$.
2. Solve the equation $(5 \cdot 3)^{2x+1} = (19 \cdot 7)^{x-1}$.
3. If $y = ax^n$ and $y = 15 \cdot 6$ when $x = 1 \cdot 7$, $y = 5 \cdot 8$ when $x = 2 \cdot 3$, determine the values of a and n.
4. Given $s = ae^{Kt}$ and $s = 21$ when $t = 1 \cdot 5$, $s = 39$ when $t = 2 \cdot 1$, find the values of a and K.
5. The time t seconds for a capacitor to discharge when charged so that the voltage between its plates is V_0, is given by

$$t = CR \log_e (V_0/V)$$

where V is the voltage at time t. Calculate t when $C = 3 \times 10^{-6}$, $R = 1 \cdot 5 \times 10^6$, $V_0 = 220$, $V = 127$.
6. Transpose the formula $P = Q(1 - e^{-at})$ to express t in terms of the other quantities.
7. (i) Rationalize: $\dfrac{3\sqrt{7} - 4\sqrt{5}}{5\sqrt{7} - 2\sqrt{5}}$.
   (ii) Solve the equation $\sqrt{(2x + 1)} + \sqrt{(x - 1)} = \sqrt{(x + 2)}$.
   (iii) Write down the solutions of $4t^2 + 3t + 1 = 0$.
8. Solve the equations $3x + 2y + 2z = 10$, $2x - y - 3z = 4$, $4x + 3y + z = 8$.
9. (i) Solve the equation $Lm^2 - Rm + \dfrac{1}{C} = 0$ for m, and hence calculate the values of m when $C = 4 \times 10^{-6}$, $R = 6 \cdot 6$, $L = 0 \cdot 03 \times 10^{-3}$.

(ii) Find p and q to satisfy the equations $p^2 - pq + q^2 = 3$; $p^2 + 3pq = 7$.

10. (i) Express $\dfrac{5x + 11}{(2x + 1)(x - 3)}$ in partial fractions.

(ii) Express $\dfrac{x^2 + 2x - 7}{(x - 1)^2(x^2 + 1)}$ in partial fractions.

27.2 Examples on Chapters 6–10

1. In an arithmetic progression, $T_{11} = 22{\cdot}3$, $T_{19} = 28{\cdot}06$. Find the A.P., the 30th term and the sum of 25 terms.

2. (i) Insert 3 geometric means between 40 and $202\frac{1}{2}$.
   (ii) Write down the 6th term of the series $200, 40, 8, \ldots$ Obtain the sum to infinity of the series. What is the percentage error if the sum of the first three terms is used as approximately the sum to infinity?

3. (i) Write down the full expansion of $(3x + y)^5$.
   (ii) Expand $1/(1 - 3x)^2$ as far as the term in x^4.
   (iii) Using a binomial expansion, find the approximate value of $(0{\cdot}95)^6$ to 3 decimal places.

4. If $F = (Wb^3\sqrt{x})/(a^4m^{3/2})$, using first order binomial approximation, find the percentage change in F when b increases by $0{\cdot}4\%$, x decreases by $0{\cdot}3\%$, a increases by $0{\cdot}8\%$ and m decreases by $1{\cdot}1\%$.

5. Solve the equation $\sec^2\theta - 6\tan\theta = 12{\cdot}4$ for values of θ between $0°$ and $360°$.

6. In the triangle ABC, $a = 12{\cdot}3$ cm, $b = 8{\cdot}2$ cm, $c = 9{\cdot}7$ cm. Solve the triangle, find its area and the radius of the circumcircle.

7. A framework of light rods, in the form of a quadrilateral ABCD has AB = 12 cm, BC = 15 cm, CD = 14 cm, DA = 9 cm. A rod of length 16 cm joins C and A to keep the framework rigid. Calculate the angles BAC, DAC and the length of BD.

8. Solve the triangle PQR in which angle QPR = $50°27'$, PQ = $9{\cdot}5$ cm, QR = $8{\cdot}1$ cm.

9. Prove the identity $(\sec\theta - 1)(\sec\theta + 1) = \sin^2\theta/\cos^2\theta$.

10. In the triangle XYZ, $x = 5{\cdot}5$ m, $y = 3{\cdot}7$ m, $z = 7{\cdot}8$ m. Using the 's formula', find the area of the triangle, and hence find $\sin X$ and the radius of the circumcircle of the triangle.

27.3 Examples on Chapters 11–15

1. By expansion and rearrangement, express $5 \sin (\theta + 20°) + 10 \cos (\theta - 40°)$ in the form $R \sin (\theta + \alpha)$, stating the values of R and α.

2. If $\sin A = 3/5$ and $\cos B = -12/13$ $(0 < A < 90°; 180° < B < 270°)$, calculate, without using trigonometric tables the numerical values of $\sin (A + B)$, $\cos (B - A)$, $\tan (A + B)$ to 3 significant figures.

3. State the expansion for $\cos 2\theta$ in terms of $\cos \theta$. Using this, calculate, without using trigonometric tables, the value of $\cos 25°$, given $\cos 50° = 0.6428$.

4. Express $7 \cos x - 5 \sin x$ in the form $R \cos (x + \alpha)$ and hence solve the equation $7 \cos x - 5 \sin x = 4.2$ for values of x between $0°$ and $360°$.

5. Obtain all the solutions between $0°$ and $360°$ of the equations:
   (i) $2 \sec^2 \theta = 3(3 - \tan \theta)$.
   (ii) $5 \cos 2\theta - 3 \sin \theta = 3.2$.

6. (i) Express $\sin 4\theta + \sin \theta$ as a product.
   (ii) Express $\cos 30° - \cos 70°$ as a product.
   (iii) Express $2 \cos 3x \cos 5x$ as a sum.
   (iv) Express $\sin 3x + \sin x$ as a product and hence solve the equation $\sin 3x + \sin x = 0$ $(0 \leqslant x \leqslant 360°)$.

7. A chord of a circle of radius r subtends an angle of 2θ (radians) at the centre of the circle. Find an expression for the area of the minor segment cut off by the chord. If $\theta = \pi/3$ and the area of the segment is 50 cm², calculate the radius of the circle.

8. A solid metal cylindrical block has a height of 10 cm and radius 2.5 cm. In the ends of the block are two central hollows in the form of spherical caps of depths 1.5 cm and base radius 2 cm. Find (i) the total surface area of the block, and (ii) the weight of the block if the metal weighs 76.8 KN/m³.

9. A metal pyramid on a square base has an altitude of 120 mm and side of base 60 mm. If the pyramid is melted down and recast in the shape of a frustum of a cone of height 60 mm and end radii in the ratio 2:1, find the end radii of the frustum and the ratio of the total surface areas of the two solids.

10. A frustum of a cone has an altitude of 20 cm and end radii of 4 cm and 7 cm. Find the area of the central and end circular sections and hence determine the volume using Simpson's rule. Verify your result using $V = \frac{1}{3}\pi h(r^2 + Rr + R^2)$.

27.4 Examples on Chapters 16–20

1. Tabulate the values of the function $f(x) = x^3 - 5x - 3$ for values of x between -3 and $+3$. Hence solve the equation $x^3 - 5x - 3 = 0$ graphically. By a suitable enlargement, determine the middle root correct to 3 significant figures.

2. By plotting a suitable graph (or graphs) between $x = 1$ and 5, obtain a solution of the equation $\log_{10} x = x - 2$. Use an enlargement to obtain the root more accurately.

3. The following experimental values of x and y are obtained. By plotting a suitable linear graph, show that the law connecting x and y is of the form $y = a/x + b$, and estimate likely values of a and b.

x	1	2	3	4	5
y	4·10	3·45	3·23	3·13	3·06

4. During an experiment with a diode valve, the following values of current (i milliamps) were obtained for various applied voltages (v volts). Show that the values of i and v obey a law of the form $i = av + bv^2$ and estimate the law.

v (volts)	0	40	80	120	160	200
i (mA)	0	3·8	14·0	30·6	53·6	83·0

5. The following values of x and y are suspected to obey a law of the form $y = ax^n$. By drawing a suitable graph, show that this is so and hence estimate likely values for a and n.

x	2·1	3·7	5·9	8·1	12·5
y	35·8	131·8	385·4	797·9	2167·0

6. During measurements for a cooling liquid, the temperature $T(°C)$ at time t (minutes) was recorded as follows:

t (min)	10	20	30	40	50
T (°F)	148·2	109·8	81·3	60·2	44·6

Show that the law connecting T and t is of the form $T = Ae^{Kt}$ and estimate values for A and K.

7. The following values of $f(x)$ are obtained from a graphical plot between $x = 0$ and $x = 5$ for intervals of 0·5 in x.

x	0	0·5	1·0	1·5	2·0	2·5	3·0	3·5	4·0	4·5	5·0
$f(x)$	17·5	16·5	14·9	12·6	10·4	8·7	7·5	6·3	5·4	4·8	4·5

Using Simpson's rule, estimate the mean and root mean square values of $f(x)$ in the given range.

8. Plot the graph of $y = x(6 - x)$ between $x = 0$ and $x = 6$. Using Simpson's rule and six equal intervals, estimate the mean value of y in the given range.

Using Simpson's rule and suitable values of y, estimate the root mean square value of y in the same range.

9. The following values of $f(x)$ are given for values of x from 1 to 8 in steps of 1 unit:

x	1	2	3	4	5	6	7	8
$f(x)$	5	23	65	137	245	395	593	845

Tabulate the finite differences as far as the fourth-order differences. Deduce that $f(x)$ is a cubic polynomial function and hence find the function.

10. (i) Given $f(1·10) = 0·7863$ and $f(1·15) = 0·7897$, use first-order finite differences to estimate $f(1·13)$.

(ii) Given $\sqrt{(35·6)} = 5·967$, $\sqrt{(35·8)} = 5·983$, use first-order finite differences to estimate $\sqrt{(35·7)}$ and $\sqrt{(35·75)}$.

(iii) Given $\sin 30° = 0·5$, $\sin 31° = 0·5150$, estimate $\sin 30°12'$, $\sin 30°30'$, $\sin 30°45'$, using first-order finite differences.

27.5 Examples on Chapters 21–26

1. Tabulate the values of $y = x^2 + 3x$ for x from 1 to 2 in steps of 0·2. Estimate the average rates of change of y with respect to x in the 5 stated intervals.

2. Tabulate the values of $\tan x$ for x in steps of 0·1 radian between $x = 0.5$ and 1·0 radian. From your table, estimate the rates of change of $\tan x$ when $x = 0.55$, 0·65, 0·75, 0·85, 0·95 radian.

3. Plot the graph of the function $y = 5/\sqrt{x}$ for values of x from 1 to 9 in steps of 1 unit. From your graph, using chords, estimate the gradient of the graph when $x = 3, 5, 7$.

4. A special car is timed over various distances from a flying start, and the distances s (metres) travelled in t (seconds) are recorded as:

t	0	5	10	15	20	25	30
s	0	108	300	575	933	1375	1900

Draw the graph of distance against time and, using chords, estimate the speeds at 5, 10, 15, 20, 25 seconds. Draw the speed–time graph. From your speed–time graph, show that the acceleration is constant, and find its value. Estimate the speed at the end of the period in Km/h.

5. Plot the graph of the function $x^3 + 2x^2 - x + 7$ for values of x between -3 and $+2$. From your graph, estimate the maximum and minimum values of the function, stating the values of x at which these occur.

6. Obtain, from first principles, the derivative of $y = 3x^2 + 4/x$.

7. Write down the derivatives of the following functions with respect to the appropriate variables:

(i) $\sqrt{(x^5)}$, (ii) $5t^3 + 3t^2 - 7$, (iii) $(2x + 3)^2$, (iv) e^{2t},

(v) $(\sqrt{x} + x)^2$, (vi) $5 \log_e x + 3e^x + x^5$, (vii) $5/x^4$.

8. Using the 'function of a function' rule, find the derivatives of:

(i) $\sqrt{(x^3 - 1)}$,   (ii) $5/(t^2 + t)^3$,   (iii) $\log_e (3x^2 + 2x + 1)$,

(iv) $10e^{5t}$,   (v) $5 \sin 3x$,   (vi) $12 \cos 4x$,

(vii) $7 \log_{10} (x^2)$,   (viii) $3 \sin 5x°$,   (ix) $12 \cos (\frac{1}{2}x)°$.

9. A cliff top is 100 metres above sea level. A shot is fired out to sea and the height h metres of the shot above sea level at time t (seconds) is given by $h = 100 + 400t - 4 \cdot 905t^2$. Find the vertical velocity at time t, and the acceleration. Calculate the vertical velocity at times $t = 25$ seconds and $t = 50$ seconds. Find the time to reach maximum height and find this height above sea level.

10. Find the maximum and minimum values of the function $x^3 - 3x^2 - 24x + 15$.

11. Find the equations of the tangents to the graph of $y = x^3 + x^2 - 7$ at the points where (i) $x = +1$, (ii) $x = -1$.

12. Given $dy/dx = x^2 - \dfrac{1}{x^2} + 1$ and $y = 4$ when $x = 1$, express y in terms of x.

13. Evaluate

   (i) $\displaystyle\int_1^3 (x - 1)^2 \, dx,$ (ii) $\displaystyle\int_1^{27} \sqrt[3]{x} \, dx,$

   (iii) $\displaystyle\int_{-1}^2 (3x^2 + 2x + 1) \, dx.$

14. Evaluate

   (i) $\displaystyle\int_0^2 5e^x \, dx,$ (ii) $\displaystyle\int_4^9 \frac{5}{x} \, dx,$

   (iii) $\displaystyle\int_0^{\pi/3} \cos x \, dx,$ (iv) $\displaystyle\int_0^{\pi} 5 \sin x \, dx.$

15. (i) Sketch the graph of $y = x^3 + 1$ and, using integration, obtain the area between the graph, the x-axis and the ordinates at $x = 1$ and $x = 4$.

   (ii) Sketch the graph of $y = 4/x$ between $x = 2$ and $x = 10$. Using integration, determine the area between the graph the x-axis and the ordinates at $x = 2$ and $x = 10$.

Answers to Examples

Examples 1

1. $324\sqrt{5} = 724\cdot4$ 2. $1/a^{1/6}b^{7/6} = 1/\sqrt[6]{(ab^7)}$ 3. q^{2y}/p^{2x}
4. $L = \dfrac{z}{X^2}\sqrt{\left(\dfrac{PY}{W}\right)}$ 5. $L = 1/4\pi^2f^2C$ 6. $1000\sqrt{10} = 3162$
7. $y/Y = (X/x)^{1/5}$ 8. $P = V^2/4d^4$ 9. $0\cdot2710$ 10. $16\cdot32$
11. $0\cdot4241$ 12. $41\cdot22$ 13. 2556 14. $254\cdot3$ 15. $127\cdot6$
16. $577\cdot5$ 17. $80\cdot08$ 18. $1\cdot746 \times 10^{-14}$
19. (i) $0\cdot7071$ (ii) $0\cdot002\ 78$ (iii) $6\cdot601$ 20. $0\cdot011\ 53$ 21. $0\cdot1220$
22. (i) $0\cdot8343$ (ii) $61\cdot24$ 23. $T = 402\cdot5$ 24. $3\cdot482$ 25. $W = 3375.$

Examples 2

1. $x = 0\cdot7591$ 2. $x = 1\cdot011$ 3. $y = 0\cdot9913$ 4. $x = 1\cdot754$
5. $t = 1\cdot206$ 6. $n = 2\cdot568$ 7. $x = 0\cdot4733$ 8. $p = 3\cdot426$
9. $n = 1\cdot98$ 10. $K = 0\cdot003\ 58, m = 2\cdot063$ 11. $a = 4, b = -0\cdot693$
12. $a = 5\cdot471, b = 1\cdot539$ 13. $a = 0\cdot696, b = 0\cdot362$
14. $T_1 = 15\cdot71, \mu = 0\cdot0805.$ 15. (i) $1\cdot9858$ (ii) $6\cdot2778$ (iii) $\bar{3}\cdot0700$ or
    $-2\cdot9300$ 16. (i) $7\cdot161$ (ii) 4256 (iii) $0\cdot001\ 785$
17. (i) $2\cdot7486$ (ii) $7\cdot4742$ (iii) $-1\cdot9805$ or $\bar{2}\cdot0195$ 18. $P = 398\cdot6$
19. $\theta = 13\cdot3$ 20. $W = 5{,}504$ 21. $t = 1\cdot292(1)$ 22. $1\cdot417$
23. $2\cdot263$ 24. $4\cdot6007$ 25. $1\cdot5387$

Examples 3

1. $A^3 - B^3$ 2. $A^3 + B^3$ 3. $(4p + q)(2p + 3q)$
4. $4\pi(R - r)(R^2 + Rr + r^2)/3$ 5. $(3m + 7n)(4m - 5n)$ 6. $(10x + 3)/(x^2 - 4)$
7. $(4a^2 + 10a - 1)/(4a^3 + 8a^2 - a - 2).$ 8. $4(x^2 - x - 1)/(x + 1)^3$
9. $x^3 + 3x^2y + 3y^2x + y^3$ 10. $x^4 - 4x^3y + 6x^2y^2 - 4xy^3 + y^4$

11. $d = 2(S - an)/n(n - 1)$ 12. $n = \left[\log \left(\dfrac{a + rS - S}{a} \right) \right] / \log r$

13. $u = vf/(v - f)$ 14. $n = (KA + 4\pi tC)/(KA)$

15. $g = 4\pi^2(K^2 + h^2)/hT^2$ 16. $p = (ft^2 + 2trf - r^3)/(t + r)^2$

17. $n = IR/(E - Ir)$ 18. $\dfrac{x - y}{1 + xy} = \dfrac{b - c}{1 + bc}$ 19. $M = \frac{1}{2}xbcd^2(1 - \frac{1}{3}x)$

20. $R = (r_1r_2r_3)/(r_2r_3 + r_1r_3 + r_1r_2)$ 21. $t = \dfrac{1}{K} \log_e \left(\dfrac{u}{u - v} \right)$

22. $t = CR \log_e (I/i)$ 23. (i) $26\sqrt{7} + 18\sqrt{5}$ (ii) $24\sqrt{2} - 29\sqrt{3}$

24. (i) $\sqrt{2} + 1$ (ii) $2 + \sqrt{3}$ (iii) $\dfrac{1}{42}(33 - 5\sqrt{15})$

25. $\dfrac{1}{25}(48 - 7\sqrt{21}) = 0.636\,76$

Examples 4

1. $x = 0, y = -2$ 2. $a = 10\frac{3}{8}, b = \frac{5}{32}$ 3. $x = 1, y = -1, z = 2$
4. $a = -5, b = 0, c = 2$ 5. $l = 9, m = -2, n = 4$
6. $P = 4, Q = -3.5, R = 2.5$ 7. $r = 2, s = -1, t = 3$
8. $p_1 = 0.54, p_2 = -0.36, p_3 = 1.45$
9. $i_1 = 53/16 = 3.31, i_2 = 189/16 = 11.81$
10. $i_1 = 0.65, i_2 = -0.54, i_3 = 0.10$ 11. $x = -2.351$ or 0.851
12. (i) $y = 1$ or $-1\frac{2}{3}$ (ii) $a = -3.1375$ or 0.6375 (iii) $t = -0.75 \pm 1.199j$
13. (i) $x = -0.5 \pm 0.866j$ (ii) $t = 1 \pm 1.414j$ (iii) $p = 1.781$ or -0.281
14. $x = -1 \pm 1.414j$ 15. $t = 1.68$ or 18.71 16. $n = 11$
17. $b = 5 \pm \sqrt{6} = 7.449$ or 2.551 18. $d = 1.8$ m
19. $x = -\dfrac{R}{2L} \pm \dfrac{1}{2}\sqrt{\left(\dfrac{R^2}{L^2} - \dfrac{4}{LC} \right)}$; roots equal if $R^2 = 4L/C$
20. $r = 5$ cm   21. $x = 1$ or 2 22. $\tan \theta = -1$ or 0.25
23. $\tan \theta = 1.28075$ or -0.78075 24. $\tan x = 4.1085$ or -0.6085
25. $u = \pm\sqrt{5}$ or $\pm\sqrt{13}$ i.e., $u = \pm2.236$ or ±3.606

Examples 5

1. $x = 3$ or $4, y = 4$ or 3 2. $a = 1$ or $35/13, b = 2$ or $-18/13$
3. $x = \pm2, y = \pm6$ 4. $x = 2, y = 5$
5. $l = \pm3, m = \pm2; l = \pm2, m = \pm1$ 6. $a = 5$ or $-2; b = 2$ or -5
7. $s = \pm\sqrt{3}$ or $\pm7, t = \mp3\sqrt{3}$ or ±2
8. $x = \pm\sqrt{2}$ or $\pm2, y = \pm3\sqrt{2}$ or ±4
9. $l = \pm1, m = \pm1; l = \pm2j/\sqrt{11}, m = \pm j/\sqrt{11}$
10. $x = \pm2, y = \mp3; x = \pm4j\sqrt{2}, y = \pm3j\sqrt{2}$
11. $x = 1$ or $41/31, y = -3$ or $-78/31$
12. $L = \pm2\sqrt{2}, M = \pm\sqrt{2}; L = \pm4\sqrt{\frac{2}{5}}, M = \pm3\sqrt{\frac{2}{5}}$

13. $a = \pm\sqrt{\frac{2}{3}}, b = \mp\dfrac{5}{\sqrt{6}}$; $a = \pm1, b = \mp2$

14. $A = \pm 1, B = \pm 2;\ A = \pm 7/\sqrt{13}, B = \pm 2/\sqrt{13}$

15. (i) $\dfrac{3}{2(x-3)} - \dfrac{1}{2(x-1)}$ (ii) $\dfrac{4}{x-3} - \dfrac{3}{x+7}$ (iii) $\dfrac{1}{x-2} - \dfrac{2}{x+1}$

16. (i) $\dfrac{1}{3(1-2x)} - \dfrac{1}{3(1+x)}$ (ii) $\dfrac{2}{x+5} + \dfrac{3}{x-4}$ (iii) $\dfrac{3}{x^2} - \dfrac{5}{x} - \dfrac{1}{1-2x}$

17. (i) $\dfrac{2}{1-x} + \dfrac{3}{1+3x}$ (ii) $\dfrac{3}{5(x-1)} + \dfrac{4}{5(2x+3)}$ (iii) $\dfrac{3}{2x-1} - \dfrac{4}{3x+1}$

18. (i) $\dfrac{1}{x} + \dfrac{4}{x-1} - \dfrac{3}{x-2}$ (ii) $\dfrac{15}{2(x-1)} - \dfrac{33}{x-2} + \dfrac{55}{2(x-3)}$

   (iii) $\dfrac{4}{3(x+1)} + \dfrac{2}{3(x-2)} - \dfrac{1}{3x-1}$

19. (i) $\dfrac{9}{x+1} - \dfrac{2}{(x+1)^2} - \dfrac{9}{x+2}$ (ii) $\dfrac{3}{4(x-1)^2} + \dfrac{5}{16(x-1)} - \dfrac{5}{16(x+3)}$

   (iii) $\dfrac{3}{(x+1)^2} + \dfrac{2}{3(x+1)} - \dfrac{4}{3(2x-1)}$

20. (i) $\dfrac{5}{9(x-2)} - \dfrac{2}{3(x+1)^2} + \dfrac{4}{9(x+1)}$ (ii) $\dfrac{3}{(x-1)^2} + \dfrac{2}{3(2x+1)} - \dfrac{1}{3(x-1)}$

   (iii) $\dfrac{5}{x-1} - \dfrac{3}{(x-1)^2} - \dfrac{4}{x-2}$

21. (i) $\dfrac{7x-8}{x^2+x-3} - \dfrac{5}{x+2}$ (ii) $\dfrac{1}{7(x-1)} - \dfrac{x-6}{7(x^2+6)}$ (iii) $\dfrac{4x+1}{x^2+x+1} - \dfrac{4}{x+1}$

22. (i) $\dfrac{3x-5}{x^2+2x+3} - \dfrac{2}{x-3}$ (ii) $\dfrac{34}{5(2x-1)} - \dfrac{17x+1}{5(x^2+1)}$

   (iii) $\dfrac{5}{3x-1} + \dfrac{2x+1}{x^2+x+3}$

23. $\dfrac{3}{x-2} + \dfrac{5}{(x-2)^2} + \dfrac{2-3x}{x^2+3x+4}$

24. $\dfrac{5}{16(x-1)} + \dfrac{3}{4(x-1)^2} - \dfrac{10x+23}{16(2x^2+x+1)}$

25. $\dfrac{1}{x+1} + \dfrac{2}{(x+1)^2} - \dfrac{3}{2x+3}$

Examples 6

1. 34, 62, 82   2. $a = 3.6, d = 0.3;\ 3.6, 3.9, 4.2, 4.5$

3. $a = 8, d = 1.2;\ T_{13} = 22.4, T_{30} = 42.8$

4. $a = 7.8, d = 0.45;\ S_{15} = 164.25, S_{21} = 258.3$ 5. $a = 9, d = 2;\ S_8 = 128$

6. $n = 13$ 7. $n = 24$ 8. $a = 3, r = 2\ T_6 = 96, T_{10} = 1,536$

9. $a = 6, r = 3;\ 6, 18, 54, 162, \ldots$

10. $a = 5, r = 2$; $T_7 = 320$; $a = -5, r = -2, T_7 = -320$
11. $a = 8, r = +3$ or -3; $a = 8, r = 3, S_7 = 8744$; $a = 8, r = -3$, $S_7 = 4376$
12. $n = 7$ 13. $r = +3$ or -3; Means are 24, 72, 216 or $-24, -72, -216$
14. (i) $a = 7.5$, $S_\infty = 11.25$ 15. (i) $S_\infty = 10\frac{2}{3}$ (ii) $S_\infty = 17\frac{1}{2}$
16. 1st piece = 100 mm, longest = 220 mm   17. (i) 31 m (ii) 335 m (iii) 25 seconds
18. 1st turn approx 50π, Last 150π; No. of turns 400; 125·5 m
19. Number of battens 20, Length = 314 mm
20. $r = \frac{3}{2}$, speeds 48, 72, 108, 162 rev/min
21. (i) 1·434 m (ii) 20·03 m (iii) 31·5 m   22. (i) 6·55(4)° (ii) 80°
23. 8·95 m   24. (i) £872·10 (ii) Just over 11 years
25. (i) £2951 (ii) 6·57(2) [7 years]

Examples 7

1. $1 + 8x + 24x^2 + 32x^3 + 16x^4$
2. $32a^5 - 80a^4b + 80a^3b^2 - 40a^2b^3 + 10ab^4 - b^5$
3. $16x^4 - 96x^3y + 216x^2y^2 - 216xy^3 + 81y^4$ 4. $1 + 6x + 6x^2 - 4x^3 + \cdots$
5. $1 + 12x + 90x^2 + 540x^3 + \cdots$ 6. $1 - 6x + 27x^2 - 108x^3 \ldots$; $-\frac{1}{3} < x < \frac{1}{3}$ 7. $4x(3 + 10x^2 + 3x^4)$ 8. $1 + 7x$
9. 1·049 to 3 dec. pl.   10. 2·013 (two terms only required)
11. $2(1 + 9x^2 + 81x^4)$ 12. 0·528

13. $\dfrac{1}{1 - x} - \dfrac{1}{1 + 2x} = 3x(1 - x + 3x^2) + \cdots$

14. $\dfrac{1}{1 + x} + \dfrac{2}{1 + 3x} = 3 - 7x + 19x^2 - 55x^3 \ldots$; $-\frac{1}{3} < x < \frac{1}{3}$

15. M increases by 5·7%   16. E increases by 1·8%   17. $E \simeq -\dfrac{3Px^2}{a^{5/2}}$

18. $1 + \frac{1}{2}x^2 + \frac{3}{8}x^4 + \frac{5}{16}x^6 + \cdots$ 19. nx^{n-1} (Proof)
20. 9·995 to 3 dec. pl.

Examples 8

1. 56/65   2. $2\frac{23}{28}$ 3. ± 0.6792 4. 0·3660
7. (i) 36°52′, 143°8′ (ii) 141°16′, 218°44′ (iii) 53°22′, 233°22′
8. (i) $1/\sqrt{2}, 1/\sqrt{2}, 1$ (ii) $\frac{1}{2}, \frac{1}{2}\sqrt{3}, 1/\sqrt{3}$ (iii) $\frac{1}{2}\sqrt{3}, \frac{1}{2}, \sqrt{3}$
9. (i) $A = 0.8038^c$ (ii) $B = 1.1755^c$ (iii) $C = 0.5376^c$
18. 51°20′, 231°20′   19. 36°52′, 90°, 270°, 143°8′
20. 32°21′, 147°39′,   21. 78°28′, 120°, 240°, 281°32′
22. 23°6′, 130°24′, 203°6′, 310°24′   23. 26°34′, 45°, 206°34′, 225°
24. 0°, 75°31′, 284°29′, 360°   25. 23°35′, 90°, 156°25′
26. 25°51′, 64°9′, 205°51′, 244°9′
27. 21°16′, 98°44′, 141°16′, 218°44′, 261°16′, 338°44′
28. 64°40′, 175°20′   29. $t = 0.236$ 30. $t = 0.001\ 76$

Examples 9

1. $25 \cdot 92 \, \text{m}^2$ 2. $51 \cdot 97 \, \text{m}^2$; $34°27'$ 3. $17 \cdot 29 \, \text{cm}$
4. $r = 7 \cdot 612 \, \text{cm}$; Area $= 182 \cdot 1 \, \text{cm}^2$ 5. Area $= 149 \cdot 1 \, \text{cm}^2$; $A = 52°15'$;
   $C = 39°4'$ 6. $39°57'$ 7. $AB = 13 \, \text{m}$; height $= 6 \cdot 15 \, \text{m}$
8. $PA = 106 \cdot 8 \, \text{m}$; $PB = 93 \cdot 0 \, \text{m}$; Shortest distance $= 85 \cdot 7 \, \text{m}$
9. $10 \cdot 18 \, \text{m}$ 10. $BC = 14 \cdot 86 \, \text{N}$; $AC = 19 \cdot 2 \, \text{N}$ 11. $12 \cdot 23 \, \text{cm}^2$
12. $235 \cdot 3 \, \text{cm}^2$; 1 to $1 \cdot 676$

Examples 10

1. $\Delta = 53 \cdot 2 \, \text{cm}^2$; $20°46'$, $41°41'$, $117°33'$
2. $a = 9 \cdot 232 \, \text{cm}$; $B = 85°23'$; $C = 47°12'$; $\Delta = 42 \cdot 34 \, \text{cm}^2$; $R = 5 \cdot 988 \, \text{cm}$
3. $YZ = 12 \cdot 87 \, \text{cm}$; $R = 7 \cdot 528 \, \text{cm}$
4. Area $= 45 \cdot 7 \, \text{cm}^2$; $PS = 7 \cdot 61 \, \text{cm}$; $RS = 5 \cdot 193 \, \text{cm}$, $PR = 9 \cdot 685 \, \text{cm}$
5. $B + D = 128°48'$; Area $= 137 \cdot 8 \, \text{cm}^2$ 6. $34 \cdot 4 \, \text{N}$ at $26°33'$ to $22 \cdot 4 \, \text{N}$
7. $67 \cdot 3 \, \text{N}$ at $45°4'$ to $75 \, \text{N}$ 8. $150 \, \text{m}$ 9. $CD = 94 \cdot 02 \, \text{m}$
10. $CD = 132 \cdot 3 \, \text{m}$; Area $= 17 \, 480 \, \text{m}^2$ 11. $113°6'$; $39°4'$; $14 \cdot 94 \, \text{cm}$
12. $P_1P_2 = 171 \cdot 94 \, \text{m}$; P_2 bears $N67°58'$ E from P_1
13. $AC = 17 \cdot 46 \, \text{cm}$; $A = 35°51'$, $C = 26°56'$, Area $= 45 \cdot 51 \, \text{cm}^2$; $R = 9 \cdot 817 \, \text{cm}$
14. Breadth $= 17 \cdot 75 \, \text{m}$ 15. Total distance $= 30 \cdot 05 \, \text{Km}$; time $2 \cdot 003 \simeq 2 \, \text{hr}$
16. $AB = 24 \cdot 69 \, \text{m}$; $BD = 19 \cdot 35 \, \text{m}$; angle $DBC = 55°6'$; Area $= 427 \cdot 2 \, \text{m}^2$
17. $AP = 422 \cdot 1 \, \text{m}$; Shortest distance $= 203 \cdot 5 \, \text{m}$; $R = 226 \cdot 8 \, \text{m}$
18. $BD = 26 \cdot 43 \, \text{cm}$; $A = 84°58'$; $B = 88°55'$; $D = 106°7'$
19. $59°18'$; $11 \cdot 41 \, \text{cm}$ 20. $43°49'$ or $136°11'$

Examples 11

1. $\frac{56}{65}$; $\frac{63}{65}$; $-\frac{16}{63}$ 2. $\frac{204}{325}$; $-\frac{323}{325}$; $\frac{36}{323}$ 3. $7\frac{1}{3}$; $\frac{13}{18}$; $\frac{3}{22}$; $\frac{18}{13}$
4. $2 \cdot 098$
5. $\sin 45° = \cos 45° = 1/\sqrt{2}$; $\tan 45° = 1$; $\sin 30° = \frac{1}{2}$, $\cos 30° = \frac{1}{2}\sqrt{3}$,
   $\tan 30° = 1/\sqrt{3}$; $\cos 15° = \dfrac{\sqrt{3} + 1}{2\sqrt{2}} = 0 \cdot 9659$; $\cos 7\frac{1}{2}° = \sqrt{0 \cdot 9829} = 0 \cdot 9914$
6. $\cos A = \sqrt{0 \cdot 3864} = 0 \cdot 6216$; $\sin B = \sqrt{0 \cdot 7148} = 0 \cdot 8455$; $0 \cdot 9440$; $0 \cdot 9944$
7. $0 \cdot 8882$ 8. $7/25 = 0 \cdot 28$; $24/25 = 0 \cdot 96$ 9. $-16/65$; $33/65$
10. $\cos 10° = \sqrt{0 \cdot 9698} = 0 \cdot 9848$; $\sin 10° = \sqrt{0 \cdot 03015} = 0 \cdot 1736$
11. $17 \cdot 32 \cos \theta + 10 \sin \theta$ 12. $14 \cdot 10 \sin \theta + 5 \cdot 13 \cos \theta$
13. $36 \cdot 3 \sin x - 15 \cdot 8 \cos x$ 14. $4 \cdot 33 \cos x + 9 \cdot 43 \sin x$
15. $R = 13$; $\alpha = 67°23'$ 16. $R = 5$; $\alpha = 36°52'$
17. $R = 7 \cdot 648$; $\alpha = 27°14'$

Examples 12

1. $0 \cdot 4283$; $0 \cdot 9036$; $0 \cdot 4740$ 2. $56/65$; $63/65$; $-119/169$; $-24/25$
3. $0 \cdot 2499$; $-0 \cdot 4242$ 4. $0 \cdot 9917$; $-0 \cdot 1288$; $-7 \cdot 70$
5. $\cos \theta = \frac{1}{4}$ or $-\frac{1}{2}$ 6. $\sin \theta = \frac{1}{3}$ or $\frac{2}{3}$
15. $-1 \cdot 360$ or $0 \cdot 735$ 16. $A = 99°35'$ 17. $8 \cdot 602 \cos (\theta + 35°32')$

18. $R = 13$; $\alpha = 67°23'$ 19. $R = 15·99$; $\alpha = 38°47'$
20. $2\sqrt{3} \sin (x - 30°)$; Max $E = 2\sqrt{3}$
21. $\sqrt{5} \cos (\theta + 63°26')$; Max $= \sqrt{5}$; Min $= -\sqrt{5}$
22. $111·8 \cos (\theta + 26°34')$ 23. $11·18 \sin (wt + 1·107)$
24. $49·12 \cos (x - 21°51')$ 25. $9·849 \sin (2x + 66°2')$

Examples 13

1. (i) $2 \sin 75° \cos 5°$ (ii) $2 \cos 55° \cos 25°$ (iii) $2 \sin 150° \cos 40°$
2. (i) $2 \cos 85° \sin 45°$ (ii) $2 \sin 45° \sin 5°$ (iii) $-2 \sin 50° \sin 25°$
3. (i) $2 \sin 4x \cos 3x$ (ii) $2 \cos 3x \sin 2x$ (iii) $2 \cos 2\theta \cos \theta$
    (iv) $2 \sin 4\theta \sin 2\theta$ (v) $2 \sin \frac{3}{2}t \cos \frac{1}{2}t$ (vi) $-2 \sin 3\pi t \sin \pi t$
4. (i) $\sin 50° + \sin 20°$ (ii) $\sin 90° - \sin 40°$ (iii) $\cos 115° + \cos 45°$
    (iv) $\cos 34° - \cos 82°$ (v) $\sin 4\theta + \sin 2\theta$ (vi) $\sin 7x - \sin x$
    (vii) $\frac{1}{2}(\sin 4t + \sin 2t)$ (viii) $\frac{1}{2}(\cos 9t + \cos t)$ (ix) $\frac{1}{2}(\cos 2\alpha - \cos 4\alpha)$
7. $60°$; $70°32'$; $289°28'$; $300°$ 8. $33°42'$, $116°34'$, $213°42'$, $296°34'$
9. $120°$, $240°$ 10. $69°35'$, $169°27'$, $249°35'$, $349°27'$ 11. $43°20'$, $136°40'$
12. $120°$, $240°$ 13. $46°40'$, $313°20'$ 14. $70°32'$, $289°28'$
15. $90°$, $210°$, $330°$ 16. $14°29'$, $165°31'$, $199°28'$, $340°32'$
17. $6°29'$, $128°31'$, $186°29'$, $308°31'$ 18. $72°19'$, $147°29'$, $252°19'$, $327°29'$
19. $11°31'$, $285°33'$ 20. $29°44'$, $259°12'$ 21. $88°37'$, $338°45'$
22. $93°12'$, $337°52'$ 23. $8°48'$, $124°28'$ 24. $24°27'$, $261°49'$
25. $4°14'$, $228°54'$ 26. $269°59'$, $323°9'$ 27. $43°32'$, $173°20'$, $223°32'$, $353°20'$
28. $126°57'$, $175°3'$, $306°57'$, $355°3'$ 29. $0°$, $90°$, $180°$, $270°$, $360°$
30. $0°$, $72°$, $144°$, $216°$, $288°$, $360°$ 31. $0°$, $45°$, $135°$, $180°$, $225°$, $315°$, $360°$
32. $36°$, $60°$, $108°$, $180°$, $252°$, $300°$, $324°$ 33. $t = 0·0162$
34. $t = 0·022$ 35. $t = 0·013$

Examples 14

1. $9·274$ cm; $23·18$ cm^2 2. 4137 m^3/hour
3. (i) $8252·2$ m^3 (ii) 3354 m^2
4. $A = \frac{1}{2}r(\pi r + 4h)$; $P = r(\pi + 2) + 2h$; $1·040(4)$ m
5. $17·3\%$; $16\,627$ cm^3; 8 cm   6. $V = \frac{1}{2}r(S - 2\pi r^2)$
7. $1·41$ cm; $7·217$ cm^2 8. $9·165$ cm
9. $3·61$ cm^2; 627 cm^2; 537 cm^2; 1140 g
10. $140·3$ Kg; 5 min 9 second

Examples 15

1. 144 cm^3; $186·8$ cm^2; $75°58'$; $70°32'$
2. $20\,780$ mm^3; 6137 mm^2; $82°41'$; $75°37'$
3. $67·17$ mm   4. $2·432$ cm; $9·728$ cm; $59·76$ cm^2
5. $156·4$ mm; $60\,359$ mm^2 6. $1:7$; 1832 cm^3 7. $10\,040$ g
8. $3589·2$ cm^2; $22\,391$ cm^3 9. $48\,060$ N   10. $1·810$ N
11. $31·42$ cm^2; $1·079$ N   12. $0·0995$ N   13. $11·92$ cm^2; $0·1814$ N
14. $4·575$ N   15. $174·2$ cm^3

Examples 16

1. (i) $-1\cdot79$, $2\cdot79$ (ii) $2\cdot3$, $-1\cdot3$
2. $-0\cdot7$, $2\cdot7$; $x = 1\cdot4$ or $-1\cdot4$, $y = -0\cdot8$ or $+4\cdot8$
3. $-2\cdot5$, $-0\cdot6$, $3\cdot1$; $3\cdot10$ 4. $-1\cdot66$, $-0\cdot55$, $2\cdot2$
5. $-1\cdot62$, $-0\cdot46$, $2\cdot07$ 6. $-3\cdot2$, $0\cdot5$, $2\cdot7$; $-3\cdot2 < x < 0\cdot5$; $x > 2\cdot7$
7. -2, 1, $1\cdot5$ 8. -1, $0\cdot4$, $2\cdot6$; $0\cdot378$ 9. $-0\cdot705$ 10. $-1\cdot1$, $0\cdot68$
11. $3\cdot38$ 12. $0\cdot34$, $2\cdot222$ rad; $19°25'$, $127°18'$ 13. $0\cdot589$
14. $0\cdot544$ 15. $x = \pm2\cdot92$, $\pm0\cdot685$, $y = \pm0\cdot685$, $\pm2\cdot92$

Examples 17

1. $a = 1\cdot42$, $b = 2\cdot6$ 2. $a = 1\cdot62$, $b = -1\cdot93$ 3. $a = 175$, $b = 4\cdot93$
4. $a = 406$, $b = -2\cdot6$ 5. $a = -8\cdot1$, $b = 9\cdot7$ 6. $a = 0\cdot02$, $b = 0\cdot0021$
7. $a = 1\cdot8$, $b = 0\cdot56$ 8. $a = 0\cdot003$, $b = 0\cdot15$ 9. $a = 0\cdot01$, $b = 0\cdot005$
10. $a = 20$, $b = 1\cdot5$ 11. $A = 15$, $B = 50$ 12. $n = 1\cdot5$, $a = 5\cdot8$

Examples 18

1. $a = 1\cdot26$, $n = 4$ 2. $a = 275\cdot4$, $K = -2\cdot96$ 3. $a = 269$, $b = -2$
4. $a = 0\cdot341$, $K = 0\cdot5$ 5. $K = 5\cdot62 \times 10^{-6}$, $n = 2\cdot98$
6. $n = 1\cdot43$, $c = 330$ 7. $a = 6\cdot14$, $n = 0\cdot47$ 8. $a = 402$, $n = 0\cdot31$
9. $A = 125$, $K = 0\cdot06$, $125°C$ 10. $a = 2\cdot7$, $n = 2$ 11. $a = 5\cdot35$, $b = 0\cdot285$
12. $a = 4\cdot77$, $K = 0\cdot02$, $9\cdot605$ millions

Examples 19

1. Area = $114\cdot8$ sq. units; $\bar{y} = 6\cdot659$; Vol: = 4804 cu. units
2. (i) $114\cdot65$ sq. units (ii) $114\cdot23$ sq. units
3. W. Done = 877 KJ Mean pressure = $175\cdot4$ KN/m²
4. Vol. = $63\cdot87$ cm³; Radius = $2\cdot016$ cm   5. $1\cdot283$ N
6. 395 coulombs; $3\cdot95$ amp; R.M.S. current = $4\cdot23$ amp
7. (i) $126\cdot6$ m (ii) $127\cdot6$ m; $15\cdot95$ m/s; $57\cdot4$ Km/h   8. $3\cdot18$
9. $32\cdot2$ sq. units; $8\cdot05$ units; 1006 cu. units   10. $11\cdot27$ N m
11. 192 Km/h; $2\cdot662$ m/s²   12. $655\cdot1$ N; 2843 cm²

Examples 20

1. 4th order differences zero   2. $y = 3x^2 + 4x - 7$
3. $f(0\cdot267) = 3\cdot78864$ 4. $\tan 20°33' = 0\cdot3749$ 5. $\sqrt{2\cdot55} = 1\cdot5970$
6. $s = 0\cdot1t^2 + 0\cdot25t + 1\cdot75$
7. 3rd order differences small (irregular). Approx. quadratic polynomial
8. $y = x^3 + x^2 - x + 2$ 9. $1\cdot16648$ 10. $\theta = 2t^2 - 5t + 4$

Examples 21

1. 0·5530(3)   2. 73·36   3. 29
4. $x^3 + 3x^2\delta x + 3x(\delta x)^2 + (\delta x)^3$; $3x^2 + 3x\delta x + (\delta x)^2$; 51·69
5. 0·140, 0·132, 0·124, 0·117, 0·111
6. −25, −8·34, −4·16, −2·5
7. 1·825, 2·230, 2·720, 3·325, 4·065; (1·822, 2·226, 2·718, 3·320, 4·055)
8. −0·523, −0·605, −0·681; equal to 3 sig. figs.
9. 2·475, 1·025, 0·785, 0·665, 0·585 m/s
10. $10x + 6 + 5\delta x$; $10x + 6$ (limit)

Examples 22

1. 3, 5, 7, 9, 11, 13, 15, 17, 19   2. 0·61, 0·75, 0·91, 1·11
3. (i) 8·15 (ii) 59·1   4. 1·45, 0·87, 0·62, 0·48
5. $v = 20·5, 15, 9, 5, 3·5, 3·0$ m/s
   $f = 5·60, 4·50, 2·60, 1·25, 0·65, 0·35$ m/s² [decelerations]
6. 6·82, 5·71, 4·95, 4·25 deg C/min
7. −5, −1·25, −0·56, −0·31
8. 13·69,   8·19,   3·28,   −1·62,   −6·52 m/s,   (i) 16·51 m   (ii) acceleration = −9·81 m/s² (constant)

Examples 23

1. y(min) $= 1$, $x = 2$.   2. y(max) $= +10$, $x = −1$; y(min) $= −22$, $x = 3$
3. $10x + 3$ 4. $−3/x^2$ 5. $6x − 2/x^3$
6. (i) $4x^3$, (ii) $\dfrac{1}{2\sqrt{x}}$, (iii) $−4/x^5$, (iv) $12x^3 − 9x^2 + 14x + 4$
7. (i) $12t^2$, (ii) $\frac{4}{3}x^{1/3}$, (iii) $3\theta^2 + 8\theta − 3$, (iv) $4u^3 − 4/u^5$
8. $x = 4$ or $−3$; $y = −203, 140$ 9. $y = 4x + 2$
10. $v = \mathrm{d}s/\mathrm{d}t = 3t^2 + 6t − 4$; $f = \mathrm{d}v/\mathrm{d}t = 6t + 6$
11. $t = 2·548$ sec; max. ht. $= 31·85$ metres
12. $y = 36x − 117$; stationary values: $−279(x = −4)$; $−53\frac{3}{4}(x = 1\frac{1}{2})$

Examples 24

1. (i) $20x^3$, (ii) $−24/x^4$, (iii) $3/2\sqrt{t}$, (iv) $1/3x^{2/3}$, (v) $2\theta + 3$
2. $8x + 4$; $4x^3 − 4x$; $2t + 1$; $9\theta^2 + 4\theta$
3. $21x^2, 42x$; $4t^3 − 4t, 12t^2 − 4$; $20\theta − 5, 20$ 4. $\frac{3}{2}\sqrt{x} − 4/x^3 + 5$
5. $12t^3 + 12t, 36t^2 + 12$ 6. $x = 0·2, 10$ 7. 10·8 m/s; 1 m/s²
8. 57 rad/s; 12 rad/s²
9. (i) −18 cm/s, 6 cm/s², (ii) $t = \frac{1}{2}$ or 3, (iii) −30 cm/s², + 30 cm/s², (iv) 1·75 seconds
10. $−1(x = 1)$, Minimum   11. $+8(x = 1)$ Maximum
12. (i) Neg. (ii) pos., $x = 0·75$ 13. Min. −264, Max. 79
14. Min. + 4, Max. − 4   15. Square of side 10 cm
16. Max. vol. when $x = 3·92$ cm

Examples 25

1. $12x^2(x^3 + 1)^3$ 2. $-30x/(x^2 - 1)^4$ 3. $t/\sqrt{(t^2 + 1)}$ 4. $5e^{5x}$

5. $-0.5e^{-0.5t}$ 6. $8x/(x^2 + 4)$ 7. $x/\sqrt{(x^2 - 1)} = 1.809$

8. $-3t^2/2(t^3 - 1)^{3/2} = -0.3241$ 9. $4e^{4x} = 5.967$

10. (i) $5\cos 5x$ (ii) $\dfrac{\pi}{36}\cos 5x$

11. (i) $(2x + 3)/2\sqrt{(x^2 + 3x)}$, (ii) $3e^{3t}$ (iii) $20x/(x^2 + 4)$

12. $-5/(t + 1)^2$; $10/(t + 1)^3$ 13. $x = 3$

14. (i) $3/(3x - 1) - 2e^{-2x}$ (ii) $2(\cos 2\theta - 3\sin 2\theta)$ (iii) $6(2t + 1)^2 + 1/t$
    (iv) $2x/(3x^2 + 1)^{2/3}$

16. $-KAe^{-Kt}$ 17. $50\pi \cos 100\pi t$

18. $t = 0.0625$; max. $s = 3\sqrt{10} = 9.486$

19. $x = 0.458(1)$; Min. $y = 0.2095$

20. $1.09, 0.434, 0.217$

Examples 26

1. $y = x^2 + 3x - 4$ 2. $v = 32t - 3t^2 + 20$

3. $y = x^3 + x^2 - x + 2$ 4. $y = \frac{1}{2}(x^2 + 2\log x + 7)$

5. $\frac{1}{4}x^4 + \frac{2}{3}x^3 - \frac{1}{2}x^2 + x + C$ 6. (i) $6\sqrt{x} + C$ (ii) $\frac{2}{5}x^{5/2} + C$

7. $12\frac{2}{3}$ 8. 250 9. $s = 45t - 6t^2$; 81 metres   10. $41\frac{1}{3}$ 11. 52

12. 0.293 13. $66\frac{2}{3}$ 14. 20 sq. units   15. 56.7

Revision Examples

Examples 27.1

1. 4.398 2. -13.04 3. $a = 88.59, n = -3.273$

4. $a = 4.468, k = 1.032$ 5. 2.473 6. $\dfrac{1}{a}\log_e\left(\dfrac{Q}{Q - P}\right)$

7. (i) $(65 - 14\sqrt{35})/155$ (ii) $x = 1$ (iii) $-0.375 \pm 0.331j$

8. $x = 4, y = -3\frac{1}{2}, z = 2\frac{1}{2}$ 9. (i) $171,370$; 48630 (ii) $p = \pm 1, \pm 7/\sqrt{13}$
    $q = \pm 2, \pm 2/\sqrt{13}$

10. (i) $\dfrac{26}{7(x - 3)} - \dfrac{17}{7(2x + 1)}$ (ii) $\dfrac{4}{x - 1} - \dfrac{2}{(x - 1)^2} - \dfrac{4x + 1}{x^2 + 1}$

Examples 27.2

1. $a = 15.1, d = 0.72$; $T_{30} = 20.88$; $S_{25} = 593.5$

2. (i) $\pm 60, +90, \pm 135$; (ii) 250; 0.8% (low)

3. (i) $243x^5 + 405x^4y + 270x^3y^2 + 90x^2y^3 + 15xy^4 + y^5$
    (ii) $1 + 6x + 27x^2 + 108x^3 + 405x^4$ (iii) 0.735

4. 0.5% (decrease)   5. $82°25', 123°24', 262°25', 300°24'$

6. $A = 86°25', B = 41°41', C = 51°54'$, Area 39.68 cm²; $R = 6.163$ cm

7. Angle BAC $= 62°53'$, CAD $= 75°50'$; BD $= 19.68$ cm

8. $R = 64°43'$ or $115°17'$; $Q = 64°50'$ or $14°16'$; $q = 9.508$ or 2.589 cm

9. Proof   10. Area $= 9.255$ m²; $\sin X = 0.6413$; $R = 4.287$ m

Examples 27.3

1. $14\cdot57 \sin(\theta + 40°5')$ 2. $-0\cdot862$, $-0\cdot969$, $1\cdot70$ 3. $0\cdot9063$
4. $8\cdot602 \cos(x + 35°32')$; $25°15'$, $263°41'$
5. (i) $51°41'$, $109°53'$, $231°41'$, $289°53'$ (ii) $140°11'$, $219°49'$
6. (i) $2 \sin \frac{5}{2}\theta \cos \frac{3}{2}\theta$ (ii) $2 \sin 50° \sin 20°$ (iii) $\cos 8x + \cos 2x$ (iv) $2 \sin 2x \cos x$; $0°$, $90°$, $180°$, $270°$, $360°$
7. $r^2(\theta - \frac{1}{2}\sin 2\theta)$; $r = 9\cdot022$ cm   8. (i) $210\cdot5$ cm² (ii) $132\cdot7$ N
9. $1\cdot809$ cm; $3\cdot618$ cm; Pyr. $184\cdot4$ cm²; Frust. $158\cdot3$ cm²; Ratio $1\cdot165$ to 1
10. Areas 16π, $30\cdot25\pi$, 49π cm²; Vol. 620π cm³

Examples 27.4

1. $-1\cdot9$, $-0\cdot6$, $2\cdot55$; $-0\cdot655$ 2. $2\cdot376$ 3. $y = 1\cdot3/x + 2\cdot8$
4. $i = 0\cdot015v + 0\cdot002v^2$ 5. $a = 6\cdot5$, $n = 2\cdot3$ 6. $A = 200$, $K = -0\cdot03$
7. Mean $= 9\cdot8$; R.M.S $= 10\cdot7$ 8. y mean $= 6$, y (R.M.S) $= 6\cdot57(3)$
9. $x^3 + 6x^2 - 7x + 5$ 10. (i) $0\cdot7883$ (ii) $5\cdot975$, $5\cdot979$,
         (iii) $0\cdot5030$, $0\cdot5075$, $0\cdot5112(5)$

Examples 27.5

1. $5\cdot2$, $5\cdot6$, $6\cdot0$, $6\cdot4$, $6\cdot8$ 2. $1\cdot380$, $1\cdot578$, $1\cdot874$, $2\cdot307$, $2\cdot975$
3. $-0\cdot481$, $-0\cdot224$, $-0\cdot135$ 4. Acc $3\cdot33$ m/s²; vel. $408\cdot3$ Km/h
5. y (Min.) $6\cdot89$ $(x = 0\cdot22)$; y (Max.) $9\cdot63$ $(x = -1\cdot55)$
6. $6x - 4/x^2$ 7. (i) $\frac{5}{2}x^{3/2}$ (ii) $15t^2 + 6t$ (iii) $4(2x + 3)$ (iv) $2e^{2t}$
         (v) $2x + 3\sqrt{x} + 1$ (vi) $5/x + 3e^x + 5x^4$ (vii) $-20/x^5$
8. (i) $3x^2/2\sqrt{(x^3 - 1)}$ (ii) $-15(2t + 1)/(t^2 + 1)^4$ (iii) $(6x + 2)/(3x^2 + 2x + 1)$

    (iv) $50e^{5t}$ (v) $15 \cos 3x$ (vi) $-48 \sin 4x$ (vii) $14/x$ (viii) $\dfrac{\pi}{12} \cos 5x°$

    (ix) $-\dfrac{\pi}{30} \sin(\frac{1}{2}x°)$

9. $400 - 9\cdot81t$ m/s; $-9\cdot81$ m/s²; $154\cdot75$ m/s; $-90\cdot5$ m/s; $40\cdot78$ s; 8256 m
10. $x = 4$, $y = -65$(min); $x = -2$, $y = 43$(max)
11. $y = 5x - 10$; $y = x - 6$ 12. $y = \frac{1}{3}x^3 + 1/x + x + 1\frac{2}{3}$
13. (i) $2\frac{2}{3}$ (ii) 60 (iii) 15 14. (i) $31\cdot95$ (ii) $4\cdot055$ (iii) $0\cdot866$ (iv) 10
15. (i) $66\cdot75$ sq. units; (ii) $6\cdot438$ sq. units

Answers to Specimen papers (APPENDIX A).

Paper I

1. (i) $0\cdot1326$ (ii) $-1\cdot277$ (iii) $7,122$ 2. (i) $n = 0\cdot486$, $K = 0\cdot526$
    (ii) $78°28'$, $120°$, $240°$, $281°32'$
3. (i) $\dfrac{3}{2x + 1} - \dfrac{1}{x - 2}$ (ii) $1 + \frac{3}{2}x - \frac{9}{8}x^2 + \frac{27}{16}x^3$; $1\cdot015$
4. (i) $12\cdot32$ (13) years (ii) $2300\cdot5$ metres

5. (i) 14·94 sin $(\theta + 36°40')$ (ii) 87°4', 346°40'
6. (i) 468·1 m^3 (ii) 81·14, 162·28 mm   7. 17·41; 64·27 cm^2
8. Cubic polynomial; Area 47·64 cm^2; mean y 3·97 cm; vol. 1173 cm^3
9. (ii) $15x^2 + 8x - 7$; $30x + 8$ (iii) 10

Paper II

1. (i) $C = 4744$ (ii) 1·176 (iii) $-0·5 \pm 0·387j$ 2. (i) $a = 0·15$, $b = -0·35$,
   $c = 0·45$ (ii) $t = \dfrac{1}{K} \log_e [(Ku - g)/(Kv - g)]$

3. (i) $\dfrac{1}{9(x - 2)} + \dfrac{11}{3(x + 1)^2} - \dfrac{1}{9(x + 1)}$ (ii) (a) 532·5 (b) 25

4. (i) $64x^6 - 192x^5y + 240x^4y^2 - 160x^3y^3 + 60x^2y^4 - 12xy^5 + y^6$
   (ii) m decreases by 2%

5. (i) Bookwork; 0·96, 0·28; 3·4286 (ii) 43°48', 270°58'
6. $m = 3·24$, $c = 0·472$ 7. (i) 168°7' (ii) 127·9 cm^2
8. (i) $45x(x^2 + 1)^{1/2}$ (ii) $3t^2 - 12t + 9$; $6t - 12$; 1 and 3 secs; 7 m, 11 m
9. (i) (a) $y = x^3 - x^2 + x + 4$ (b) $12\frac{2}{3}$ (ii) 42 Kg

Appendix A

General Instructions
Attempt SIX questions only.
All questions carry equal marks.

1. (i) Use logarithms to evaluate $(0\cdot876)^{1\cdot4} \times (13\cdot76)^{-0\cdot7}$.
    (ii) Solve the equation $5^{2x+1} = 3^{x-1}$.
    (iii) Find the value of $W = p_1 v_1 \log_e (v_2/v_1)$ when $p_1 = 2,880$, $v_1 = 1\cdot5$, $v_2 = 7\cdot8$.

2. (i) The frictional resistance P in KN/m^2 in a bearing running at v m/min is proportional to v^n, i.e. $P = Kv^n$ (K a constant). If $P = 2\cdot835$ when $v = 32$ and $P = 5\cdot075$ when $v = 106$, determine possible values of K and n.
    (ii) State the expansion for $\cos 2\theta$ in terms of $\cos \theta$. Hence solve the equation $5 \cos 2\theta + 3 \cos \theta + 4 = 0$ for θ between $0°$ and $360°$.

3. (i) Factorize the function $2x^2 - 3x - 2$. Hence express $\dfrac{x - 7}{2x^2 - 3x - 2}$ in partial fractions.
    (ii) Write down the binomial expansion of $(1 + 3x)^{1/2}$ as far as the term in x^3. Using a suitable value of x, find the value of $\sqrt{(1\cdot03)}$ correct to 3 places of decimals.

4. (i) The capital value of a machine tool is £5500. If depreciation is allowed at the rate of 10% per annum, find how long (to the nearest year) it will take for the capital value to depreciate to £1500.
    (ii) The distance fallen by a body during each second increases by a constant amount. If the body falls $110\cdot12$ m during the tenth second and $149\cdot36$ m during the fourteenth second, find the total distance fallen in 20 seconds.

5. (i) By expansion express $5 \sin (\theta + 30°) + 10 \cos (\theta - 50°)$ in the form $R \sin (\theta + \alpha)$.
    (ii) Using a suitable method, find the solutions of the equation $3 \sin \theta + 4 \cos \theta = 3\cdot2$ for values of θ between $0°$ and $360°$.

6. (i) The cross-section of a channel is a minor segment of a circle. The width of the channel is 600 mm and its maximum depth is 200 mm. If the channel runs full, find the volume of water carried past a section in 30 minutes, if the velocity of flow is 3 metres/s.

(ii) A metal sphere of radius 120 mm is melted down and recast in the form of a frustum of a cone. The height of the frustum is 150 mm and the end radii are in the ratio of 2 to 1. Find the radii of the ends of the frustum.

7. A triangle marked on a metal plate has sides of 50 mm, 70 mm and 90 mm. Calculate the area of the triangle. If a circle is drawn on the plate to circumscribe the triangle, calculate the area of the circle.

8. Corresponding ordinates y cm for steps of 2 cm in x are read off from a graph as follows:

x	0	2	4	6	8	10	12
y	0·07	0·33	1·07	2·53	4·95	8·57	13·63

Tabulate the finite differences for y up to the fourth order. What form of function would y be in terms of x?

Use Simpson's rule to obtain the area under the graph, and estimate the mean value of y. If the area were rotated through $360°$ about the x-axis, what would be the approximate volume swept out? ($\bar{y} = 3·918$ cm.)

9. (i) Show, from first principles, that the derivative of y with respect to x, when $y = x^2 + 3x - 4$, is $2x + 3$.

(ii) Write down the first and second derivatives of the function

$$y = 5x^3 + 4x^2 - 7x + 5.$$

(iii) Evaluate $\int_1^3 (2x + 1)\, dx$.

Paper II

General Instructions   Time Allowed: $2\frac{1}{2}$ hours
Attempt SIX questions only.
All questions carry equal marks.

1. (i) Using logarithms, find the value of c if $c = pv^n$ when $p = 2,156$, $v = 1·75$, $n = 1·41$.

(ii) Solve the equation $5^{2x-1} = e^{x+1}$ ($e = 2·718$).

(iii) Obtain the solutions of the equation

$$\frac{2m + 1}{m + 1} = \frac{m - 1}{3m + 1} \text{ in the form } a + b\text{j} \quad (\text{j} = \sqrt{-1}).$$

2. (i) Solve the simultaneous equations

$$3a + 4b - 2c = -1·85; \quad 5a + 2b + 3c = 1·40; \quad 4a - 3b + c = 2·10.$$

(ii) The equation connecting the initial velocity u m/s with the velocity v m/s at time t seconds is

$$v = \frac{g}{K} - \left(\frac{g}{K} - u\right) e^{-Kt}$$

where g is the acceleration due to gravity and K is a constant. Transpose the formula to obtain t in terms of the other quantities.

3. (i) Express $\dfrac{4x - 7}{(x + 1)^2(x - 2)}$ in partial fractions.

(ii)(a) The fifth term of an arithmetic progression is 10·9, and the ninth term is 16·1. Find the sum of the first 25 terms of the progression.

   (b) The first term of a geometric progression is 15 and the second term is 6. Find the sum to infinity of the progression.

4. (i) Write down the full expansion of $(2x - y)^6$ in ascending powers of y.

  (ii) The ratio of loss of energy to input energy m when water is transmitted along a pipe is given by

$$m = \frac{BU^2L}{p^3r^5}$$

Using first-order binomial approximations, find the percentage change in m if U increases by 0·5%, L increases by 1%, p increases by 2% and r decreases by 0·4%.

5. (i) Write down the expansions of $\sin(A + B)$, $\cos(A + B)$. Deduce the expansions of $\sin 2\theta$ and $\cos 2\theta$, and hence obtain the expansion of $\tan 2\theta$ in terms of $\tan \theta$. If $\tan \theta = \frac{3}{4}(\theta$ acute), calculate, without using trigonometric tables, the numerical values of $\sin 2\theta$, $\cos 2\theta$, $\tan 2\theta$.

  (ii) Solve the equation $12 \cos \theta - 5 \sin \theta = 5.2$ for values of θ between 0° and 360°.

6. A steamship at a speed of V Km/h uses the following indicated power (KW) H. Show, by means of a suitable graph that the law connecting H and V is approximately of the form $H = cV^m$, and estimate possible values of c and m

V (Km/h)	10	12	14	16	18	20
H (KW)	820	1454	2424	3729	5518	7756

7. A framework of light rods ABCD, in the form of a plane quadrilateral, is kept rigid by a light rod BD.
If AB = 9 cm, BC = 14 cm, CD = 12 cm, DA = 11 cm, BD = 15 cm, calculate: (i) the sum of the angles BAD and BCD, (ii) the area of the quadrilateral ABCD.

8. (i) Using the 'function of a function' rule, obtain the derivative of y with respect to x when $y = 15(x^2 + 1)^{3/2}$.

  (ii) The distance s metres, travelled by a body in time t seconds, is given by $s = t^3 - 6t^2 + 9t + 7$.
Write down expressions for the velocity and acceleration. At what times is the velocity zero? Show that the distance is a maximum or minimum at these times, and calculate the maximum and minimum distances.

9. (i) (a) If $dy/dx = 3x^2 - 2x + 1$ and $y = 5$ when $x = 1$, express y in terms of x.

    (b) Evaluate $\int_4^9 \sqrt{x}\, dx$.

  (ii) A casting is in the form of a frustum of a cone of end radii 80 mm and 120 mm, and height 200 mm. A cylindrical hole of radius 40 mm runs through the frustum and its axis coincides with the axis of the frustum. If the metal density is 7830 Kg/m³, find the mass of the casting to the nearest Kilogramme.

Appendix B
Tables of Constants, Conversion Factors, and Formulae

Constants and Conversion Factors

$\pi = 3\frac{1}{7}$ (approx.); $\pi = 3\cdot1416$ or $3\cdot142$ to 4 sig. figs.

$\log_{10} \pi = 0\cdot4972$, $\sqrt{\pi} = 1\cdot773$, $\log_{10} \sqrt{\pi} = 0\cdot2486$

$e = 2\cdot718$, $\log_{10} e = 0\cdot4343$, $\log_e 10 = 2\cdot3026$ ($2\cdot303$)

$\pi/4 = 0\cdot7854$, $\log_{10} \pi/4 = \bar{1}\cdot8951$, $\log_{10} 1728 = 3\cdot2375$

$\log_b N = \log_a N/\log_a b$; $\log_a b = 1/\log_b a$

$\log_e N = 2\cdot303 \log_{10} N$; $\log_{10} N = 0\cdot4343 \log_e N$

$\log_a x^n = n \log_a x$; $\log_a \sqrt[n]{x} = \dfrac{1}{n} \log_a x$

1 in. $= 2\cdot54$ cm; 1 cm $= 0\cdot3937$ in., 1 metre $= 1\cdot094$ yd $= 3\cdot281$ ft

1 yd $= 0\cdot9144$ metre, 1 mile $= 1760$ yd $= 5280$ ft

1 mile $= 1\cdot609$ km, 5 miles (approx.) $= 8$ km

1 litre $= 1000$ cm³, 1 kg $= 2\frac{1}{5}$ lb

1 nautical mile $= 6080$ feet

π radians $= 180°$; 1 radian $= 57\cdot3°$

$\pi/6 = 30°$, $\pi/4 = 45°$, $\pi/3 = 60°$, $\pi/2 = 90°$

1 ft³ of fresh water weighs $62\cdot3$ lbf

1 ft³ of sea water weighs $62\cdot5$ lbf

Densities in Kg/m³ (mass)

Cast iron 7200, Wrought iron 7690, Steel 7830, Aluminium 2700
Brass 8570, Copper 8940, Lead 11 300, Tin 7450, Zinc 7190 Water 1001

Useful Formulae

Triangle area $\triangle = \frac{1}{2}bh = \frac{1}{2}bc \sin A = \sqrt{[s(s-a)(s-b)(s-c)]}$
Trapezium area $= \frac{1}{2}h$(sum of parallel sides)
Circle: Area $= \pi r^2 = \frac{1}{4}\pi d^2$; Circumference $= 2\pi r = \pi d$
Sector of circle (angle θ radians); Arc $= s = r\theta$; Area $= \frac{1}{2}r^2\theta$
Segment of circle (minor) Area $= \frac{1}{2}r^2(\theta - \sin \theta)$
Sine rule $a/\sin A = b/\sin B = c/\sin C$
Cosine rule $a^2 = b^2 + c^2 - 2bc \cos A$; Circumradius $R = a/(2 \sin A)$
Volumes: Cylinder $\pi r^2 h$; Cone $\frac{1}{3}\pi r^2 h$, Sphere $\frac{4}{3}\pi R^3$, Frustum of cone
     $\frac{1}{3}\pi h(r^2 + Rr + R^2)$, Cap (sphere) $\frac{1}{3}\pi h^2(3R - h)$
Surface areas: Cylinder (curved) $2\pi rh$; Cone (curved) πrl, Frustum of cone
    $\pi l(r + R)$; Zone (of sphere) $2\pi Rh$
Simpson's Rule: Area $= \frac{1}{3}h$[First + Last + 4(evens) + 2(odds)]
Binomial expansion:

$$(1 + x)^n = 1 + nx + \frac{n(n-1)}{1 \times 2} x^2 + \frac{n(n-1)(n-2)}{1 \times 2 \times 3} x^3 + \ldots$$

First order approximation $(1 + x)^n \simeq 1 + nx$
A.P:$T_n = a + (n-1)d$; $S_n = \frac{1}{2}n[2a + (n-1)d]$
G.P:$T_n = ar^{n-1}$; $S_n = \dfrac{a(1-r^n)}{1-r}$; $S_\infty = \dfrac{a}{1-r}$

$\dfrac{dy}{dx} = \lim_{\delta x \to 0}\left(\dfrac{\delta y}{\delta x}\right)$; $\dfrac{d}{dx}(x^n) = nx^{n-1}$; $\dfrac{d}{dx}(e^x) = e^x$; $\dfrac{d}{dx}(\log_e x) = \dfrac{1}{x}$

$\dfrac{d}{dx}(\sin x) = \cos x$; $\dfrac{d}{dx}(\cos x) = -\sin x$ (x in radians)

$\displaystyle\int x^n \, dx = \dfrac{x^{n+1}}{n+1}$; $\displaystyle\int \dfrac{1}{x} \, dx = \log_e x$; $\displaystyle\int e^x \, dx = e^x$; $\displaystyle\int \cos x \, dx = \sin x$;

$\displaystyle\int \sin x \, dx = -\cos x$; $\displaystyle\int_a^b f(x) \, dx = [F(x)]_a^b = F(b) - F(a)$

$$\text{Sin } (A + B) = \sin A \cos B + \cos A \sin B$$
$$\cos (A + B) = \cos A \cos B - \sin A \sin B$$
$$\sin 2\theta = 2 \sin \theta \cos \theta$$
$$\cos 2\theta = \cos^2 \theta - \sin^2 \theta = 2 \cos^2 \theta - 1$$
$$= 1 - 2 \sin^2 \theta$$
$$a \sin \theta + b \cos \theta = R \sin (\theta + \alpha)$$

where

$$R = \sqrt{(a^2 + b^2)},$$
$$\tan \alpha = b/a$$

Weight per unit volume (on earth)

These are given in KN/m³. Water 9·81 KN/m³
Other substances:—Weight per unit volume = Specific gravity × 9·81 KN/m³
e.g. Steel: weight per unit volume = 7·830 × 9·81 KN/m³ = 76·83 KN/m³.

Appendix C
Mathematical Tables

LOGARITHMS

	0	1	2	3	4	5	6	7	8	9	1	2	3	4	5	6	7	8	9
10	0000	0043	0086	0128	0170	0212	0253	0294	0334	0374	4	8	12	17	21	25	29	33	37
11	0414	0453	0492	0531	0569	0607	0645	0682	0719	0755	4	8	11	15	19	23	26	30	34
12	0792	0828	0864	0899	0934	0969	1004	1038	1072	1106	3	7	10	14	17	21	24	28	31
13	1139	1173	1206	1239	1271	1303	1335	1367	1399	1430	3	6	10	13	16	19	23	26	29
14	1461	1492	1523	1553	1584	1614	1644	1673	1703	1732	3	6	9	12	15	18	21	24	27
15	1761	1790	1818	1847	1875	1903	1931	1959	1987	2014	3	6	8	11	14	17	20	22	25
16	2041	2068	2095	2122	2148	2175	2201	2227	2253	2279	3	5	8	11	13	16	18	21	24
17	2304	2330	2355	2380	2405	2430	2455	2480	2504	2529	2	5	7	10	12	15	17	20	22
18	2553	2577	2601	2625	2648	2672	2695	2718	2742	2765	2	5	7	9	12	14	16	19	21
19	2788	2810	2833	2856	2878	2900	2923	2945	2967	2989	2	4	7	9	11	13	16	18	20
20	3010	3032	3054	3075	3096	3118	3139	3160	3181	3201	2	4	6	8	11	13	15	17	19
21	3222	3243	3263	3284	3304	3324	3345	3365	3385	3404	2	4	6	8	10	12	14	16	18
22	3424	3444	3464	3483	3502	3522	3541	3560	3579	3598	2	4	6	8	10	12	14	15	17
23	3617	3636	3655	3674	3692	3711	3729	3747	3766	3784	2	4	6	7	9	11	13	15	17
24	3802	3820	3838	3856	3874	3892	3909	3927	3945	3962	2	4	5	7	9	11	12	14	16
25	3979	3997	4014	4031	4048	4065	4082	4099	4116	4133	2	3	5	7	9	10	12	14	15
26	4150	4166	4183	4200	4216	4232	4249	4265	4281	4298	2	3	5	7	8	10	11	13	15
27	4314	4330	4346	4362	4378	4393	4409	4425	4440	4456	2	3	5	6	8	9	11	13	14
28	4472	4487	4502	4518	4533	4548	4564	4579	4594	4609	2	3	5	6	8	9	11	12	14
29	4624	4639	4654	4669	4683	4698	4713	4728	4742	4757	1	3	4	6	7	9	10	12	13
30	4771	4786	4800	4814	4829	4843	4857	4871	4886	4900	1	3	4	6	7	9	10	11	13
31	4914	4928	4942	4955	4969	4983	4997	5011	5024	5038	1	3	4	6	7	8	10	11	12
32	5051	5065	5079	5092	5105	5119	5132	5145	5159	5172	1	3	4	5	7	8	9	11	12
33	5185	5198	5211	5224	5237	5250	5263	5276	5289	5302	1	3	4	5	6	8	9	10	12
34	5315	5328	5340	5353	5366	5378	5391	5403	5416	5428	1	3	4	5	6	8	9	10	11
35	5441	5453	5465	5478	5490	5502	5514	5527	5539	5551	1	2	4	5	6	7	9	10	11
36	5563	5575	5587	5599	5611	5623	5635	5647	5658	5670	1	2	4	5	6	7	8	10	11
37	5682	5694	5705	5717	5729	5740	5752	5763	5775	5786	1	2	3	5	6	7	8	9	10
38	5798	5809	5821	5832	5843	5855	5866	5877	5888	5899	1	2	3	5	6	7	8	9	10
39	5911	5922	5933	5944	5955	5966	5977	5988	5999	6010	1	2	3	4	5	7	8	9	10
40	6021	6031	6042	6053	6064	6075	6085	6096	6107	6117	1	2	3	4	5	6	8	9	10
41	6128	6138	6149	6160	6170	6180	6191	6201	6212	6222	1	2	3	4	5	6	7	8	9
42	6232	6243	6253	6263	6274	6284	6294	6304	6314	6325	1	2	3	4	5	6	7	8	9
43	6335	6345	6355	6365	6375	6385	6395	6405	6415	6425	1	2	3	4	5	6	7	8	9
44	6435	6444	6454	6464	6474	6484	6493	6503	6513	6522	1	2	3	4	5	6	7	8	9
45	6532	6542	6551	6561	6571	6580	6590	6599	6609	6618	1	2	3	4	5	6	7	8	9
46	6628	6637	6646	6656	6665	6675	6684	6693	6702	6712	1	2	3	4	5	6	7	7	8
47	6721	6730	6739	6749	6758	6767	6776	6785	6794	6803	1	2	3	4	5	5	6	7	8
48	6812	6821	6830	6839	6848	6857	6866	6875	6884	6893	1	2	3	4	4	5	6	7	8
49	6902	6911	6920	6928	6937	6946	6955	6964	6972	6981	1	2	3	4	4	5	6	7	8
50	6990	6998	7007	7016	7024	7033	7042	7050	7059	7067	1	2	3	3	4	5	6	7	8
51	7076	7084	7093	7101	7110	7118	7126	7135	7143	7152	1	2	3	3	4	5	6	7	8
52	7160	7168	7177	7185	7193	7202	7210	7218	7226	7235	1	2	2	3	4	5	6	7	7
53	7243	7251	7259	7267	7275	7284	7292	7300	7308	7316	1	2	2	3	4	5	6	6	7
54	7324	7332	7340	7348	7356	7364	7372	7380	7388	7396	1	2	2	3	4	5	6	6	7
	0	1	2	3	4	5	6	7	8	9	1	2	3	4	5	6	7	8	9

LOGARITHMS

	0	1	2	3	4	5	6	7	8	9	1	2	3	4	5	6	7	8	9
55	7404	7412	7419	7427	7435	7443	7451	7459	7466	7474	1	2	2	3	4	5	5	6	7
56	7482	7490	7497	7505	7513	7520	7528	7536	7543	7551	1	2	2	3	4	5	5	6	7
57	7559	7566	7574	7582	7589	7597	7604	7612	7619	7627	1	2	2	3	4	5	5	6	7
58	7634	7642	7649	7657	7664	7672	7679	7686	7694	7701	1	1	2	3	4	4	5	6	7
59	7709	7716	7723	7731	7738	7745	7752	7760	7767	7774	1	1	2	3	4	4	5	6	7
60	7782	7789	7796	7803	7810	7818	7825	7832	7839	7846	1	1	2	3	4	4	5	6	6
61	7853	7860	7868	7875	7882	7889	7896	7903	7910	7917	1	1	2	3	4	4	5	6	6
62	7924	7931	7938	7945	7952	7959	7966	7973	7980	7987	1	1	2	3	3	4	5	6	6
63	7993	8000	8007	8014	8021	8028	8035	8041	8048	8055	1	1	2	3	3	4	5	5	6
64	8062	8069	8075	8082	8089	8096	8102	8109	8116	8122	1	1	2	3	3	4	5	5	6
65	8129	8136	8142	8149	8156	8162	8169	8176	8182	8189	1	1	2	3	3	4	5	5	6
66	8195	8202	8209	8215	8222	8228	8235	8241	8248	8254	1	1	2	3	3	4	5	5	6
67	8261	8267	8274	8280	8287	8293	8299	8306	8312	8319	1	1	2	3	3	4	5	5	6
68	8325	8331	8338	8344	8351	8357	8363	8370	8376	8382	1	1	2	3	3	4	4	5	6
69	8388	8395	8401	8407	8414	8420	8426	8432	8439	8445	1	1	2	2	3	4	4	5	6
70	8451	8457	8463	8470	8476	8482	8488	8494	8500	8506	1	1	2	2	3	4	4	5	6
71	8513	8519	8525	8531	8537	8543	8549	8555	8561	8567	1	1	2	2	3	4	4	5	5
72	8573	8579	8585	8591	8597	8603	8609	8615	8621	8627	1	1	2	2	3	4	4	5	5
73	8633	8639	8645	8651	8657	8663	8669	8675	8681	8686	1	1	2	2	3	4	4	5	5
74	8692	8698	8704	8710	8716	8722	8727	8733	8739	8745	1	1	2	2	3	4	4	5	5
75	8751	8756	8762	8768	8774	8779	8785	8791	8797	8802	1	1	2	2	3	3	4	5	5
76	8808	8814	8820	8825	8831	8837	8842	8848	8854	8859	1	1	2	2	3	3	4	5	5
77	8865	8871	8876	8882	8887	8893	8899	8904	8910	8915	1	1	2	2	3	3	4	4	5
78	8921	8927	8932	8938	8943	8949	8954	8960	8965	8971	1	1	2	2	3	3	4	4	5
79	8976	8982	8987	8993	8998	9004	9009	9015	9020	9025	1	1	2	2	3	3	4	4	5
80	9031	9036	9042	9047	9053	9058	9063	9069	9074	9079	1	1	2	2	3	3	4	4	5
81	9085	9090	9096	9101	9106	9112	9117	9122	9128	9133	1	1	2	2	3	3	4	4	5
82	9138	9143	9149	9154	9159	9165	9170	9175	9180	9186	1	1	2	2	3	3	4	4	5
83	9191	9196	9201	9206	9212	9217	9222	9227	9232	9238	1	1	2	2	3	3	4	4	5
84	9243	9248	9253	9258	9263	9269	9274	9279	9284	9289	1	1	2	2	3	3	4	4	5
85	9294	9299	9304	9309	9315	9320	9325	9330	9335	9340	1	1	2	2	3	3	4	4	5
86	9345	9350	9355	9360	9365	9370	9375	9380	9385	9390	1	1	2	2	3	3	4	4	5
87	9395	9400	9405	9410	9415	9420	9425	9430	9435	9440	0	1	1	2	2	3	3	4	4
88	9445	9450	9455	9460	9465	9469	9474	9479	9484	9489	0	1	1	2	2	3	3	4	4
89	9494	9499	9504	9509	9513	9518	9523	9528	9533	9538	0	1	1	2	2	3	3	4	4
90	9542	9547	9552	9557	9562	9566	9571	9576	9581	9586	0	1	1	2	2	3	3	4	4
91	9590	9595	9600	9605	9609	9614	9619	9624	9628	9633	0	1	1	2	2	3	3	4	4
92	9638	9643	9647	9652	9657	9661	9666	9671	9675	9680	0	1	1	2	2	3	3	4	4
93	9685	9689	9694	9699	9703	9708	9713	9717	9722	9727	0	1	1	2	2	3	3	4	4
94	9731	9736	9741	9745	9750	9754	9759	9763	9768	9773	0	1	1	2	2	3	3	4	4
95	9777	9782	9786	9791	9795	9800	9805	9809	9814	9818	0	1	1	2	2	3	3	4	4
96	9823	9827	9832	9836	9841	9845	9850	9854	9859	9863	0	1	1	2	2	3	3	4	4
97	9868	9872	9877	9881	9886	9890	9894	9899	9903	9908	0	1	1	2	2	3	3	4	4
98	9912	9917	9921	9926	9930	9934	9939	9943	9948	9952	0	1	1	2	2	3	3	4	4
99	9956	9961	9965	9969	9974	9978	9983	9987	9991	9996	0	1	1	2	2	3	3	3	4
	0	1	2	3	4	5	6	7	8	9	1	2	3	4	5	6	7	8	9

ANTILOGARITHMS

	0	1	2	3	4	5	6	7	8	9	1	2	3	4	5	6	7	8	9
·00	1000	1002	1005	1007	1009	1012	1014	1016	1019	1021	0	0	1	1	1	1	2	2	2
·01	1023	1026	1028	1030	1033	1035	1038	1040	1042	1045	0	0	1	1	1	1	2	2	2
·02	1047	1050	1052	1054	1057	1059	1062	1064	1067	1069	0	0	1	1	1	1	2	2	2
·03	1072	1074	1076	1079	1081	1084	1086	1089	1091	1094	0	0	1	1	1	1	2	2	2
·04	1096	1099	1102	1104	1107	1109	1112	1114	1117	1119	0	1	1	1	1	2	2	2	2
·05	1122	1125	1127	1130	1132	1135	1138	1140	1143	1146	0	1	1	1	1	2	2	2	2
·06	1148	1151	1153	1156	1159	1161	1164	1167	1169	1172	0	1	1	1	1	2	2	2	2
·07	1175	1178	1180	1183	1186	1189	1191	1194	1197	1199	0	1	1	1	1	2	2	2	2
·08	1202	1205	1208	1211	1213	1216	1219	1222	1225	1227	0	1	1	1	1	2	2	2	3
·09	1230	1233	1236	1239	1242	1245	1247	1250	1253	1256	0	1	1	1	1	2	2	2	3
·10	1259	1262	1265	1268	1271	1274	1276	1279	1282	1285	0	1	1	1	1	2	2	2	3
·11	1288	1291	1294	1297	1300	1303	1306	1309	1312	1315	0	1	1	1	2	2	2	2	3
·12	1318	1321	1324	1327	1330	1334	1337	1340	1343	1346	0	1	1	1	2	2	2	3	3
·13	1349	1352	1355	1358	1361	1365	1368	1371	1374	1377	0	1	1	1	2	2	2	3	3
·14	1380	1384	1387	1390	1393	1396	1400	1403	1406	1409	0	1	1	1	2	2	2	3	3
·15	1413	1416	1419	1422	1426	1429	1432	1435	1439	1442	0	1	1	1	2	2	2	3	3
·16	1445	1449	1452	1455	1459	1462	1466	1469	1472	1476	0	1	1	1	2	2	2	3	3
·17	1479	1483	1486	1489	1493	1496	1500	1503	1507	1510	0	1	1	1	2	2	2	3	3
·18	1514	1517	1521	1524	1528	1531	1535	1538	1542	1545	0	1	1	1	2	2	2	3	3
·19	1549	1552	1556	1560	1563	1567	1570	1574	1578	1581	0	1	1	1	2	2	3	3	3
·20	1585	1589	1592	1596	1600	1603	1607	1611	1614	1618	0	1	1	1	2	2	3	3	3
·21	1622	1626	1629	1633	1637	1641	1644	1648	1652	1656	0	1	1	2	2	2	3	3	3
·22	1660	1663	1667	1671	1675	1679	1683	1687	1690	1694	0	1	1	2	2	2	3	3	3
·23	1698	1702	1706	1710	1714	1718	1722	1726	1730	1734	0	1	1	2	2	2	3	3	4
·24	1738	1742	1746	1750	1754	1758	1762	1766	1770	1774	0	1	1	2	2	2	3	3	4
·25	1778	1782	1786	1791	1795	1799	1803	1807	1811	1816	0	1	1	2	2	2	3	3	4
·26	1820	1824	1828	1832	1837	1841	1845	1849	1854	1858	0	1	1	2	2	3	3	3	4
·27	1862	1866	1871	1875	1879	1884	1888	1892	1897	1901	0	1	1	2	2	3	3	3	4
·28	1905	1910	1914	1919	1923	1928	1932	1936	1941	1945	0	1	1	2	2	3	3	4	4
·29	1950	1954	1959	1963	1968	1972	1977	1982	1986	1991	0	1	1	2	2	3	3	4	4
·30	1995	2000	2004	2009	2014	2018	2023	2028	2032	2037	0	1	1	2	2	3	3	4	4
·31	2042	2046	2051	2056	2061	2065	2070	2075	2080	2084	0	1	1	2	2	3	3	4	4
·32	2089	2094	2099	2104	2109	2113	2118	2123	2128	2133	0	1	1	2	2	3	3	4	4
·33	2138	2143	2148	2153	2158	2163	2168	2173	2178	2183	0	1	1	2	2	3	3	4	4
·34	2188	2193	2198	2203	2208	2213	2218	2223	2228	2234	1	1	2	2	3	3	4	4	5
·35	2239	2244	2249	2254	2259	2265	2270	2275	2280	2286	1	1	2	2	3	3	4	4	5
·36	2291	2296	2301	2307	2312	2317	2323	2328	2333	2339	1	1	2	2	3	3	4	4	5
·37	2344	2350	2355	2360	2366	2371	2377	2382	2388	2393	1	1	2	2	3	3	4	4	5
·38	2399	2404	2410	2415	2421	2427	2432	2438	2443	2449	1	1	2	2	3	3	4	4	5
·39	2455	2460	2466	2472	2477	2483	2489	2495	2500	2506	1	1	2	2	3	3	4	5	5
·40	2512	2518	2523	2529	2535	2541	2547	2553	2559	2564	1	1	2	2	3	4	4	5	5
·41	2570	2576	2582	2588	2594	2600	2606	2612	2618	2624	1	1	2	2	3	4	4	5	5
·42	2630	2636	2642	2649	2655	2661	2667	2673	2679	2685	1	1	2	2	3	4	4	5	6
·43	2692	2698	2704	2710	2716	2723	2729	2735	2742	2748	1	1	2	3	3	4	4	5	6
·44	2754	2761	2767	2773	2780	2786	2793	2799	2805	2812	1	1	2	3	3	4	4	5	6
·45	2818	2825	2831	2838	2844	2851	2858	2864	2871	2877	1	1	2	3	3	4	5	5	6
·46	2884	2891	2897	2904	2911	2917	2924	2931	2938	2944	1	1	2	3	3	4	5	5	6
·47	2951	2958	2965	2972	2979	2985	2992	2999	3006	3013	1	1	2	3	3	4	5	5	6
·48	3020	3027	3034	3041	3048	3055	3062	3069	3076	3083	1	1	2	3	4	4	5	6	6
·49	3090	3097	3105	3112	3119	3126	3133	3141	3148	3155	1	1	2	3	4	4	5	6	6
	0	1	2	3	4	5	6	7	8	9	1	2	3	4	5	6	7	8	9

ANTILOGARITHMS

	0	1	2	3	4	5	6	7	8	9	1	2	3	4	5	6	7	8	9
·50	3162	3170	3177	3184	3192	3199	3206	3214	3221	3228	1	1	2	3	4	.4	5	6	7
·51	3236	3243	3251	3258	3266	3273	3281	3289	3296	3304	1	2	2	3	4	5	5	6	7
·52	3311	3319	3327	3334	3342	3350	3357	3365	3373	3381	1	2	2	3	4	5	5	6	7
·53	3388	3396	3404	3412	3420	3428	3436	3443	3451	3459	1	2	2	3	4	5	6	6	7
·54	3467	3475	3483	3491	3499	3508	3516	3524	3532	3540	1	2	2	3	4	5	6	6	7
·55	3548	3556	3565	3573	3581	3589	3597	3606	3614	3622	1	2	2	3	4	5	6	7	7
·56	3631	3639	3648	3656	3664	3673	3681	3690	3698	3707	1	2	3	3	4	5	6	7	8
·57	3715	3724	3733	3741	3750	3758	3767	3776	3784	3793	1	2	3	3	4	5	6	7	8
·58	3802	3811	3819	3828	3837	3846	3855	3864	3873	3882	1	2	3	4	4	5	6	7	8
·59	3890	3899	3908	3917	3926	3936	3945	3954	3963	3972	1	2	3	4	5	5	6	7	8
·60	3981	3990	3999	4009	4018	4027	4036	4046	4055	4064	1	2	3	4	5	6	6	7	8
·61	4074	4083	4093	4102	4111	4121	4130	4140	4150	4159	1	2	3	4	5	6	7	8	9
·62	4169	4178	4188	4198	4207	4217	4227	4236	4246	4256	1	2	3	4	5	6	7	8	9
·63	4266	4276	4285	4295	4305	4315	4325	4335	4345	4355	1	2	3	4	5	6	7	8	9
·64	4365	4375	4385	4395	4406	4416	4426	4436	4446	4457	1	2	3	4	5	6	7	8	9
·65	4467	4477	4487	4498	4508	4519	4529	4539	4550	4560	1	2	3	4	5	6	7	8	9
·66	4571	4581	4592	4603	4613	4624	4634	4645	4656	4667	1	2	3	4	5	6	7	9	10
·67	4677	4688	4699	4710	4721	4732	4742	4753	4764	4775	1	2	3	4	5	7	8	9	10
·68	4786	4797	4808	4819	4831	4842	4853	4864	4875	4887	1	2	3	4	6	7	8	9	10
·69	4898	4909	4920	4932	4943	4955	4966	4977	4989	5000	1	2	3	5	6	7	8	9	10
·70	5012	5023	5035	5047	5058	5070	5082	5093	5105	5117	1	2	4	5	6	7	8	9	11
·71	5129	5140	5152	5164	5176	5188	5200	5212	5224	5236	1	2	4	5	6	7	8	10	11
·72	5248	5260	5272	5284	5297	5309	5321	5333	5346	5358	1	2	4	5	6	7	9	10	11
·73	5370	5383	5395	5408	5420	5433	5445	5458	5470	5483	1	3	4	‎	6	8	9	10	11
·74	5495	5508	5521	5534	5546	5559	5572	5585	5598	5610	1	3	4	5	6	8	9	10	12
·75	5623	5636	5649	5662	5675	5689	5702	5715	5728	5741	1	3	4	5	7	8	9	10	12
·76	5754	5768	5781	5794	5808	5821	5834	5848	5861	5875	1	3	4	5	7	8	9	11	12
·77	5888	5902	5916	5929	5943	5957	5970	5984	5998	6012	1	3	4	5	7	8	10	11	12
·78	6026	6039	6053	6067	6081	6095	6109	6124	6138	6152	1	3	4	6	7	8	10	11	13
·79	6166	6180	6194	6209	6223	6237	6252	6266	6281	6295	1	3	4	6	7	9	10	11	13
·80	6310	6324	6339	6353	6368	6383	6397	6412	6427	6442	1	3	4	6	7	9	10	12	13
·81	6457	6471	6486	6501	6516	6531	6546	6561	6577	6592	2	3	5	6	8	9	11	12	14
·82	6607	6622	6637	6653	6668	6683	6699	6714	6730	6745	2	3	5	6	8	9	11	12	14
·83	6761	6776	6792	6808	6823	6839	6855	6871	6887	6902	2	3	5	6	8	9	11	13	14
·84	6918	6934	6950	6966	6982	6998	7015	7031	7047	7063	2	3	5	6	8	10	11	13	15
·85	7079	7096	7112	7129	7145	7161	7178	7194	7211	7228	2	3	5	7	8	10	12	13	15
·86	7244	7261	7278	7295	7311	7328	7345	7362	7379	7396	2	3	5	7	8	10	12	13	15
·87	7413	7430	7447	7464	7482	7499	7516	7534	7551	7568	2	3	5	7	9	10	12	14	16
·88	7586	7603	7621	7638	7656	7674	7691	7709	7727	7745	2	4	5	7	9	11	12	14	16
·89	7762	7780	7798	7816	7834	7852	7870	7889	7907	7925	2	4	5	7	9	11	13	14	16
·90	7943	7962	7980	7998	8017	8035	8054	8072	8091	8110	2	4	6	7	9	11	13	15	17
·91	8128	8147	8166	8185	8204	8222	8241	8260	8279	8299	2	4	6	8	9	11	13	15	17
·92	8318	8337	8356	8375	8395	8414	8433	8453	8472	8492	2	4	6	8	10	12	14	15	17
·93	8511	8531	8551	8570	8590	8610	8630	8650	8670	8690	2	4	6	8	10	12	14	16	18
·94	8710	8730	8750	8770	8790	8810	8831	8851	8872	8892	2	4	6	8	10	12	14	16	18
·95	8913	8933	8954	8974	8995	9016	9036	9057	9078	9099	2	4	6	8	10	12	15	17	19
·96	9120	9141	9162	9183	9204	9226	9247	9268	9290	9311	2	4	6	8	11	13	15	17	19
·97	9333	9354	9376	9397	9419	9441	9462	9484	9506	9528	2	4	7	9	11	13	15	17	20
·98	9550	9572	9594	9616	9638	9661	9683	9705	9727	9750	2	4	7	9	11	13	16	18	20
·99	9772	9795	9817	9840	9863	9886	9908	9931	9954	9977	2	5	7	9	11	14	16	18	20
	0	1	2	3	4	5	6	7	8	9	1	2	3	4	5	6	7	8	9

NATURAL SINES (left-hand column and top)

	0'	6'	12'	18'	24'	30'	36'	42'	48'	54'	—	1'	2'	3'	4'	5'	
0°	·0000	0017	0035	0052	0070	0087	0105	0122	0140	0157	·0175	3	6	9	12	15	89°
1	·0175	0192	0209	0227	0244	0262	0279	0297	0314	0332	·0349	3	6	9	12	15	88
2	·0349	0366	0384	0401	0419	0436	0454	0471	0488	0506	·0523	3	6	9	12	15	87
3	·0523	0541	0558	0576	0593	0610	0628	0645	0663	0680	·0698	3	6	9	12	15	86
4	·0698	0715	0732	0750	0767	0785	0802	0819	0837	0854	·0872	3	6	9	12	14	85
5	·0872	0889	0906	0924	0941	0958	0976	0993	1011	1028	·1045	3	6	9	12	14	84
6	·1045	1063	1080	1097	1115	1132	1149	1167	1184	1201	·1219	3	6	9	12	14	83
7	·1219	1236	1253	1271	1288	1305	1323	1340	1357	1374	·1392	3	6	9	12	14	82
8	·1392	1409	1426	1444	1461	1478	1495	1513	1530	1547	·1564	3	6	9	12	14	81
9	·1564	1582	1599	1616	1633	1650	1668	1685	1702	1719	·1736	3	6	9	11	14	80
10	·1736	1754	1771	1788	1805	1822	1840	1857	1874	1891	·1908	3	6	9	11	14	79
11	·1908	1925	1942	1959	1977	1994	2011	2028	2045	2062	·2079	3	6	9	11	14	78
12	·2079	2096	2113	2130	2147	2164	2181	2198	2215	2233	·2250	3	6	9	11	14	77
13	·2250	2267	2284	2300	2317	2334	2351	2368	2385	2402	·2419	3	6	8	11	14	76
14	·2419	2436	2453	2470	2487	2504	2521	2538	2554	2571	·2588	3	6	8	11	14	75
15	·2588	2605	2622	2639	2656	2672	2689	2706	2723	2740	·2756	3	6	8	11	14	74
16	·2756	2773	2790	2807	2823	2840	2857	2874	2890	2907	·2924	3	6	8	11	14	73
17	·2924	2940	2957	2974	2990	3007	3024	3040	3057	3074	·3090	3	6	8	11	14	72
18	·3090	3107	3123	3140	3156	3173	3190	3206	3223	3239	·3256	3	6	8	11	14	71
19	·3256	3272	3289	3305	3322	3338	3355	3371	3387	3404	·3420	3	5	8	11	14	70
20	·3420	3437	3453	3469	3486	3502	3518	3535	3551	3567	·3584	3	5	8	11	14	69
21	·3584	3600	3616	3633	3649	3665	3681	3697	3714	3730	·3746	3	5	8	11	14	68
22	·3746	3762	3778	3795	3811	3827	3843	3859	3875	3891	·3907	3	5	8	11	13	67
23	·3907	3923	3939	3955	3971	3987	4003	4019	4035	4051	·4067	3	5	8	11	13	66
24	·4067	4083	4099	4115	4131	4147	4163	4179	4195	4210	·4226	3	5	8	11	13	65
25	·4226	4242	4258	4274	4289	4305	4321	4337	4352	4368	·4384	3	5	8	11	13	64
26	·4384	4399	4415	4431	4446	4462	4478	4493	4509	4524	·4540	3	5	8	10	13	63
27	·4540	4555	4571	4586	4602	4617	4633	4648	4664	4679	·4695	3	5	8	10	13	62
28	·4695	4710	4726	4741	4756	4772	4787	4802	4818	4833	·4848	3	5	8	10	13	61
29	·4848	4863	4879	4894	4909	4924	4939	4955	4970	4985	·5000	3	5	8	10	13	60
30	·5000	5015	5030	5045	5060	5075	5090	5105	5120	5135	·5150	3	5	8	10	13	59
31	·5150	5165	5180	5195	5210	5225	5240	5255	5270	5284	·5299	2	5	7	10	12	58
32	·5299	5314	5329	5344	5358	5373	5388	5402	5417	5432	·5446	2	5	7	10	12	57
33	·5446	5461	5476	5490	5505	5519	5534	5548	5563	5577	·5592	2	5	7	10	12	56
34	·5592	5606	5621	5635	5650	5664	5678	5693	5707	5721	·5736	2	5	7	10	12	55
35	·5736	5750	5764	5779	5793	5807	5821	5835	5850	5864	·5878	2	5	7	9	12	54
36	·5878	5892	5906	5920	5934	5948	5962	5976	5990	6004	·6018	2	5	7	9	12	53
37	·6018	6032	6046	6060	6074	6088	6101	6115	6129	6143	·6157	2	5	7	9	12	52
38	·6157	6170	6184	6198	6211	6225	6239	6252	6266	6280	·6293	2	5	7	9	11	51
39	·6293	6307	6320	6334	6347	6361	6374	6388	6401	6414	·6428	2	4	7	9	11	50
40	·6428	6441	6455	6468	6481	6494	6508	6521	6534	6547	·6561	2	4	7	9	11	49
41	·6561	6574	6587	6600	6613	6626	6639	6652	6665	6678	·6691	2	4	7	9	11	48
42	·6691	6704	6717	6730	6743	6756	6769	6782	6794	6807	·6820	2	4	6	9	11	47
43	·6820	6833	6845	6858	6871	6884	6896	6909	6921	6934	·6947	2	4	6	8	11	46
44	·6947	6959	6972	6984	6997	7009	7022	7034	7046	7059	·7071	2	4	6	8	10	45
—	54'	48'	42'	36'	30'	24'	18'	12'	6'	0'		1'	2'	3'	4'	5'	

NATURAL COSINES (right-hand column and bottom)

NATURAL SINES (left-hand column and top)

	0'	6'	12'	18'	24'	30'	36'	42'	48'	54'	—	1'	2'	3'	4'	5'	
45°	·7071	7083	7096	7108	7120	7133	7145	7157	7169	7181	·7193	2	4	6	8	10	44°
46	·7193	7206	7218	7230	7242	7254	7266	7278	7290	7302	·7314	2	4	6	8	10	43
47	·7314	7325	7337	7349	7361	7373	7385	7396	7408	7420	·7431	2	4	6	8	10	42
48	·7431	7443	7455	7466	7478	7490	7501	7513	7524	7536	·7547	2	4	6	8	10	41
49	·7547	7559	7570	7581	7593	7604	7615	7627	7638	7649	·7660	2	4	6	8	9	40
50	·7660	7672	7683	7694	7705	7716	7727	7738	7749	7760	·7771	2	4	6	7	9	39
51	·7771	7782	7793	7804	7815	7826	7837	7848	7859	7869	·7880	2	4	5	7	9	38
52	·7880	7891	7902	7912	7923	7934	7944	7955	7965	7976	·7986	2	4	5	7	9	37
53	·7986	7997	8007	8018	8028	8039	8049	8059	8070	8080	·8090	2	3	5	7	9	36
54	·8090	8100	8111	8121	8131	8141	8151	8161	8171	8181	·8192	2	3	5	7	8	35
55	·8192	8202	8211	8221	8231	8241	8251	8261	8271	8281	·8290	2	3	5	7	8	34
56	·8290	8300	8310	8320	8329	8339	8348	8358	8368	8377	·8387	2	3	5	6	8	33
57	·8387	8396	8406	8415	8425	8434	8443	8453	8462	8471	·8480	2	3	5	6	8	32
58	·8480	8490	8499	8508	8517	8526	8536	8545	8554	8563	·8572	2	3	5	6	8	31
59	·8572	8581	8590	8599	8607	8616	8625	8634	8643	8652	·8660	1	3	4	6	7	30
60	·8660	8669	8678	8686	8695	8704	8712	8721	8729	8738	·8746	1	3	4	6	7	29
61	·8746	8755	8763	8771	8780	8788	8796	8805	8813	8821	·8829	1	3	4	6	7	28
62	·8829	8838	8846	8854	8862	8870	8878	8886	8894	8902	·8910	1	3	4	5	7	27
63	·8910	8918	8926	8934	8942	8949	8957	8965	8973	8980	·8988	1	3	4	5	6	26
64	·8988	8996	9003	9011	9018	9026	9033	9041	9048	9056	·9063	1	3	4	5	6	25
65	·9063	9070	9078	9085	9092	9100	9107	9114	9121	9128	·9135	1	2	4	5	6	24
66	·9135	9143	9150	9157	9164	9171	9178	9184	9191	9198	·9205	1	2	3	5	6	23
67	·9205	9212	9219	9225	9232	9239	9245	9252	9259	9265	·9272	1	2	3	4	6	22
68	·9272	9278	9285	9291	9298	9304	9311	9317	9323	9330	·9336	1	2	3	4	5	21
69	·9336	9342	9348	9354	9361	9367	9373	9379	9385	9391	·9397	1	2	3	4	5	20
70	·9397	9403	9409	9415	9421	9426	9432	9438	9444	9449	·9455	1	2	3	4	5	19
71	·9455	9461	9466	9472	9478	9483	9489	9494	9500	9505	·9511	1	2	3	4	5	18
72	·9511	9516	9521	9527	9532	9537	9542	9548	9553	9558	·9563	1	2	3	4	4	17
73	·9563	9568	9573	9578	9583	9588	9593	9598	9603	9608	·9613	1	2	2	3	4	16
74	·9613	9617	9622	9627	9632	9636	9641	9646	9650	9655	·9659	1	2	2	3	4	15
75	·9659	9664	9668	9673	9677	9681	9686	9690	9694	9699	·9703	1	1	2	3	4	14
76	·9703	9707	9711	9715	9720	9724	9728	9732	9736	9740	·9744	1	1	2	3	3	13
77	·9744	9748	9751	9755	9759	9763	9767	9770	9774	9778	·9781	1	1	2	3	3	12
78	·9781	9785	9789	9792	9796	9799	9803	9806	9810	9813	·9816	1	1	2	2	3	11
79	·9816	9820	9823	9826	9829	9833	9836	9839	9842	9845	·9848	1	1	2	2	3	10
80	·9848	9851	9854	9857	9860	9863	9866	9869	9871	9874	·9877	0	1	1	2	2	9
81	·9877	9880	9882	9885	9888	9890	9893	9895	9898	9900	·9903	0	1	1	2	2	8
82	·9903	9905	9907	9910	9912	9914	9917	9919	9921	9923	·9925	0	1	1	2	2	7
83	·9925	9928	9930	9932	9934	9936	9938	9940	9942	9943	·9945	0	1	1	1	2	6
84	·9945	9947	9949	9951	9952	9954	9956	9957	9959	9960	·9962	0	1	1	1	1	5
85	·9962	9963	9965	9966	9968	9969	9971	9972	9973	9974	·9976	0	0	1	1	1	4
86	·9976	9977	9978	9979	9980	9981	9982	9983	9984	9985	·9986	0	0	1	1	1	3
87	·9986	9987	9988	9989	9990	9990	9991	9992	9993	9993	·9994						2
88	·9994	9995	9995	9996	9996	9997	9997	9997	9998	9998	·9998						1
89	·9998	9999	9999	9999	9999	1·000	1·000	1·000	1·000	1·000	1·0000						0
—	54'	48'	42'	36'	30'	24'	18'	12'	6'	0'		1'	2'	3'	4'	5'	

The bold type indicates that the integer changes.

NATURAL COSINES (right-hand column and bottom)

NATURAL TANGENTS (left-hand column and top)

Differences (ADD)

	0'	6'	12'	18'	24'	30'	36'	42'	48'	54'	—	1'	2'	3'	4'	5'	
0	0·0000	0017	0035	0052	0070	0087	0105	0122	0140	0157	0·0175	3	6	9	12	15	**89**
1	0·0175	0192	0209	0227	0244	0262	0279	0297	0314	0332	0·0349	3	6	9	12	15	**88**
2	0·0349	0367	0384	0402	0419	0437	0454	0472	0489	0507	0·0524	3	6	9	12	15	**87**
3	0·0524	0542	0559	0577	0594	0612	0629	0647	0664	0682	0·0699	3	6	9	12	15	**86**
4	0·0699	0717	0734	0752	0769	0787	0805	0822	0840	0857	0·0875	3	6	9	12	15	**85**
5	0·0875	0892	0910	0928	0945	0963	0981	0998	1016	1033	0·1051	3	6	9	12	15	**84**
6	0·1051	1069	1086	1104	1122	1139	1157	1175	1192	1210	0·1228	3	6	9	12	15	**83**
7	0·1228	1246	1263	1281	1299	1317	1334	1352	1370	1388	0·1405	3	6	9	12	15	**82**
8	0·1405	1423	1441	1459	1477	1495	1512	1530	1548	1566	0·1584	3	6	9	12	15	**81**
9	0·1584	1602	1620	1638	1655	1673	1691	1709	1727	1745	0·1763	3	6	9	12	15	**80**
10	0·1763	1781	1799	1817	1835	1853	1871	1890	1908	1926	0·1944	3	6	9	12	15	**79**
11	0·1944	1962	1980	1998	2016	2035	2053	2071	2089	2107	0·2126	3	6	9	12	15	**78**
12	0·2126	2144	2162	2180	2199	2217	2235	2254	2272	2290	0·2309	3	6	9	12	15	**77**
13	0·2309	2327	2345	2364	2382	2401	2419	2438	2456	2475	0·2493	3	6	9	12	15	**76**
14	0·2493	2512	2530	2549	2568	2586	2605	2623	2642	2661	0·2679	3	6	9	12	16	**75**
15	0·2679	2698	2717	2736	2754	2773	2792	2811	2830	2849	0·2867	3	6	9	13	16	**74**
16	0·2867	2886	2905	2924	2943	2962	2981	3000	3019	3038	0·3057	3	6	9	13	16	**73**
17	0·3057	3076	3096	3115	3134	3153	3172	3191	3211	3230	0·3249	3	6	10	13	16	**72**
18	0·3249	3269	3288	3307	3327	3346	3365	3385	3404	3424	0·3443	3	6	10	13	16	**71**
19	0·3443	3463	3482	3502	3522	3541	3561	3581	3600	3620	0·3640	3	7	10	13	16	**70**
20	0·3640	3659	3679	3699	3719	3739	3759	3779	3799	3819	0·3839	3	7	10	13	17	**69**
21	0·3839	3859	3879	3899	3919	3939	3959	3979	4000	4020	0·4040	3	7	10	13	17	**68**
22	0·4040	4061	4081	4101	4122	4142	4163	4183	4204	4224	0·4245	3	7	10	14	17	**67**
23	0·4245	4265	4286	4307	4327	4348	4369	4390	4411	4431	0·4452	3	7	10	14	17	**66**
24	0·4452	4473	4494	4515	4536	4557	4578	4599	4621	4642	0·4663	4	7	11	14	18	**65**
25	0·4663	4684	4706	4727	4748	4770	4791	4813	4834	4856	0·4877	4	7	11	14	18	**64**
26	0·4877	4899	4921	4942	4964	4986	5008	5029	5051	5073	0·5095	4	7	11	15	18	**63**
27	0·5095	5117	5139	5161	5184	5206	5228	5250	5272	5295	0·5317	4	7	11	15	18	**62**
28	0·5317	5340	5362	5384	5407	5430	5452	5475	5498	5520	0·5543	4	8	11	15	19	**61**
29	0·5543	5566	5589	5612	5635	5658	5681	5704	5727	5750	0·5774	4	8	12	15	19	**60**
30	0·5774	5797	5820	5844	5867	5890	5914	5938	5961	5985	0·6009	4	8	12	16	20	**59**
31	0·6009	6032	6056	6080	6104	6128	6152	6176	6200	6224	0·6249	4	8	12	16	20	**58**
32	0·6249	6273	6297	6322	6346	6371	6395	6420	6445	6469	0·6494	4	8	12	16	20	**57**
33	0·6494	6519	6544	6569	6594	6619	6644	6669	6694	6720	0·6745	4	8	13	17	21	**56**
34	0·6745	6771	6796	6822	6847	6873	6899	6924	6950	6976	0·7002	4	9	13	17	21	**55**
35	0·7002	7028	7054	7080	7107	7133	7159	7186	7212	7239	0·7265	4	9	13	18	22	**54**
36	0·7265	7292	7319	7346	7373	7400	7427	7454	7481	7508	0·7536	5	9	14	18	23	**53**
37	0·7536	7563	7590	7618	7646	7673	7701	7729	7757	7785	0·7813	5	9	14	18	23	**52**
38	0·7813	7841	7869	7898	7926	7954	7983	8012	8040	8069	0·8098	5	9	14	19	24	**51**
39	0·8098	8127	8156	8185	8214	8243	8273	8302	8332	8361	0·8391	5	10	15	20	24	**50**
40	0·8391	8421	8451	8481	8511	8541	8571	8601	8632	8662	0·8693	5	10	15	20	25	**49**
41	0·8693	8724	8754	8785	8816	8847	8878	8910	8941	8972	0·9004	5	10	16	21	26	**48**
42	0·9004	9036	9067	9099	9131	9163	9195	9228	9260	9293	0·9325	5	11	16	21	27	**47**
43	0·9325	9358	9391	9424	9457	9490	9523	9556	9590	9623	0·9657	6	11	17	22	28	**46**
44	0·9657	9691	9725	9759	9793	9827	9861	9896	9930	9965	1·0000	6	11	17	23	29	**45**
—		54'	48'	42'	36'	30'	24'	18'	12'	6'	0'	1'	2'	3'	4'	5'	

The bold type indicates that the integer changes.

Differences (SUBTRACT)

NATURAL COTANGENTS (right-hand column and bottom)

286

Differences (ADD)

	0'	6'	12'	18'	24'	30'	36'	42'	48'	54'	—	1'	2'	3'	4'	5'	
45°	1·0000	0035	0070	0105	0141	0176	0212	0247	0283	0319	1·0355	6	12	18	24	30	44°
46	1·0355	0392	0428	0464	0501	0538	0575	0612	0649	0686	1·0724	6	12	18	25	31	43
47	1·0724	0761	0799	0837	0875	0913	0951	0990	1028	1067	1·1106	6	13	19	25	32	42
48	1·1106	1145	1184	1224	1263	1303	1343	1383	1423	1463	1·1504	7	13	20	26	33	41
49	1·1504	1544	1585	1626	1667	1708	1750	1792	1833	1875	1·1918	7	14	21	28	34	40
50	1·1918	1960	2002	2045	2088	2131	2174	2218	2261	2305	1·2349	7	14	22	29	36	39
51	1·2349	2393	2437	2482	2527	2572	2617	2662	2708	2753	1·2799	8	15	23	30	38	38
52	1·2799	2846	2892	2938	2985	3032	3079	3127	3175	3222	1·3270	8	16	24	31	39	37
53	1·3270	3319	3367	3416	3465	3514	3564	3613	3663	3713	1·3764	8	16	25	33	41	36
54	1·3764	3814	3865	3916	3968	4019	4071	4124	4176	4229	1·4281	9	17	26	34	43	35
55	1·4281	4335	4388	4442	4496	4550	4605	4659	4715	4770	1·4826	9	18	27	36	45	34
56	1·4826	4882	4938	4994	5051	5108	5166	5224	5282	5340	1·5399	10	19	29	38	48	33
57	1·5399	5458	5517	5577	5637	5697	5757	5818	5880	5941	1·6003	10	20	30	40	50	32
58	1·6003	6066	6128	6191	6255	6319	6383	6447	6512	6577	1·6643	11	21	32	43	53	31
59	1·6643	6709	6775	6842	6909	6977	7045	7113	7182	7251	1·7321	11	23	34	45	56	30
60	1·7321	7391	7461	7532	7603	7675	7747	7820	7893	7966	1·8040	12	24	36	48	60	29
61	1·8040	8115	8190	8265	8341	8418	8495	8572	8650	8728	1·8807	13	26	38	51	64	28
62	1·8807	8887	8967	9047	9128	9210	9292	9375	9458	9542	1·9626	14	27	41	55	68	27
63	1·9626	9711	9797	9883	9970	**0057**	**0145**	**0233**	**0323**	**0413**	2·0503	15	29	44	58	73	26
64	2·0503	0594	0686	0778	0872	0965	1060	1155	1251	1348	2·1445	16	31	47	63	78	25
65	2·1445	1543	1642	1742	1842	1943	2045	2148	2251	2355	2·2460	17	34	51	68	85	24
66	2·2460	2566	2673	2781	2889	2998	3109	3220	3332	3445	2·3559	18	37	55	73	91	23
67	2·3559	3673	3789	3906	4023	4142	4262	4383	4504	4627	2·4751	20	40	60	79	99	22
68	2·4751	4876	5002	5129	5257	5386	5517	5649	5782	5916	2·6051	22	43	65	87	108	21
69	2·6051	6187	6325	6464	6605	6746	6889	7034	7179	7326	2·7475	24	47	71	95	119	20
70	2·7475	7625	7776	7929	8083	8239	8397	8556	8716	8878	2·9042	26	52	78	104	130	19
71	2·9042	9208	9375	9544	9714	9887	**0061**	**0237**	**0415**	**0595**	3·0777	29	58	87	116	144	18
72	3·0777	0961	1146	1334	1524	1716	1910	2106	2305	2506	3·2709	32	64	97	129	161	17
73	3·2709	2914	3122	3332	3544	3759	3977	4197	4420	4646	3·4874	36	72	108	144	180	16
74	3·4874	5105	5339	5576	5816	6059	6305	6554	6806	7062	3·7321	41	81	122	163	203	15
75	3·7321	7583	7848	8118	8391	8667	8947	9232	9520	9812	4·0108	46	93	139	186	232	14
76	4·0108	0408	0713	1022	1335	1653	1976	2303	2635	2972	4·3315	53	107	160	214	267	13
77	4·3315	3662	4015	4373	4737	5107	5483	5864	6252	6646	4·7046	62	124	186	248	310	12
78	4·7046	7453	7867	8288	8716	9152	9594	**0045**	**0504**	**0970**	5·1466	73	146	220	293	366	11
79	5·1446	1929	2422	2924	3435	3955	4486	5026	5578	6140	5·671	87	175	263	350	438	10
80	5·671	5·730	5·789	5·850	5·912	5·976	6·041	6·107	6·174	6·243	6·314						9
81	6·314	6·386	6·460	6·535	6·612	6·691	6·772	6·855	6·940	7·026	7·115						8
82	7·115	7·207	7·300	7·396	7·495	7·596	7·700	7·806	7·916	8·028	8·144						7
83	8·144	8·264	8·386	8·513	8·643	8·777	8·915	9·058	9·205	9·357	9·514						6
84	9·514	9·677	9·845	10·02	10·20	10·39	10·58	10·78	10·99	11·20	11·43	UNTRUSTWORTHY					5
85	11·43	11·66	11·91	12·16	12·43	12·71	13·00	13·30	13·62	13·95	14·30						4
86	14·30	14·67	15·06	15·46	15·89	16·35	16·83	17·34	17·89	18·46	19·08						3
87	19·08	19·74	20·45	21·20	22·02	22·90	23·86	24·90	26·03	27·27	28·64						2
88	28·64	30·14	31·82	33·69	35·80	38·19	40·92	44·07	47·74	52·08	57·29						1
89	57·29	63·66	71·62	81·85	95·49	114·6	143·2	191·0	286·5	573·0	∞						0
—	54'	48'	42'	36'	30'	24'	18'	12'	6'	0'		1'	2'	3'	4'	5'	

The bold type indicates that the integer changes.

Differences (SUBTRACT)

NATURAL COTANGENTS (right-hand column and bottom)

287

Index